THE HOLE IN OUR GOSPEL

RICHARD STEARNS

THOMAS NELSON
Since 1798

NASHVILLE   DALLAS   MEXICO CITY   RIO DE JANEIRO

At the author's request, all royalties due to the author
will benefit World Vision's work with children in need.

Published in Nashville, Tennessee, by Thomas Nelson. Thomas Nelson is a registered trademark of Thomas Nelson, Inc.

Author is represented by the literary agency of Alive Communications, Inc., 7680 Goddard Street, Suite 200, Colorado Springs, CO 80920, www.alivecommunications.com.

In some cases, names and locations have been changed to protect the privacy of individuals whose stories are told in these pages.

Thomas Nelson, Inc., titles may be purchased in bulk for educational, business, fund-raising, or sales promotional use. For information, please e-mail SpecialMarkets@ThomasNelson.com.

Unless otherwise indicated, Scripture quotations are taken from the Holy Bible, New International Version (NIV). © 1973, 1978, 1984 by International Bible Society. Used by permission of Zondervan Publishing House. All rights reserved.

Scriptures marked NKJV are taken from THE NEW KING JAMES VERSION. © 1982 by Thomas Nelson, Inc. Used by permission. All rights reserved.

Scriptures marked KJV are from the Holy Bible, King James Version.

Scriptures marked MSG are taken from *The Message* by Eugene H. Peterson. © 1993, 1994, 1995, 1996, 2000, 2001, 2002. Used by permission of NavPress Publishing Group.

ISBN 978-0-8499-4690-5 (SE)
ISBN 978-0-8499-4700-1 (paperback)
ISBN 978-0-8499-4676-9 (IE)
ISBN 978-0-8499-4863-3 (WV Ed)

Library of Congress Cataloging-in-Publication Data

Stearns, Richard (Richard E.)
  The hole in our Gospel / By Richard Stearns.
    p. cm.
Includes bibliographical references (p.   ).
ISBN 978-0-7852-2918-6 (hardcover)
  1. Church work with the poor. 2. Christian life. 3. Stearns, Richard (Richard E.) 4. World Vision International. I. Title.
BV639.P6S74 2009
248.4—dc22   2008039768

Printed in the United States of America

11 12 13 14 QG 7 6 5 4 3 2 1

To Reneé . . .

My precious wife and partner—my faithful source of strength—the anchor of our family, who is the very model of the Proverbs 31 woman. She is the gift God gave me, that I might become the man He desired me to be.

> *A wife of noble character who can find?*
> > *She is worth far more than rubies.*
> *Her husband has full confidence in her*
> > *and lacks nothing of value.*
> *She brings him good, not harm,*
> > *all the days of her life.*

> *She opens her arms to the poor*
> > *and extends her hands to the needy.*

> *She is clothed with strength and dignity;*
> > *she can laugh at the days to come.*
> *She speaks with wisdom,*
> > *and faithful instruction is on her tongue.*
> *She watches over the affairs of her household*
> > *and does not eat the bread of idleness.*
> *Her children arise and call her blessed;*
> > *her husband also, and he praises her:*
> *"Many women do noble things,*
> > *but you surpass them all."*
> *Charm is deceptive, and beauty is fleeting;*
> > *but a woman who fears the LORD is to be praised.*
> *Give her the reward she has earned,*
> > *and let her works bring her praise at the city gate.*

—Proverbs 31

CONTENTS

Acknowledgments   xiii
Introduction   1
Prologue   7

PART 1: THE HOLE IN MY GOSPEL—AND MAYBE YOURS

Chapter 1: A Hole in the Whole   15
Chapter 2: A Coward for God   25
Chapter 3: You Lack One Thing   36

PART 2: THE HOLE GETS DEEPER

Chapter 4: The Towering Pillars of Compassion and Justice   53
Chapter 5: The Three Greatest Commandments   64
Chapter 6: A Hole in Me   73
Chapter 7: The Stick in Your Hand   88

PART 3: A HOLE IN THE WORLD

Chapter 8: The Greatest Challenge of the New Millennium   97
Chapter 9: One Hundred Crashing Jetliners   106
Chapter 10: What's Wrong with This Picture?   114
Chapter 11: Caught in the Web   125
Chapter 12: The Horsemen of the Apocalypse   132
Chapter 13: Spiders, Spiders, and More Spiders   151
Chapter 14: Finally, the Good News   161

PART 4: A HOLE IN THE CHURCH

Chapter 15: A Tale of Two Churches   171
Chapter 16: The Great Omission   181
Chapter 17: AWOL for the Greatest Humanitarian Crisis of All Time   190
Chapter 18: Putting the American Dream to Death   203
Chapter 19: Two Percent of Two Percent   210

Chapter 20: A Letter to the Church in America   221
Chapter 21: Why We're Not So Popular Anymore   226
Chapter 22: A Tale of Two Real Churches   231

PART 5: REPAIRING THE HOLE

Chapter 23: What Are You Going to Do about It?   243
Chapter 24: How Many Loaves Do You Have?   250
Chapter 25: Time, Talent, and Treasure   257
Chapter 26: A Mountain of Mustard Seeds   274

To Learn More   280
Q&A with Reneé Stearns   281
What Are You Going to Do About It?   287
Can Poverty Be Defeated?   300
Resources for Your Journey   303
Study Guide   305
Notes   314
Scripture Index   325
General Index   327
About the Author   335
About World Vision   336

ACKNOWLEDGMENTS

This book might not have been written without the encouragement of people who felt I had a message that needed to be heard. Perhaps first to prod me was Dale Hanson-Bourke, a World Vision board member at the time and an author herself. Not one year after I was hired, Dale kept asking when I would write my book. I told her that the last thing the world needed was yet another book, and that when I had something to say that was important—then I'd write a book. My colleague Joan Mussa, World Vision's senior vice president of Advocacy and Communications, was another encouraging voice. She saw both the importance of and the opportunity for a book that lifted up what is perhaps God's "greatest cause"—responding to the poorest of the poor with compassion. More importantly, she believed I had such a book in me. Joan enlisted Laurie Delgatto, another World Vision colleague, to read every speech I had given over ten years and to organize them into possible book concepts. Poor Laurie slogged through dozens of scribbled and typed talks, trying to make some sense out of them all. Laurie and Joan brought others in to form a kind of "book support group." Dean Owen, Roger Flessing, Jane Sutton-Redner, and Milana McLead formed the nucleus of the group that cheered me on, helped me brainstorm, shaped my ideas, and read my early manuscripts with a red pen. A book began to take form.

I have the blessing of a wonderful, godly, and visionary board of directors, who saw the importance of this message and granted me a six-month sabbatical so I would be able to complete the project without the endless interruptions of running World Vision U.S. Larry Probus, another of my senior VPs, stepped up as acting president while I was gone and carried a double burden so that I could write. In fact, the rest of my incredibly talented senior leadership team—Atul Tandon, Mike Veitenhans, Julie Regnier, Kathy Evans, and George Ward—carried on magnificently in my absence.

Many others along the way were there to compensate for my shortcomings by helping with a host of important details. Among them were Steve Hayner, a World Vision board member and former president of InterVarsity; and Steve Haas, World Vision's VP for church partnerships. Both of these friends read the manuscript with a special eye out for any theological gaffes I might have made, and they made valuable suggestions to keep me on the right course. Also included were Beth Dotson-Brown and Wendy Chin, who did much of the extensive research; Sally Zamadics on project management; Brian Vasey on contracts; and Hilary Whitman, Arlene Mitsui, and Selena Koosmann on cover designs. Shelley Liester and Cheryl Plantenberg scheduled my meetings and assembled early copies of the manuscript. Kari Costanza, a World Vision journalist, traveled with me on many occasions and took copious notes about the people we met. Thanks, too, to my agent, Beth Jusino, and Alive Communications for helping a first-time author navigate the world of publishing. Renée Chavez was an amazing copy editor provided to me by Thomas Nelson. She combed the manuscript, catching every error; improved my grammar; and added valuable conceptual perspective at critical places. Let me also thank the staff at Thomas Nelson who invested in this project and encouraged me along the way: Mary Graham, Matt Baugher, Joey Paul, Julie Faires, Emily Sweeney, Jennifer McNeil, and Stephanie Newton.

Last of all, let me acknowledge just a few who changed my life so that there could even be a story to tell.

My sister, Karen, instilled in me a love for learning and encouraged me to rise above our family circumstances through education. She has always believed in me.

Merold Stern, my first pastor back in 1974, and his amazing wife, Margaret, laid the foundation in my spiritual life for all that would come later. Merold's wise understanding of Scripture, his amazing preaching, and his godly character have influenced me more than he will ever know.

Rob Stevenson was more than the executive recruiter who brought me to World Vision back in 1998. He was the spiritual guide who challenged me and led me down a path I did not want to take. Without Rob's gentle guidance, I certainly would not have followed God's call.

My friend Bill Bryce has always been able to see in me not what was, but what might be. He first saw in me a heart for the poor and was the first to envision me leaving the corporate world. Bill's discernment and his own commitment to the poor have been a steady influence on my life for more than twenty-five years.

My dear wife, Reneé, and my five terrific children—Sarah, Andy, Hannah, Pete, and Grace—had to leave their friends and lives behind and accept my frequent absences when we all moved to Seattle to become part of World Vision. They, too, have sacrificed to help the brokenhearted.

Finally, I need to acknowledge Lorraine Pierce, the spiritual "birth mother" of World Vision, who, along with her husband and family, sacrificed almost everything to serve the poorest of the poor in obedience to the gospel.

INTRODUCTION

What does God expect of us? That's what this book is about. It's a simple question, really. But is the answer so simple? What is the Christian faith about? Going to church every Sunday, saying grace before meals, and avoiding the most serious sins—or does God expect more?

I am a Christian—perhaps you are too. But what does that mean exactly? To even *be* Christians, we must first believe that Jesus Christ is the Son of God. That in itself is no small idea. If it is true, it changes everything, because if Christ is God, then all that He said and did is deeply significant to how we live our lives. So we believe. But God expects more.

And so the question, "What does God expect of me?" is a very profound one—not just for me, but for everyone who claims to follow Christ. Jesus had a lot to say about it. Yes, He did give us deep insights into the character of God and our relationship with Him as well, but He also spoke at length about God's expectations, our values, and how we are to live in the world. So how are we to live? What kind of relationship are we to have with a holy God? What is God asking for, really, from you and me? Much more than church attendance. More than prayer too. More than belief, and even more than self-denial. God asks us for *everything*. He requires a total life commitment from those who would be His followers. In fact, Christ calls us to be His partners in changing our world, just as He called the Twelve to change their world two thousand years ago.

Certainly the twenty-first-century world is in need of change. It is hard to read the headlines each day without a growing sense of alarm. We hear about terrorism, ethnic and religious tensions, wars and conflicts, widespread hunger and poverty, global economic turmoil, brutal dictators, corrupt governments, massive natural disasters, climate change, nuclear intimidations, and even child trafficking and slavery. Our post-9/11 world seems both frightening and threatening, and the majority of us struggle to understand it, let alone do something about it. The world's problems just seem too big and too hard for most of us; it's so much easier to retreat from them than to take them on. On Sunday morning, safe in our church pews and surrounded by friends, it can be all too easy to leave the world's violence, suffering, and turmoil outside—out of sight, out of mind.

But wait—as Christians, are we really given the option of turning away from the world's problems? Does God permit that?

I write this book from a very biased perspective. I believe that "God so loved the world that he gave his one and only Son, that whoever believes in him shall not perish but have eternal life" (John 3:16). And if Jesus was willing to die for this troubled planet, maybe I need to care about it too. Maybe I should love the people who live on it more. Maybe I have a responsibility to do my part to love the world that Jesus loves so much.

The idea behind *The Hole in Our Gospel* is quite simple. It's basically the belief that being a Christian, or follower of Jesus Christ, requires much more than just having a *personal* and transforming relationship with God. It also entails a *public* and transforming relationship with the world.

If your personal faith in Christ has no positive outward expression, then your faith—and mine—has a hole in it. As Johnny Cash sang, "You're so heavenly minded, you're no earthly good."[1] The apostle James felt strongly about this type of person. "Show me your faith without deeds," he challenged, "and I will show you my faith by what I do" (James 2:18). In other words, *make your faith public.*

Embracing the gospel, or good news, proclaimed by Jesus is so much more than a private transaction between God and us. The gospel itself was born of God's vision of a changed people, challenging and transforming the prevailing values and practices of our world. Jesus called the resulting new world order the "kingdom of God" (see Matt. 12:28; 19:24; 21:32, 43; and Mark 1:15, among others) and said that it would become a reality through the lives and deeds of His followers. Jesus asked a great deal of those who followed Him. He expected much more from them than just believing He was God's Son. He challenged them to embrace radically different standards, to love their neighbors *and* their enemies, to forgive those who wronged them, to lift up the poor and downtrodden, to share what they had with those who had little, and to live lives of sacrifice. Then He likened their effect on the world around them to that which light has on darkness. Light dispels darkness; it reverses it. Likewise, truth dispels falsehood, and goodness reverses evil.

This is not easy stuff. Anyone who has tried to follow Jesus knows that the journey is fraught with setbacks, challenges, and failures—two steps forward and one step back. Those who choose to follow Christ have struggled since the very beginning to live differently in a world that often rejects their values and mocks their beliefs. The temptation to retreat from it and to keep our faith private has befallen every generation of Christians.

Yet we are the carriers of the gospel—the good news that was meant to *change* the world. Belief is not enough. Worship is not enough. Personal morality is not enough. And Christian community is not enough. God has always demanded *more*. When we committed ourselves to following Christ, we also committed to living our lives in such a way that a watching world would catch a glimpse of God's character—His love, justice, and mercy—through our words, actions, and behavior. "We are . . . Christ's ambassadors," wrote the apostle Paul, "as though God were making his appeal through us" (2 Cor. 5:20).[2] God chose us to be His representatives. He called us to go out, to proclaim the "good news"—to *be* the "good news"—and to change the world. Living out our faith privately was never meant to be an option.

I write this book unapologetically from the perspective of one who holds a Christian worldview. And because more than three-quarters of all Americans call themselves "Christians," it is obviously a worldview held by a large majority. I quote the Old and New Testaments frequently because I believe them to be God's inspired words to us, and as such, they carry great authority. But if you are not a Christian, I hope you will read this book anyway. You will find it to be both self-critical and judicial of the shortcomings readily found in the Christian community. As a group, we are far from perfect. But Christian or not, you must not read this book dispassionately, as if you are somehow exempt from caring. All of us who live in this world share responsibility for tackling the world's problems and showing compassion to our fellow man.

I have woven my own story into this book because it is the tale of an ordinary person with whom God has been patient. It is an account like many others—of one person trying to be faithful to God while also trying to make the world a little better by the life he lived. Since the day I committed my life to following Christ, I have struggled to understand what God expects of me. To the best of my ability, though, I have endeavored to live out my faith, both privately—through prayer, Scripture study, and worship—and publicly, by demonstrating God's love to others through my actions and words, not just within my small circle of relationships but in the broader community as well. I have tried to appreciate the mystery of the good news we Christians call the "gospel" and its power to change the world by changing the human heart. I have stumbled many times on this journey and do not claim to have figured it all out.

You might imagine the author of a book challenging you to respond to the great needs of the poorest people in our world—an author who, in fact, leads a large, global humanitarian organization that feeds the hungry, assists disaster victims, and cares for widows and orphans across the planet—to be some kind of spiritual hero or saint. You might even be inclined to think of me as a "Mother Teresa" in a business suit. But if you have any of those impressions, you are sorely mistaken. Let me clear that up right at the outset. I, too, have had a lifelong battle trying to "walk the talk." I am certainly no saint or hero, and I never set out to "save the world"—I didn't have that kind of courage or imagination. I was a most reluctant recruit to this cause—in many ways a coward. But as you read a little more about my story, my hope is that you'll learn from my mistakes and laugh a little at my failures. That God still chooses to use flawed human beings like me is both astonishing and encouraging. And if He can use me, He can use you.

This book asks the question, What if? What if each of us decided with renewed commitment to truly embrace the good news, the whole gospel, and demonstrate it through our lives—not even in big ways, but in small ones? What if we each said to God, "Use me; I want to change the world"? There are now two billion people on earth who claim to be Christian. That's almost one in three. Have we changed the world? Certainly, but our critics would be quick to point out that the changes have not always been good. So have we changed the world the way *God* intended? Have we been effective ambassadors for the good news that we call the "gospel"? The Lord's Prayer, repeated in churches the world over, contains the phrase "Thy kingdom come, Thy will be done *on earth*, as it is in heaven" (Matt. 6:10; emphasis added). Do we believe what we pray?

The whole gospel is a vision for ushering in God's kingdom—now, not in some future time, and here, on earth, not in some distant heaven. What if two billion people embraced this vision of God transforming our world—through *them*? Imagine it. Indeed, what if even two *thousand* people took their faith to the next level—what might God do? Two thousand years ago, the world was changed forever by just twelve.

It can happen again.

—Rich Stearns
Bellevue, Washington
December, 2008

AUTHOR'S NOTE FOR PAPERBACK EDITION

The original edition of *The Hole in Our Gospel* has challenged and inspired many readers to put their faith and convictions into action. I'm grateful for all those who have helped make this book a success. Even so, we knew that there was something missing—in fact, a handful of things—that we believed would make the book more useful to readers. So in this new edition we've included a sixteen-page photo insert; a Q&A with my wife, Reneé (everyone who reads the book says they want to hear from my amazing wife); a "What Are You Going to Do About It?" section to help you start making a difference today; a Q&A exploring the question "Can Poverty Be Defeated?"; and Scripture and general indexes that make the book a more handy resource. Thank you for purchasing this book. I look forward to hearing about the many ways God is moving you to take His gospel to a lost and hurting world.

"I am not ashamed of the gospel, because it is the power of God for the salvation of everyone who believes." —Romans 1:16

> "Whoever heard me spoke well of me,
>   and those who saw me commended me,
> because I rescued the poor who cried for help,
>   and the fatherless who had none to assist him.
> The man who was dying blessed me;
>   I made the widow's heart sing.
> I put on righteousness as my clothing;
>   justice was my robe and my turban.
> I was eyes to the blind
>   and feet to the lame.
> I was a father to the needy;
>   I took up the case of the stranger.
> I broke the fangs of the wicked
>   and snatched the victims from their teeth."
> —Job 29:11–17

PROLOGUE

*But the angel said to them, "Do not be afraid. I bring you
good news of great joy that will be for all the people."*

—LUKE 2:10

Rakai, Uganda, August 1998

His name was Richard, the same as mine. I sat inside his meager thatch hut, listening to his story, told through the tears of an orphan whose parents had died of AIDS. At thirteen, Richard was trying to raise his two younger brothers by himself in this small shack with no running water, electricity, or even beds to sleep in. There were no adults in their lives—no one to care for them, feed them, love them, or teach them how to become men. There was no one to hug them either, or to tuck them in at night. Other than his siblings, Richard was alone, as no child should be. I try to picture my own children abandoned in this kind of deprivation, fending for themselves without parents to protect them, and I cannot.

I didn't want to be there. I wasn't *supposed* to be there, so far out of my comfort zone—not in that place where orphaned children live by themselves in their agony. There, poverty, disease, and squalor had eyes and faces that stared back, and I had to see and smell and touch the pain of the poor. That particular district, Rakai, is believed to be ground zero for the Ugandan AIDS pandemic.[1] There, the deadly virus has stalked its victims in the dark for decades. Sweat trickled down my face as I sat awkwardly with Richard and his brothers while a film crew captured every tear—mine and theirs.

I much preferred living in my bubble, the one that, until that moment, had safely contained my life, family, and career. It kept difficult things like this out, insulating me from anything too raw or upsetting. When such things intruded, as they rarely did, a channel could be changed, a newspaper page turned, or a check written to keep the poor at a safe distance. But not in Rakai. There, "such things" had faces and names—even my name, Richard.

Not sixty days earlier I had been CEO of Lenox, America's finest tableware company, producing and selling luxury goods to those who could afford them. I lived with my wife and five children in a ten-bedroom house on five acres just outside of Philadelphia. I drove a Jaguar to work every day, and my business travel took me to places such as Paris, Tokyo, London, and Florence. I flew first-class and stayed in the best hotels. I was respected in my community, attended a venerable suburban church, and sat on the board of my kids' Christian school. I was one of the good guys—you might say a "poster child" for the successful Christian life. I had never heard of Rakai, the place where my bubble would burst. But in just sixty days, God turned my life inside out, and it would never be the same.

Quite unexpectedly, eight months earlier, I had been contacted by World Vision, the Christian relief and development organization, during their search for a new president. Why me? It wasn't something I had sought after. In fact, you might say I had been minding my own business when the phone rang that day. But it was a phone call that had been twenty-four years in the planning. You see, in 1974, at the age of twenty-three, in my graduate school dormitory, I knelt down beside my bed and dedicated my life to Christ. This was no small decision for me, and it came only after months of reading, studying, conversations with friends, and the important witness of Reneé, the woman who would later become my wife. While at the time I knew very little about the implications of that decision, I knew this: nothing would ever be quite the same again, because I had made a promise to follow Christ—no matter what.

THE MAN WHO WOULDN'T BUY CHINA . . .

Several months after becoming a Christian, I was newly engaged to Reneé. As we were planning our wedding and our life together, she suggested that we go to a department store to register for our china, crystal, and silver. My self-righteous response was an indication of just how my newfound faith was integrating into my life: "As long as there are children starving in the world, we're not going to own fine china, crystal, and silver." Perhaps you can see God's sense of irony in my becoming president of America's premier fine tableware company a couple of decades later. So when I answered that phone call from World Vision in January 1998, I knew that God was on the other end of the line. It was His voice I heard, not the recruiter's: *Rich, do you remember that idealistic young man in 1974 who was so passionate about starving children that he would not even fill out a wedding registry? Take a good look at yourself now. Do you see what you've become? But, Rich, if you still care about those children, I have a job I want you to do.*

In my prayers over the weeks leading up to my appointment as World Vision's president, I begged God to send someone else to do it, much as Moses had done. Surely this was a mistake. I was no Mother Teresa. I remember praying that God would send me anywhere else, "but, please, God, not to the poor—not into the pain and alienation of poverty and disease, not there." I didn't *want* to go there.

> "Let my heart be broken by the things that break the heart of God."
>
> —a prayer by Bob Pierce, founder of World Vision

Yet here I was, the new president of World Vision, sent by knowing staff to get a "baptism by fire" for my new calling, with a film crew to document every moment.

Bob Pierce, the founder of World Vision, once prayed, "Let my heart be broken by the things that break the heart of God." But who *really* wants his heart broken? Is this something to ask of God? Don't we pray that God will *not* break our hearts? But as I look at the life of Jesus, I see that He was, as Isaiah described him, "a Man of sorrows . . . acquainted with grief" (53:3 NKJV). Jesus' heart was continually moved to compassion as He encountered the lame, the sick, the widow, and the orphan. I try to picture God's broken heart as He looks today upon the broken world for which He died. Surely Richard's story breaks His heart.

Two crude piles of stones just outside the door mark the graves of Richard's parents. It disturbs me that he must walk past them every day. He and his brothers must have watched first their father and then their mother die slow and horrible deaths. I wondered if the boys were the ones who fed them and bathed them in their last days. Whatever the case, Richard, a child himself, is now the head of household.

Child-headed household, words never meant to be strung together. I tried to wrap my mind around this new phrase, one that describes not only Richard's plight but that of tens of thousands, even millions more. I'm told that there are sixty thousand orphans just in Rakai, twelve million orphans due to AIDS in sub-Saharan Africa.[2] How can this be true? Awkwardly I asked Richard what he hopes to be when he grows up, a ridiculous question to ask a child who has lost his childhood. "A doctor," he said, "so I can help people who have the disease."

"Do you have a Bible?" I asked. He ran to the other room and returned with his treasured book with gold-gilt pages. "Can you read it?"

"I love to read the book of John, because it says that Jesus loves the children."

This overwhelmed me, and my tears started to flow. *Forgive me, Lord, forgive me. I didn't know.* But I did know. I knew about poverty and suffering in the world. I was aware that children die daily from starvation and lack of clean water. I also knew about AIDS and the orphans it leaves behind, but I kept these things outside of my insulating bubble and looked the other way.

Yet this was to be the moment that would ever after define me. Rakai was what God wanted me to see. My sadness that day was replaced by repentance. Despite what the Bible had told me so clearly, I had turned a blind eye to the poor. Now my heart was filled with anger, first at myself, and then toward the world. Why wasn't Richard's story being told? The media overflowed with celebrity dramas, stock market updates, and Bill Clinton's impending impeachment hearings. But where were the headlines and magazine covers about Africa? Twelve million orphans, and no one noticed? But what sickened me most was this question: where was the Church? Indeed, where *were* the followers of Jesus Christ in the midst of perhaps the greatest humanitarian crisis of our time? Surely the Church should have been caring for these "orphans and widows in their distress" (James 1:27). Shouldn't the pulpits across America have flamed with exhortations to rush to the front lines of compassion? Shouldn't they be flaming today? Shouldn't churches be reaching out to care for children in such desperate need? How could the great tragedy of these orphans get drowned out by choruses of praise music in hundreds of thousands of churches across our country? Sitting in a hut in Rakai, I remember thinking, *How have we missed it so tragically, when even rock stars and Hollywood actors seem to understand?*

Ten years later I know. Something fundamental has been missing in our understanding of the gospel.

The word *gospel* literally means "good news." Jesus declared that He had come to "preach good news to the poor" (Luke 4:18). But what good news, what *gospel*, did the Church have for Richard and his brothers in Rakai? What "good news" have God's people brought to the world's three billion poor?[3] What "gospel" have millions of Africa's AIDS orphans seen?[4] What gospel have most of us embraced in the twenty-first century?

The answer is found in the title of this book: a gospel with a *hole* in it.

PART 1

THE HOLE IN MY GOSPEL—AND MAYBE YOURS

Christ has no body on earth but yours,
no hands but yours,
no feet but yours.
Yours are the eyes through which
Christ's compassion for the world is to look out;
yours are the feet with which He is to go about doing good;
and yours are the hands with which He is to bless us now.

—SAINT TERESA OF AVILA

Kindness has converted more sinners than zeal, eloquence, or learning.

—FREDERICK W. FABER

CHAPTER ONE

A Hole in the Whole

*Faith today is treated as something that only should make us
different, not that actually does or can make us different. In reality
we vainly struggle against the evils of this world, waiting to die and
go to heaven. Somehow we've gotten the idea that the essence of
faith is entirely a mental and inward thing.*

—DALLAS WILLARD

Where Is the Hole?

So how can our gospel have a hole in it? As I mentioned in the prologue, the word *gospel* literally means glad tidings, or good news. It is shorthand, meant to convey the coming of the kingdom of God through the Messiah. One dictionary has this definition:

> *Gospel*—glad tidings, esp. concerning salvation and the kingdom of God as announced to the world by Christ.[1]

The amazing news of the gospel is that men and women, through Christ's atoning death, can now be reconciled to God. But the good news Jesus proclaimed had a fullness beyond salvation and the forgiveness of sins; it also signified the coming of God's kingdom on earth. This new kingdom, characteristics of which were captured in the Beatitudes, would turn the existing world order upside down.

> Blessed are the poor in spirit,
>> for theirs is the kingdom of heaven.
> Blessed are those who mourn,
>> for they will be comforted.
> Blessed are the meek,
>> for they will inherit the earth.
> Blessed are those who hunger and thirst for righteousness,
>> for they will be filled.
> Blessed are the merciful,
>> for they will be shown mercy.
> Blessed are the pure in heart,
>> for they will see God.
> Blessed are the peacemakers,
>> for they will be called sons of God.
> Blessed are those who are persecuted because of righteousness,
>> for theirs is the kingdom of heaven. (Matt. 5:3–10)

The kingdom of which Christ spoke was one in which the poor, the sick, the grieving, cripples, slaves, women, children, widows, orphans, lepers, and aliens—the "least of these" (Matt. 25:40 NKJV)—were to be lifted up and embraced by God. It was a world order in which justice was to become a reality, first in the hearts and minds of Jesus' followers, and then to the wider society through their influence. Jesus' disciples were to be "salt" and "light" to the world (see Matthew 5:13–14). They were to be the "yeast" that leavens the whole loaf of bread (see Matthew 13:33). His was not intended to be a far-off and distant kingdom to be experienced only in the afterlife; no, Christ's proclamation of the "kingdom of heaven" was a call for a redeemed world order populated by redeemed people—*now*. In other words, the perfect kingdom of God that I just described was to begin *on earth*. That was the vision first proclaimed by Jesus, and it was good news for our world. But this does not seem to square with our twenty-first-century view of the gospel. Somehow this grand vision from God has been dimmed and diminished.

THE "BINGO CARD" GOSPEL

Because of the service by which you have proved yourselves, men will

*praise God for the obedience that accompanies your confession of the
gospel of Christ, and for your generosity in sharing with them and with
everyone else.* —2 Corinthians 9:13

More and more, our view of the gospel has been narrowed to a simple
transaction, marked by checking a box on a bingo card at some prayer breakfast, registering a decision for Christ, or coming forward during an altar
call. I have to admit that my own view of evangelism, based on the Great
Commission, amounted to just that for many years. It was about saving as
many people from hell as possible—for the *next* life. It minimized any concern for those same people in *this* life. It
wasn't as important that they were poor
or hungry or persecuted, or perhaps rich,
greedy, and arrogant; we just had to get
them to pray the "sinner's prayer" and
then move on to the next potential convert. In our evangelistic efforts to make
the good news accessible and simple to
understand, we seem to have boiled it
down to a kind of "fire insurance" that
one can buy. Then, once the policy is in
effect, the sinner can go back to whatever
life he was living—of wealth and suc-

> In our evangelistic efforts
> to make the good news
> accessible and simple to
> understand, we seem to
> have boiled it down to a
> kind of "fire insurance"
> that one can buy.

cess, or of poverty and suffering. As long as the policy is in the drawer, the
other things don't matter as much. We've got our "ticket" to the next life.

There is a real problem with this limited view of the kingdom of God;
it is not the whole gospel. Instead, it's a gospel with a gaping hole. First,
focusing almost exclusively on the afterlife reduces the importance of what
God expects of us in this life. The kingdom of God, which Christ said is
"within you" (Luke 17:21 NKJV), was intended to change and challenge
everything in our fallen world in the here and now. It was not meant to be a
way to leave the world but rather the means to actually redeem it. Yes, it first
requires that we repent of our own sinfulness and totally surrender our
individual lives to follow Christ, but then we are also commanded to go into
the world—to bear fruit by lifting up the poor and the marginalized, challenging injustice wherever we find it, rejecting the worldly values found

within every culture, and loving our neighbors as ourselves. While our "joining" in the coming kingdom of God may begin with a decision, a transaction, it requires so much more than that.

I believe that we have reduced the gospel from a dynamic and beautiful symphony of God's love *for* and *in* the world to a bare and strident monotone. We have taken this amazing good news from God, originally presented in high definition and Dolby stereo, and reduced it to a grainy, black-and-white, silent movie. In doing so, we have also stripped it of much of its power to change not only the human heart but the world. This is especially reflected in our limited view of evangelism. Jesus commanded His followers to take the good news of reconciliation and forgiveness to the ends of the earth. The dictate is the same today.

Christianity is a faith that was meant to spread—but not through coercion. God's love was intended to be demonstrated, not dictated. Our job is not to manipulate or induce others to agree with us or to leave their religion and embrace Christianity. Our charge is to both proclaim and embody the gospel so that others can see, hear, and feel God's love in tangible ways. When we are living out our faith with integrity and compassion in the world, God can use us to give others a glimpse of His love and character. It is God—not us—who works in the hearts of men and women to forgive and redeem. Coercion is not necessary or even particularly helpful. God is responsible for the harvest—but we *must* plant, water, and cultivate the seeds.

Let's look more closely at this metaphor, used often in the New Testament to describe evangelism (see, for example, Matthew 9:37–38; Mark 4:1–20, 26–29; Luke 10:1–3; and John 4:35–38). For most of the twentieth century, American evangelists really honed in on this idea of the harvest, believing that the fruit was already ripe and just needed to be picked. This was the essence of Billy Graham's great global crusades, Campus Crusade's pamphlet *The Four Spiritual Laws*, *The JESUS Film*, and *Evangelism Explosion*. All of these tools and efforts were highly effective at proclaiming the good news that our sins could be forgiven if we committed our lives to Christ. Many millions of people did commit their lives to Him. In fact, my own life was influenced by both *The Four Spiritual Laws* and a Billy Graham Crusade, so I can personally attest to how successful these "harvest techniques" are at harvesting fruit that has already ripened.

But what about the fruit that *hasn't* ripened? For most of us who made our first-time commitments to Christ as adults, our stories were not of instant conversion the first time we ever heard about Jesus. In fact, according to the Barna Research Group, only about 6 percent of people who are not Christians by the age of eighteen will become Christians later in life.[2] It is rare that a simple recitation of the gospel will cause people to instantly change their minds. It usually takes much more than that. Our own narratives typically involve a journey of discovery marked by relationships with respected friends and loved ones, reading, discussions, learning about the basis for the Christian faith, seeing the difference faith made in the lives of people we knew, and witnessing genuine faith demonstrated through acts of love and kindness toward others. In other words, before we became "ripe" for harvest, a lot of other things had to happen first.

Think about all the things that must happen before there can be a good harvest of crops. First, someone has to go and prepare the land. This is backbreaking work that involves felling trees, pulling massive stumps out of the ground, extracting rocks and boulders from the field, and moving them aside. But there's no harvest yet. Next the soil has to be broken up. The earth needs to be plowed, fertilizer churned in with the soil, and orderly rows tilled to prepare for the seed. Then the seeds must be carefully planted and covered. But still no harvest. Perhaps a fence needs to be built to protect the plants from animals that might devour them. And always, the seedlings must be carefully watered, nurtured, and fed over the long growing season.

There are sometimes setbacks—bad weather, blights, floods, and insects—that can jeopardize the harvest. But if all of the hard work is done faithfully and with perseverance, and if God provides good seed and favorable weather, finally a glorious harvest is the result.

Haven't we heard the stories of faithful missionaries who dedicated their whole lives in another country without seeing even one person embrace Christ as Savior—only to learn that fifty years later there was a tremendous harvest? In our instant-gratification society, we would prefer to go directly to the harvest. Who wants to do all of that hard work of stump pulling and boulder moving? But isn't all of that "other" work the essence of the coming of the kingdom of God in its fullness? When we become involved in people's lives, work to build relationships, walk with them through their sorrows and their joys, live with generosity toward others, love and care for them unconditionally, stand up for the defenseless, and pay particular attention to the poorest and most vulnerable, we are *showing* Christ's love to those around us, not just talking about it. These are the things that plant the seeds of the gospel in the human heart.

> The gospel means much more than the personal salvation of individuals. It means a *social* revolution.

Didn't Jesus always care about the *whole* person—one's health, family, work, values, relationships, behavior toward others—and his or her soul? Jesus' view of the gospel went beyond a bingo card transaction; it embraced a revolutionary new view of the world, an earth transformed by transformed people, His "disciples of all the nations" (Matt. 28:19 NKJV), who would usher in the revolutionary kingdom of God. Those words from the Lord's Prayer, "your kingdom come, your will be done on earth, as it is in heaven" were and are a clarion call to Jesus' followers not just to proclaim the good news but to *be* the good news, here and now (Matt. 6:10). This gospel—the *whole* gospel—means much more than the personal salvation of individuals. It means a *social revolution*.

JESUS HAD A MISSION STATEMENT

I have come that they may have life, and have it to the full. —John 10:10

The revolution began in Nazareth, where Jesus grew up.

Picture for a moment your neighbor's son being asked to speak at the Sunday service at your church. Can you imagine your shock if he stood up, read the scriptures pertaining to the second coming of Christ, and then said, "Today this scripture is fulfilled in your hearing"? That is exactly what Jesus did in the synagogue in Nazareth, except He referred to the Messiah's first coming. This happened at the very start of Jesus' public ministry, immediately after His baptism by John the Baptist and the forty days in the wilderness, facing the temptations of Satan. Listen to this remarkable passage:

Jesus returned to Galilee in the power of the Spirit, and news about him spread through the whole countryside. He taught in their synagogues, and everyone praised him.

He went to Nazareth, where he had been brought up, and on the Sabbath day he went into the synagogue, as was his custom. And he stood up to read. The scroll of the prophet Isaiah was handed to him. Unrolling it, he found the place where it is written:

"The Spirit of the Lord is on me,
   because he has anointed me
   to preach good news to the poor.
He has sent me to proclaim freedom for the prisoners
   and recovery of sight for the blind,
   to release the oppressed,
   to proclaim the year of the Lord's favor."

Then he rolled up the scroll, gave it back to the attendant and sat down. The eyes of everyone in the synagogue were fastened on him, and he began by saying to them, "Today this scripture is fulfilled in your hearing." (Luke 4:14–21)

The passage Jesus read was a messianic prophecy that envisioned a future messiah who would be both a king and a servant. As perhaps Jesus' first public statement of His identity as the Messiah, what He said in Nazareth was a declaration both of who He was and why He had come. It was in essence Jesus' *mission statement*, and it laid out the great promises of God to those who receive the Messiah and His coming kingdom. In this mission statement, we see three main components.

First, we see the *proclamation of the good news* of salvation. Take note that the recipients of this good news were to be, first and foremost, the poor, just as Jesus promised in the Beatitudes. When we talk today about proclaiming the gospel, we typically mean evangelism, a verbal proclamation of the good news of salvation and how it can be received by anyone by asking God's forgiveness and committing his or her life to Christ. But this is not the whole gospel.

Second, we see a reference to "recovery of sight for the blind" (v. 18).

In the original text from Isaiah 61, there is also a promise to "bind up the brokenhearted" (v. 1). These references indicate that the good news includes a *compassion for the sick and the sorrowful*—a concern not just for our spiritual condition but for our physical well-being also. We see this same concern time after time in the ministry of Jesus as He healed the diseased and the lame, showed empathy for the poor, fed the hungry, and literally restored sight to the blind. Jesus clearly cared about addressing poverty, disease, and human brokenness in tangible ways.

Third, we see a majestic *commitment to justice*. Jesus has come to "proclaim freedom for the prisoners," "to release the oppressed," and "to proclaim the year of the Lord's favor" (Luke 4:18–19). In the first century, the allusion to prisoners and the oppressed would have certainly meant those living under the occupation of Rome but also, in a broader sense, anyone who had been the victim of injustice, whether political, social, or economic. The proclamation of "the year of the Lord's favor" was a clear reference to the Old Testament year of Jubilee, when slaves were set free, debts were forgiven, and all land was returned to its original owners. The year of Jubilee was God's way of protecting against the rich getting too rich and the poor getting too poor.

Proclaiming the whole gospel, then, means much more than evangelism in the hopes that people will hear and respond to the good news of salvation by faith in Christ. It also encompasses tangible compassion for the sick and the poor, as well as biblical justice, efforts to right the wrongs that are so prevalent in our world. God is concerned about the spiritual, physical, and social dimensions of our being. This *whole gospel* is truly good news for the poor, and it is the foundation for a social revolution that has the power to change the world. And if this was Jesus' mission, it is also the mission of all who claim to follow Him. It is my mission, it is your mission, and it is the mission of the Church.

THE POWER OF THE WHOLE

About six months after the terrible earthquake that killed twenty thousand people in Gujarat, India, in 2001,[3] I visited there. The region had been flattened; nearly every house and building had collapsed. Several of my colleagues and I were there to dedicate the first of hundreds of new houses built through a partnership between World Vision, Habitat for Humanity, and USAID. The resilient Indian people, with some help from outsiders, were beginning to put their lives back together and move on, even though their human losses had been unimaginable to most of us in the West.

During the dedication proceedings, a group of village elders sat just a few yards behind us, observing everything. They looked like majestic and dignified figures from the pages of *National Geographic*, with deeply lined faces; long, white beards and mustaches; and turbaned heads. As the event wore on, they were having quite a lively conversation in their local dialect. They could not have known that one of my colleagues, Atul Tandon,[4] had grown up in that very region and understood every word they were saying.

After the ceremony, Atul shared with me what he had overheard. He said that the men were speculating as to why "these Christians" had traveled thousands of miles across the ocean to help their community rebuild. They wondered what motivated complete strangers to help them. They were experiencing the love of God and the kingdom of God in profound ways through the concrete love and action demonstrated by Christians, acting through the Habitat for Humanity and World Vision organizations.

Saint Francis of Assisi understood the power of faith put into action to change the human heart, for it was he who said, "Preach the gospel always; when necessary use words." We had not yet spoken a word in their language, but the village elders had already "heard" the gospel.

A Bible Full of Holes

I am astonished that you are so quickly deserting the one who called you by the grace of Christ and are turning to a different gospel—which is really no gospel at all. —Galatians 1:6–7

We have shrunk Jesus to the size where He can save our soul but now don't believe He can change the world. —Anonymous

Luke 4 is not the only place in the Bible that speaks to the issues of poverty and justice. God's Word is replete with such passages, from Genesis to Revelation—but do we heed them?

When my friend Jim Wallis[5] was a seminary student at Trinity Evangelical

Divinity School outside of Chicago, he and some of his classmates did a little experiment. They went through all sixty-six books of the Bible and underlined every passage and verse that dealt with poverty, wealth, justice, and oppression. Then one of Jim's fellow students took a pair of scissors and physically cut every one of those verses out of the Bible. The result was a volume in tatters that barely held together. Beginning with the Mosaic books, through the books of history, the Psalms and Proverbs, and the Major and Minor Prophets, to the four Gospels, the book of Acts, the Epistles and into Revelation, so central were these themes to Scripture that the resulting Bible was in shambles. (According to *The Poverty and Justice Bible*, there are almost two *thousand* verses in Scripture that deal with poverty and justice.[6]) When Jim would speak on these issues, he would hold his ragged book in the air and proclaim, "Brothers and sisters, this is our American Bible; it is full of holes. Each one of us might as well take our Bibles, a pair of scissors, and begin cutting out all the scriptures we pay no attention to, all the biblical texts that we just ignore."[7] Jim's Bible was literally full of holes.

Hole (hōl) n.—A hollowed place in something solid[8]

The gospel Jesus described in Luke 4 is indeed something solid. If there is a hole in our gospel, in our understanding of the nature of God's call upon us, His followers, it is not because Scripture is unclear about these issues. Rather, it is because we have chosen, as Jim Wallis suggests, to pay little attention to God's unmistakable message to bring the whole gospel to the whole world. We'll come back to the scriptural basis for a fuller understanding of the "whole gospel" in the next section. But any *head* analysis of what Jesus expects of those who choose to follow Him must be accompanied by the *heart*, and the *hands and feet* as well. In my own case, getting what I knew in my head into my heart and out to my hands and feet was the challenge. Walking the walk was a lot harder than talking the talk. Isn't it always that way?

CHAPTER TWO

A Coward for God

To know what is right and not do it is the worst cowardice.

—CONFUCIUS

The true gospel is a call to self-denial.
It is not a call to self-fulfillment.

—JOHN MACARTHUR

Let me take you back a few years to help you understand how this luxury-goods CEO ended up in the jungles of Uganda in the first place. One of the lowest points in my life was a Friday afternoon in Seattle. After a nine-month search, the World Vision board of directors had selected me and offered me the opportunity to become World Vision's U.S.-based president. I had flown to Seattle with my wife and my teenage son, Andy, to meet the key leaders, learn about the challenges of the job, and decide whether I would accept the board's invitation. As I shared in the prologue, I had not sought this position. In fact, I had prayed that God would send someone *else* to do it—anyone but me. Yet the board (and presumably God) had inexplicably called *me*, and this was the hour of decision.

I wish I could tell you that I accepted this call with a sense of spiritual excitement and passion to help the broken people of our world. I'd like to say that I boldly prayed, "Here I am, Lord. Send me"—that I was eager to seize the opportunity to serve. But that would be a lie.

That Friday, at the end of two days of meetings and interviews with

World Vision's top leaders, I had sunk deeper and deeper into a spiritual and emotional funk. I had been bombarded with wrenching stories of human suffering, confronted with the considerable challenges that would face the new president, and introduced to a language full of jargon and acronyms I didn't even understand. Surely this was a mistake. What did I know about any of this? After all, I was a guy who had spent the last eleven years selling dishes—expensive ones. There had to be someone better qualified than me.

> At every point of decision, every fork in the road, we're supposed to ask, "W.W.J.D.?" or, "What would Jesus do?"

Returning to Reneé and Andy that afternoon, I was at the end of my emotional and spiritual rope. I had run out of time, and now I had a decision to make. Would I accept the board's invitation, leave my twenty-three-year career behind, and move my wife and five kids across the country, or would I turn down the job and stay at Lenox? This was one of those life decisions that changes everything, and I didn't want to make it. I was afraid. When Reneé asked how the day had gone, I said I couldn't talk about it just yet; I needed to rest and be alone. I was an emotional basket case. And so, at 4 p.m., I slipped into my pajamas, crawled into bed, pulled the covers over my head, and began to weep and pray, crying out to God to "take this cup" from me. It was pretty pathetic. Andy, sixteen at the time, came into my room a few minutes later, patted me on the shoulder, and said, "Everything will be okay, Dad. Mom and I are going out for a few hours to get something to eat. Get some sleep." There I was, blubbering in front of my teenager—quite the spiritual role model!

W.W.J.D.?

Whoever claims to live in him must walk as Jesus did. —1 John 2:6

When I was a kid, I used to plan "coin flip" bike rides with some of my friends. The idea was that we would all start riding our bikes down the street, and when we came to a major fork or intersection, we would stop and flip a coin. "If it's heads, we go straight," we'd say. "If it's tails, we turn right." And then we would do whatever the coin flip told us to. For a bunch of ten-year-olds, this could be a pretty exciting adventure, and it sometimes took us places we had never been, quite far from our safe little neighborhood. The only rule was, you *had* to do what the coin flip said.[1]

As followers of Christ, we're supposed to do the *very same thing*: at every point of decision, every fork in the road, we're supposed to ask, "W.W.J.D.?" or, "What would Jesus do?"—and then do exactly that. And much like my childhood bike rides, that kind of commitment will inevitably take us out of our safety zones, but, oh, what an adventure for the person who actually does it!

The day I committed my life to Christ, I understood what it meant— following Christ no matter what. I was determined to not become one of those hypocrites who talked the talk but didn't walk the walk. After Reneé and I married, she and I worked together to live intentionally for Christ. We moved to Boston and showed up at Park Street Church on the Boston Common that very first Sunday. We led the kids' youth group, tithed our income faithfully, and got involved in Bible studies and fellowship groups whenever we could. Park Street was an amazing "missions church," and Reneé and I eagerly attended every annual missions conference, giving our money liberally to support the cause. We were excited about spreading the good news about Christ across the world. I even became the church's youngest elder, at age twenty-seven. And at work, as I started my climb up the corporate ladder, I witnessed to people unashamedly and never shrank from an argument about faith or Christianity. In fact, when I was twenty-six and working at Parker Brothers (yes, the Monopoly, Clue, and Nerf Ball manufacturer), I almost got fired for leaving an hour early every Friday afternoon to work with the kids at our church. I was told that success at Parker Brothers required nothing less than a 110 percent commitment, and leaving early didn't make a good impression on senior management. I remember asking my boss, "Isn't Parker Brothers supposed to be all about kids?" and then asking why actually working with real kids was such a bad thing. I survived that shaky performance review and promised to work harder.

Reneé enrolled in law school at Boston College, determined to follow her own dream to help the poor with their legal problems. With our first baby, Sarah, in tow, she graduated with distinction, passed the bar, and began serving the poor in rural Massachusetts. Our marriage, family, church involvement, and jobs were completely integrated with our understanding of what it meant to follow Jesus. So how did it happen that twenty years later I found myself weeping in my pj's, with the covers pulled over my head and begging God to let me off the hook?

TWO PHONE CALLS THAT CHANGED MY LIFE

Over two decades, a lot happened. For one thing we had five children. Reneé knew she couldn't manage five kids and a full-time legal career, so she made the difficult decision to stay home with the kids. I stayed at Parker Brothers for nine years and became president at age thirty-three. (I guess leaving early on Fridays to help kids wasn't such a bad decision after all.) My career took off in ways I couldn't explain. It seemed as though everything I touched turned to gold, and I was at the right place at the right time *every* time. On average, I had been promoted every twelve months for nine straight years.

But then, as sometimes happens in corporate America, Parker Brothers went through a change of ownership, and I was told my services were no longer required. This was quite a traumatic shock after so many years of unbridled success, and I took the news hard. But I promptly picked myself up and started my search for a new job with diligence, trusting that God had something new for us.

After about five months of searching, I managed to find a position with the Franklin Mint in Pennsylvania, making even more money than I had at Parker Brothers. At first, things were looking up. I moved Reneé and our then three kids from Boston to Philadelphia—and then the unthinkable happened: I got fired again after just nine months. This time God had my full attention.

Looking back, I believe now that He wanted me to see that I had come to depend more on myself than on Him, confusing my success with His approval. I had now been fired twice in just over a year and would spend a total of fourteen months unemployed. This period of humbling and reflection, more than any other time in my life, helped me understand what it meant to put my relationship with God above all else. As I arose each morning and began my day unhurried by meetings and obligations, I spent long sessions with my Bible, praying and asking God for His direction for my life. And as I read the story of Moses and the Israelites wandering through the desert for forty years, I prayed that my own wilderness experience wouldn't last quite so long. I understood more clearly that God's daily provision of manna—bread that literally fell from heaven—was a forty-year lesson to His people that they were totally and completely dependent on Him for their very lives. They were helpless in the wilderness without God's constant care, and I was learning the hard way that I was too. When you are unemployed, you feel helpless. You can't just go get a job; someone has to offer you one. For a former CEO, this powerlessness was excruciating, but it drove home the message that all we are and all we have come from God's hand.

If I were to summarize all I learned during those "wilderness" months, I would point back to a catechism lesson I learned when I was five or six. As a child I had to memorize simple questions and answers about God. One of the questions was, why did God make me? The answer? To love, serve, and obey Him. That's what I now understood for the first time. No matter where I was or what my circumstances were, I was made to love, serve, and obey God. I could do all three whether unemployed or as a CEO—my situation didn't matter. When I was eventually offered a job, I took that lesson with me and began each day asking, how can I love, serve, and obey God today, in this place with these people?

I was finally offered a job as head of a small division of Lenox, the fine china company. I can't begin to tell you how grateful I was to God for that job after so many months out of work. God does indeed use our most painful seasons to deepen our faith and conform us to His will. Though painful, my period of unemployment was one of the richest spiritual times of my life.

At Lenox, good things began to happen again. The division I led tripled in size over the next three years. Senior management noticed, and I got promotion after promotion, becoming president and CEO of Lenox in 1995. But this time I had my priorities straight, and I knew on whom I depended.

You have to understand how amazing it was for a kid raised in relative poverty to become the CEO of two large corporations. My childhood had been fraught with insecurity. My parents divorced, my father declared bankruptcy, and the bank had foreclosed on our home. I grew up always knowing we were one paycheck away from broke. Just getting through college had been a financial miracle made up of loans, scholarships, and a string of summer jobs. For two summers I drove a taxi. I remember, as I picked up businessmen at the airport and eavesdropped on their conversations, dreaming, not of becoming an executive someday, but of riding in the backseat of a taxi, something I had never in my life done. That's why being unemployed was so traumatic for me—I had an insecurity that traced back to my childhood. So becoming a corporate CEO, not once but twice, was the American Dream come true. I had made it to the top against formidable odds—twice now—and this time, God willing, I hoped to stay there.

Several years later, that phrase, "God willing," overshadowed all of the events that ultimately led me to leave Lenox and join World Vision. I was sitting in my rather posh corner office one day in 1997 when the phone rang. My good friend Bill Bryce was calling from Massachusetts. Bill and I and our wives had been friends for many years. We had met Bill at Park Street Church in 1975, and after he and Annette married, we met weekly in a couples Bible study.

In 1984, Bill came to the Bible study group with a dilemma. At the time he was working as a fund-raiser for Gordon-Conwell Theological Seminary, and he had just been offered a job at World Vision, helping raise money for their ministry to the poor. With this decision to make, Bill was asking us for prayer and advice. At that time I had never heard of World Vision, but its mission seemed so inspiring. "Are you nuts?" I said. "You can't decide whether to raise money for some dusty old seminary or to help save the lives of starving children? Is that a *hard* choice to make?" (Gordon-Conwell is one of the finest seminaries in the country, turning out amazing graduates who are, in fact, changing the world. My rash comment to Bill at the time was not very mature or thoughtful, as I'm sure you'll agree.) So Bill quit his job to join World Vision, and I, big mouth that I was, became his first donor.

Now, thirteen years later, Bill was calling me at Lenox. World Vision's U.S. president, Bob Seiple,[2] had told the board of directors that he wished to leave within the next year and that they should begin the search for a successor. "Wow!" I said. "*Now* what is World Vision going to do? How do you replace a guy like Bob Seiple?"

Bill paused a moment, then said, "That's the reason I called." What he said next was somewhat stunning. He told me that since he first heard of Bob's decision a couple of weeks earlier, he had been praying that God would lead the right person to take his place. And then he just blurted it out: "Don't ask me to explain it, but God told me that *you* are going to be the next president of World Vision." He went on to say that God didn't make a habit of speaking to him in this way, but every time he had prayed about the vacancy, he heard God say that it was going to be Rich—his friend Rich. To top it off, Bill said he had never been *so certain* that God was speaking to him.

What, you might ask, did I do with this momentous news? I laughed out loud. I told Bill it was a ridiculous notion and that he had been drinking too much strong tea. Just how was I going to become president of World Vision? First, I wasn't even interested or available. I had made it to the top, loved my job, loved my house and community, and had five young kids who attended a great Christian school, and I had no intention of uprooting them. After my time in the "wilderness" a few years earlier, I wasn't eager to have any other major disruptions in my life.

Second, I had no qualifications for such a job—I couldn't find most African countries on a map, let alone know how to help the people who lived there. I didn't even read the international section of the newspaper— just the local news, sports, and entertainment sections. And I was, after all, running a luxury tableware company, selling mostly to the rich.

Third, I did not know one person on the World Vision board of directors, and they didn't know me, so just how was I supposed to become president?

"I'm going to tell you where to send your résumé," Bill told me.

"Bill," I said, "have you not been listening? I am not sending my résumé to anyone. This is a preposterous idea."

Flustered but undeterred, Bill said, "How are you going to get the job if you won't send your résumé?"

"Exactly," I replied. "I'm *not* going to get the job. That's what I've been trying to tell you." I think he then told me I was hopeless and I was not listening to God's plan. I still remember my last words to him: "If God wants me, He knows where to find me."

Months passed, and Bill gave me periodic updates on the search for

World Vision's next president. They had hired a recruiting firm, were doing a national search, and had formed a committee to guide the search process. Each time Bill would ask if I'd changed my mind. I hadn't and still thought he was nuts.

About six months after Bill's "prophecy," I was again sitting at my desk, this time going through some mail, when I found a handwritten note from one of my Lenox VPs, who worked about twenty minutes down the road, in the collectibles division. The note said:

> *Rich, I was reading the Wall Street Journal today and looking at the employment section. When I saw this ad, it made me think of you. I have always thought that someday you'd do something like this. So here it is. Didn't know if you had seen it.*
>
> *—Bob*
>
> *P.S. This was kind of a dumb thing to do. Don't get the wrong idea. You're a great CEO and we wouldn't want to lose you!*

I turned the page to see a copy of a small ad that read, PRESIDENT, WORLD VISION, and went on to describe the job. I learned much later that the search firm had run the ad just once in the *Wall Street Journal*, to cast a wider net and see if any "business types" might see it and apply. I will admit: reading that note sent a bit of a shiver up my spine. Bob had no idea about my conversations with my friend Bill. It was kind of eerie. But I thought I'd have a little fun with Bill, so I picked up the phone and called him.

When he heard what had happened, he was quite excited. "See, I told you so. If that isn't a message from God, I don't know what is. Now do you believe me?" I told him I doubted it was any message from God and that it was now in my wastebasket; it was just a crazy coincidence. God would have to speak a little more clearly than that.

It was January 1998, about seven months after Bill's first call to me, when the next life-changing phone call came. Again, as I sat at my battleship-sized desk, my assistant indicated that a recruiter was on the line and asked if I wanted to speak with him.

"Sure," I said. I always spoke with recruiters, because, well, you never know. The conversation went something like this:

"Hello, Rich. My name is Rob Stevenson, and I have been retained by World Vision's board to help find their next president. Do you have a few minutes to talk?" The minute he said, "World Vision," a shiver went down my spine. The series of coincidences were beginning to get a little creepy.

"How did you get my name?" I asked. "Did Bill Bryce put you up to this?"

The recruiter said he didn't know any Bill Bryce and that he had gotten my name from a donor list.

"Okay," I said, relieved. "How can I help you?"

Mr. Stevenson then spent the next few minutes describing the work of World Vision, with which I was already familiar from so many conversations with Bill. After a fairly long monologue covering the job description and qualifications, he asked me the standard question: "Do you know anyone who might be a good fit for this position?"

"I don't think so," I said. "The way I see it, you seem to be looking for someone who is part CEO, part Mother Teresa, and part Indiana Jones, and I don't know anyone like that. You might find two out of three, but probably not all three. But I'll keep my eyes and ears open, and if I think of someone, I'll be sure to call you." I was kind of hoping to keep this call as short as possible. It was dangerous. But then came the other standard question headhunters tend to ask:

"What about you?" he said. "Would you have an interest in this job?"

"Me?" I laughed uncomfortably. "I don't think so. I am not qualified, not interested, and not really available." What did I know about the poor anyway—didn't this guy remember I was running a *luxury* goods company? This was crazy.

Undaunted, Rob continued: "I really think I need to meet you. As we've been talking, I have sensed the Holy Spirit prompting me to arrange a meeting. I've spoken to two hundred people about this job, and you are the first one I've had this spiritual confirmation about. Would you be willing to meet me for dinner to discuss this further?"

Did he say that to all the candidates? It was really starting to freak me out. I remember thinking, *I need to get off this call.*

"I don't think so, Rob," I answered. "It would be a waste of your time and mine. I'm busy and you're busy. Besides, you're in Minneapolis, and I'm in Philadelphia."

"I'll fly to you," he said. "Would you just keep an open mind?"

Not really. In fact, my mind was totally closed. This was not going to happen. I almost said, "I'll pray about it, but the answer is no." But then, just as I was about to excuse myself, he added, "Let me ask you a different question . . ."

"Are you willing to be open to God's will for your life?"

And then it came.

"Are you willing to be open to God's will for your life?"

Ouch! What a terrible question to ask someone. What a *rude* question to ask someone! And what an uncomfortable question for someone to answer. That one question really put me at a loss for words. I think there was a long pause; then slowly I started to answer. "Well . . . yes . . . I *do* want to be open to God's will. But . . ." And, you see, as I thought about my answer, there were a lot of buts:

- But I'm not qualified. You don't really want me in this job.
- But I don't know anything about global poverty, or relief and development, or fund-raising. Surely this would be a huge mistake.

And then there were the more selfish buts:

- But I have worked more than twenty years to get to the top of the corporate ladder. You can't be suggesting that I give all of that up. This would be career suicide.
- But I love being the CEO of Lenox, and I am just on the brink of making a lot of money. We'll be set for life in just a few more years.
- But we live in a two-hundred-year-old stone farmhouse with ten bedrooms on five acres; it's the house of our dreams, that we waited years for. You can't expect us to sell it.
- But what about my brand-new company car, the royal blue Jaguar XK-8? I'd have to give that back.
- But I have five kids, who love their friends and their school, and we would have to move them to the other side of the

country. And how could we put them all through college on a
World Vision salary? And what is the salary anyway?

Then, deeper still, were my greatest fears, spiritual and emotional . . .

- But, Lord, I don't *want* to do this. This will wreck my life.
  Don't send me to the poor, Lord—anywhere but there.
- But I *can't* do this, God. Not poverty, slums, hunger, disease,
  dying children, grieving parents—don't ask me to go there,
  Lord. Not into so much pain and suffering and despair.

In those few seconds, all of those issues flashed through my head,
because, you see, in my heart I knew what was at stake. God was asking me
that day to choose. He was challenging me to decide what kind of disciple
I was willing to be. Two decades earlier I had "bet the farm" on Jesus
Christ, and now He was asking me to hand over the deed. What was the
most important thing in my life? He wanted to know. Was it my career, my
financial security, my family, my stuff? Or was I committed to following
Him regardless of the cost—no matter what?

Why did God make me?

To love, serve, and obey Him . . .

"Are you willing to be open to God's will for your life?"

I heard Rob's voice again on the phone.

"Well . . . yes . . . I do want to be open to God's will for my life—but
I'm pretty sure this is not it, Rob."

"Let's find out," he said. "Have dinner with me."

CHAPTER THREE

You Lack One Thing

*The place God calls you to is the place where your deep gladness
and the world's deep hunger meet.*

—FREDERICK BUECHNER

*Choose for yourselves this day whom you will serve . . .
But as for me and my household, we will serve the LORD.*

—JOSHUA 24:15

During my "dark night of the soul"—caused by a call from World Vision—I began reading my Bible with greater intensity. But when I came to Matthew 19 and the story of the rich young ruler, I wanted to run for the scissors and cut it out of my Bible. You remember the scene. A man variously described in three different gospel accounts as young, rich, and a ruler approached Jesus with this question: "Teacher, what good thing must I do to get eternal life?" (v. 16). Now, as I read this passage, I saw myself in this man. He was young and prosperous. He was likely held in esteem by his peers and his community. He seemed to exemplify the epitome of Jewish respectability. I imagined that he was successful in everything he did, that he went to temple regularly, tithed his income, observed all the holy days and feasts, and read his Torah. He had worked the whole system and had ended up at the top. That was me in spades. Everyone who knew me would have said that I was a poster boy for the successful Christian life—church every Sunday, great marriage, five attractive (and above-average) kids, a corporate CEO with a Bible on his desk, a faithful supporter of Christian causes—the whole Christian enchilada. So I could really relate to this guy's frame of mind. I sometimes imagine that he might have actually approached Jesus that day filled with a bit of pride, asking his question and expecting a nice pat on the back, perhaps thinking Jesus would point to him in front of the crowd and say, "This, my friends, is exactly the kind of follower I am looking for." But Jesus' reply was rather disappointing: "If you want to enter life, obey the commandments" (v. 17).

That was not what the man had wanted to hear. So, trying to pin Jesus down a bit more, he asked, "Which ones?" (v. 18).

Jesus' reply was conventional: "Do not murder, do not commit adultery, do not steal, do not give false testimony, honor your father and mother,' and 'love your neighbor as yourself'" (v. 18).

The young man now seemed more pleased. "All these I have kept," he said (v. 20). In other words, *Check me out, Jesus. Check out my reputation. Ask my rabbi. You'll find that I have got all these bases covered.* Now, as I see it, this is where the young man should have stopped—no harm, no foul. He should have just said thank you to Jesus, shaken His hand, and walked away. But no, he decided to push it just a little further. "What do I still lack?" (Translation: *Come on, Rabbi, this is too easy. Give me a tougher test.*)

And this is when Jesus nailed him. "One thing you lack," He told the self-righteous young man. "Go, sell everything you have and give to the poor, and you will have treasure in heaven. Then come, follow me" (Mark 10:21).

Whoa, Jesus, time out! Can you imagine what must have been going through the young man's mind just then? *Be serious, Jesus. Isn't that a tad extreme? I've worked pretty hard to get where I am, and I have obligations. Sell everything I have and give it away? I can't just pick up and leave. I've got a wife and kids to support, workers that depend on me, and some big financial deals that are pending—I own a lot of land here. Let's not be too radical about all of this. Aren't You taking this a little too far? I tell You what: maybe I could just write a little bigger check to help the poor . . .*

But Jesus' words hung in the air: "*One thing you lack . . . Go, sell everything you have and give to the poor . . . Then come, follow me.*" Devastating. Jesus had looked into the man's soul and diagnosed the condition of his heart. You see, on the outside he was doing all the right things, but on the inside his heart was divided. His possessions and his position were competing with God for primacy. He had surrendered his outward behavior to God, but his commitment to Him was not absolute. He had not made a total surrender of self; he had not "bet the farm." I don't believe Jesus was saying that all of us have to sell everything we have and give it to the poor. No, Jesus was looking into the heart of this particular young man, and He saw that he had not relinquished his life unconditionally. For him, his status and stuff had become idols. Most troubling of all was the very next line in Matthew's account: "When the young man heard this, he went away sad, because he had great wealth" (19:22). He couldn't do it. At the moment of decision, he simply could not surrender everything. He turned his back on Jesus and walked away.

> When we say that we want to be His disciple, yet attach a list of conditions, Jesus refuses to accept our terms. His terms involve unconditional surrender.

———

Are you willing to be open to God's will for your life? That was the question Rob asked me, quite simply, but it cut much deeper than that. Jesus wanted everything; He always has. *You lack one thing, Rich. Sell your possessions and give to the poor, and you will have treasure in heaven. Then come, follow Me.* Quitting my job, selling my house, and moving my family to serve at World Vision was uncomfortably equivalent to what Jesus had asked of this other rich young man. Can you see why I wanted to run for the scissors when I read this story in the Bible?

Over the past few years I have spoken with quite a few men and women who have heard my story and called me because they, too, want to go from success to significance,[1] by serving God more directly. Often they have decided that they want to move into ministry of some sort and invest themselves full-time in Christian work. So I ask them a few questions: Will you relocate? How important is title and salary? Are you willing to work where most needed? Invariably they reply with a list of conditions. Usually it sounds something like this: "Well, we're very committed to staying in the

Atlanta area. All of our friends are here, and we have spent years getting our house just right. Our kids are in a very special private school, and we don't want to move them. We waited six years to join the country club, and now we're members. We couldn't take too big of a pay cut and still maintain our lifestyle . . . But other than that, we're wide open to serve." I really understand where they are coming from, because these are many of the same issues that weighed heavily on my mind as I wrestled with my call to World Vision. But the lesson I learned was that God expects us to serve Him on His terms—not ours. In fact, He dealt with this clearly in Luke:

> As they were walking along the road, a man said to him, "I will follow you wherever you go."
> Jesus replied, "Foxes have holes and birds of the air have nests, but the Son of Man has no place to lay his head."
> He said to another man, "Follow me."
> But the man replied, "Lord, first let me go and bury my father."
> Jesus said to him, "Let the dead bury their own dead, but you go and proclaim the kingdom of God."
> Still another said, "I will follow you, Lord; but first let me go back and say good-by to my family."
> Jesus replied, "No one who puts his hand to the plow and looks back is fit for service in the kingdom of God." (9:57–62)

Consistent with His encounter with the rich young ruler, Jesus was requiring an absolute surrender. To be a disciple means forsaking everything to follow Jesus, unconditionally, putting our lives completely in His hands. When we say that we want to be His disciple, yet attach a list of conditions, Jesus refuses to accept our terms. His terms involve unconditional surrender.

> "Then he called the crowd to him along with his disciples and said: 'If anyone would come after me, he must deny himself and take up his cross and follow me. For whoever wants to save his life will lose it, but whoever loses his life for me and for the gospel will save it. What good is it for a man to gain the whole world, yet forfeit his soul?'" (Mark 8:34–36)

These are tough words. No "prosperity gospel" here.

THE PRAYER OF JABEZ REVISITED

*Then he said to them all: "If anyone would come after me, he must deny himself and take up his cross daily and follow me. For whoever wants to save his life will lose it, but whoever loses his life for me will save it." —*Luke 9:23–24

A few years ago, when the phenomenal book *The Prayer of Jabez*² was published, I was eager to read it to see what everyone was talking about. The book is based on an obscure prayer found in the middle of a long section of genealogies in 1 Chronicles 4: "Oh, that you would bless me and enlarge my territory! Let your hand be with me, and keep me from harm so that I will be free from pain" (vv. 9–10).

The gist of the book was that if we would truly pray for God to bless us in this way, to be used by Him for the kingdom, good things would happen—God would "enlarge our territory," and we would be able to serve Him in a deeper and expanded way. Nothing wrong with that. But many who read the book interpreted it differently. Their understanding was that God intends to bless us with *things*, such as career success, financial gains, and other outward signs of prosperity—all we have to do is ask. For many, in fact, the book became a celebration of the "prosperity gospel"—the belief that God rewards faithful and sincere Christians with success, good health, and material prosperity.

But wait, I remember thinking. *If we truly pray for God to "enlarge our territory," does it follow that He will always bless us in ways that bring happiness, fulfillment, and material blessings? What about that verse about taking up our cross daily, or the one about dying to self? Look at the apostle Paul. Talk about having your territory enlarged! God made him Apostle to the Gentiles, used him to write half of the New Testament and to build and strengthen the early church in astounding ways—but it sure didn't result in a life of "sugar and spice and everything nice."*

True. Listen to what *really* happened to Paul when God expanded his territory:

I have worked much harder, been in prison more frequently, been flogged more severely, and been exposed to death again and again. Five times I received from the Jews the forty lashes minus one. Three times I was beaten with rods, once I was stoned, three times I was shipwrecked, I spent a night and a day in the open sea, I have been constantly on the move. I have been in danger from rivers, in danger from bandits, in danger from my own countrymen, in danger from Gentiles; in danger in the city, in danger in the country, in danger at sea; and in danger from false brothers. I have labored and toiled and have often gone without sleep; I have known hunger and thirst and have often gone without food; I have been cold and naked. (2 Cor. 11:23–27)

We might want to think twice before we ask God for that kind of blessing. The Bible is replete with those God used to do His will but who paid a great price. Ten of the twelve disciples died as martyrs for their faith. John the Baptist was beheaded by Herod. Isaiah was sawed in two. Over the centuries millions have been martyred for their faith in Jesus Christ, and many others have been afflicted. Joni Eareckson Tada, who now ministers to thousands, began her greatest ministry *after* her territory was enlarged— by a diving accident that paralyzed her. Chuck Colson, dynamic Christian speaker and founder of Prison Fellowship, got his "enlarged territory" only after he was convicted and sent to prison for crimes he committed during the Watergate scandal. Thousands of missionaries have lived difficult lives of sacrifice in relative poverty and deprivation as God expanded their work and ministries in the places where they served. God doesn't promise that all of His followers will be protected from hardship and suffering. Christians get cancer, lose loved ones, and suffer financial setbacks just like everyone else. But God can also use our tragedies to expand our territory in ways that show a skeptical world a different way to live.

Does God bless those of us who commit our lives to following Him? Of course He does. Sometimes He does bless us in material ways, with money, success, good health, and happy families, but those things are not guaranteed. Yet we are always blessed by God's love for us and the meaning He brings to our lives, whether in hardship or prosperity. God also blesses us through our sacrifices for Him as we feel the privilege of being a tool in His hand.

The Prayer of Jabez sold millions of copies to people who wanted to believe that Christians will not experience hardship or suffering. I don't believe this was the author's meaning. Nevertheless, I wanted to add another chapter to that little book, entitled "Counting the Cost," to help people understand that sometimes, in fact often, God's blessings come through our sufferings, not through our bank accounts—and I have the verses to prove it: "Dear friends, do not be surprised at the painful trial you are suffering, as though something strange were happening to you. But rejoice that you participate in the sufferings of Christ, so that you may be overjoyed when his glory is revealed. If you are insulted because of the name of Christ, you are *blessed*, for the Spirit of glory and of God rests on you" (1 Peter 4:12–14; emphasis added).

FRODO AND THE RING OF POWER

If money be not thy servant, it will be thy master. The covetous man cannot so properly be said to possess wealth, as that may be said to possess him. —Sir Francis Bacon

So here I was, the story of the rich young ruler burning in my head, with an uncomfortably similar decision to make. Now, remember, I hadn't even been offered the job at World Vision at this point; I had just been asked to allow my name to be considered as a candidate. By now you are probably thinking, *What is wrong with this guy? How hard could it be just to agree to be considered for a job that actually sounds like a phenomenal opportunity? Who wouldn't want to be president of World Vision?* I also want to acknowledge here, with some humility, how shallow this all seems even to me as I look back. Few people would have much sympathy for a fat-cat CEO who had to give up his bloated salary, oversized house, and fancy car. I wasn't being asked to give up everything and move to Sudan to live in a mud hut—I was being invited to move to Seattle to live in a very nice house and to undertake an exciting job with a generous salary. The "sacrifice" I was asked to make was significant only in my head. But you see, when things have become precious to us—whether our possessions, our work, our status and positions, or even our friends and families—we really don't want to let go of them. They can become idols that compete with God in our lives.

I am a huge *Lord of the Rings* fan. I have read the books several times and have watched the movies more than once as well. In the story, the Ring of Power has magical powers that, among other things, allow its wearer to become invisible. Ironically, though, whoever possesses the Ring ultimately finds that the Ring possesses him, as the allure of its power becomes too great to resist. The more one wears it and experiences its power, the harder it is to remove it or to part with it. The miserable Gollum, once so possessed by desire for it, had been reduced to a shriveled and pathetic creature who thought of nothing else but his "precious"—the One Ring. He had all but lost his humanity. Perhaps you can see the metaphor. There are things in our lives that can also "possess" us in an unwholesome way. For the follower of Christ, anything that becomes more precious to us than our relationship with the Lord becomes destructive. And like the Ring, these are often things that seem beautiful and shiny, that is, good and positive in our lives: career advancement, a growing bank account, our spouses and children. And these things may, indeed, be good, but they become stumbling blocks when they begin to possess us, when they divide our hearts and compromise our commitment to the Lord. "For where your treasure is, there your heart will be also" (Matt. 6:21).

In my own life, success, the prestige of my career, the admiration I felt from others because of it, and the financial prosperity that had come with it had become more and more important to my identity. Those things were especially appealing perhaps in part because of my financial insecurity as a child. Letting go of my own American Dream was not an easy thing for me to think about. But this was never something that was very noticeable—that is, until God asked me to lay my idols down at His feet. *Rich, are you willing to be open to God's will for your life?* Only then did I realize how controlling they had become.

In *The Lord of the Rings*, Gandalf the wizard tells Frodo, the story's hero, about the dangers he will face as the one who must bear the Ring of Power on a perilous journey. He warns Frodo of the great power the Ring has to possess the one who carries it. Frodo, of course, is skeptical; it's just a ring, after all. So, as a test, Gandalf challenges him to give up the Ring, to destroy it.

> "Try!" said Gandalf. "Try now!"
> Frodo drew the Ring out of his pocket again and looked at it . . . The gold looked very fair and pure, and Frodo thought how rich and beautiful was its colour, how perfect was its roundness. It was an admirable thing and altogether precious. When he took it out he had intended

to fling it from him into the very hottest part of the fire. But he found now that he could not do so, not without a great struggle. He weighed the Ring in his hand, hesitating, and forcing himself to remember all that Gandalf had told him; and then with an effort of will he made a movement, as if to cast it away—but he found that he had put it back in his pocket.

Gandalf laughed grimly. "You see?"[3]

That is how it was with the rich young ruler. He had gotten quite attached to his identity and his status, to the point that when Jesus asked him to sell everything he had and give to the poor, he could not. And that is how it was with me. The "Ring" had been on my finger for quite a few years, and I liked it. "Go, sell your possessions and give to the poor . . . Then come, follow me"—easier said than done.

SECOND PRIZE IN A BEAUTY CONTEST

Growth demands a temporary surrender of security. —Gail Sheehy

That phone call with Rob the recruiter did result in the two of us having dinner a couple of weeks later. We talked for four hours, covering every imaginable topic related to World Vision and me. At the end, Rob said he believed, contrary to my own opinion, that I would be a good candidate for consideration. He asked if he could add my name to his short list of fifteen candidates and present my background to the board of directors. "If this is God's will for your life, we'll find out. If it's not, we'll find that out as well. What've you got to lose?" Easy for him to say.

The next few months are a blur to me as I look back. It seemed that every few weeks Rob would call and say something like, "We're down to twelve, and you're one of the twelve." Then it was eight, and then it was four. I was getting nervous. Never had I wanted to finish second so badly in my life. Having once been president of Parker Brothers, I kept thinking of that Community Chest card in Monopoly that reads, "You have won second prize in a beauty contest! Collect $10." Then I could walk away with my head up and feel like quite the disciple for throwing my hat in the ring. I could show God that I was available to Him without having to actually do anything. The final four candidates (ironic, since the March Final

Four college basketball tournament was under way) were asked to fly to Chicago to be interviewed by members of the search committee.

I remember in every interview that day carefully explaining all of the reasons I was a bad choice and didn't have the experience necessary. In one session, Bill Hybels, a board member and the well-known pastor of Willow Creek Church, soberly informed me, "Rich, if you are selected for this job, you will have to travel to some of the worst places in the world. You will be exposed to heartbreaking things: children living in garbage dumps, women who have lost their children to disease, people on their deathbeds with AIDS. Are you comfortable with that?"

"Comfortable?" I gasped. "I am so *un*comfortable with that, I can't even express it! I am terrified! I am not the guy you want at your bedside in the midst of your suffering. I don't think God gave me the gift of mercy. Don't get me wrong; I have a tender heart—and cry at Disney movies. My heart breaks for children in need. But *comfortable?* No way. If you think you're hiring Mother Teresa, you need to know that you have the wrong guy."[4]

I was pretty sure that had done it. They would never pick me now. And so, I flew home, quite certain I had won second prize, maybe even third or fourth. You can imagine my surprise when Rob called me the next morning. He said that he had gathered the six board members together at the end of the day and asked them simply to write just their first choice on a slip of paper, fold it, and pass it to him with no discussion. He had then opened all six ballots—and found my name on all of them.

"What does that mean?" I asked incredulously.

"Congratulations!" he said. "You've got the job!"

"I *what?* But I don't want the job. I can't do this job. This can't be right." I should have known that something like this might happen. God never picks the person you or I would choose. He chose a posse of fishermen, tax collectors, and insurgents to be His disciples. He picked Paul, the greatest persecutor of Christians, to be Apostle to the Gentiles and to write most of the New Testament. He selected David, the runt of Jesse's litter, to be king over Israel, and Moses, a shepherd, to confront the most powerful man on earth, the Pharaoh, and to lead several hundred thousand Israelites out of slavery. God really seems to have a sense of humor about these things, so why not choose a guy selling luxury tableware to help the poor? Makes sense, right?

This verse from 1 Corinthians has become my life verse: "But God chose the foolish things of the world to shame the wise; God chose the weak things of the world to shame the strong" (1:27).

I remember saying to Rob that he had better keep their second choice on the hook because their first choice wasn't so sure this was going to happen. We then decided that Reneé and I would need to fly to Seattle for a series of fact-finding meetings and discussions before I made a final decision. World Vision had spent several months checking me out, but I had done almost nothing to check them out—denial, I guess. Now I needed to go out to World Vision's Seattle headquarters for my own due diligence. I had a thousand questions to ask before I was going to turn my life upside down.

But before I finish my story, I need to relate to you one more amazing thing that happened—the *same* day as our flight to Seattle. I had gone to the office early because, months earlier, I had invited an industry colleague who lived in London to visit and tour our Lenox offices. His name was Keith, and he was a wealthy investor who owned one of the prestigious British tableware companies. With so much on my mind, and the flight later that day to Seattle, I was distracted as I showed Keith around Lenox and then brought him back to my office for coffee. That's when he got up and closed the door, telling me he had a private matter to discuss with me.

With growing amazement I listened as Keith explained that he was planning to buy another large British tableware company and combine the two companies. The new company would be the largest of its kind in the world. And then he dropped the bombshell: he wanted me to join him as CEO. He said that he didn't want to bother hiring a recruiting firm because he knew that I was the best candidate for the job. I started to speak, but he stopped me and said that I needed to know one more thing: he would make me rich. He said he would offer me 10 percent ownership in this new enterprise, a stake easily worth $25 to $50 million, if I would agree to leave Lenox and serve as his CEO.

As you might imagine, events like this didn't happen every day in my life. I immediately remembered something Reneé had said to me about two months earlier, just as I had begun talking with World Vision. She said she believed that at the moment of decision, a great temptation would be put in my path—a financial lure—that would threaten to prevent me from going to World Vision. Now, remember, just six hours later I was going to be on a plane to Seattle to make my final decision.

I told Keith that I was stunned by his offer but that there was a complication. Even though no one at Lenox was aware of my discussions with World Vision, I decided to share my dilemma with Keith. Without naming the organization, I told him that my wife and I were committed Christians and that over the past few weeks I had been in discussions with a large charitable organization about becoming their president. I said that if I accepted the offer, it would be an opportunity for my wife and me to put our faith into action in a more direct way. And I told him that later that day I was flying out for my final interviews. Then I told him that if it didn't work out with the charity, I would be incredibly interested in his offer, but I had to finish the process with them first.

Keith seemed a bit taken aback and said that he was amazed that I would actually consider leaving my career at Lenox to work for a charity but that he admired me for considering such a move. And then he told me a story that became a direct message from God to Rich Stearns.

He confided that decades earlier, he and his wife were unable to have children, and they finally adopted a little girl from India. They raised her as their own until very suddenly, they lost her at the age of ten. He never told me how she died. The grief tore them apart, he lost interest in his businesses, and ultimately he and his wife separated. But then he told me that one day as he was going through his mail, he found an appeal from an organization called World Vision, which invited him to sponsor a child for twenty pounds a month. (I felt that shiver go up my spine again.) With excitement he wrote them a letter explaining the loss of his daughter and asking if it would be possible to sponsor a ten-year-old girl from the same region of India where his daughter had been born. Two weeks later he received a photo of his new "daughter," and for the next few years, he wrote to her and sent her presents regularly.

"Rich," he said, "somehow, by sponsoring that little girl, I was finally able to let go of my grief." Then he told me that the point of his story was that over the years he had become so impressed with this World Vision organization—that it wasn't easy to help the poor, but that he could see that they had solid experience, a thoughtful strategy, and people with the right skills to do it effectively. "So," he said, "I can see why a big charity like that might benefit from someone like you, Rich. But selfishly I hope you decide to come work with me."

Perhaps you can imagine my shock about what had just happened. This could be no coincidence. God was speaking to me through this amazing temptation, saying, *Do you see, Rich? Through World Vision I can touch the poorest of the poor, but also the richest of the rich. Are you willing to be open to My will for your life?* Somewhat hesitantly I told Keith that it was World Vision who wanted me to be their next U.S. president. The color seemed to drain from his face as we both realized what a bizarre happenstance this was. We ended our meeting, and I promised to call him in a few weeks, after my decision had been made. And then I left for the airport.

So that's how I ended up on a Friday afternoon, cowering beneath the blankets and whimpering.

After two days of meetings and a Saturday spent with a realtor, looking at potential neighborhoods where we might live—also depressing—we flew back home Sunday. I was so upset and conflicted about my decision that I actually called Rob's office that Sunday night and left him a voice mail. I was too much of a coward to talk to him. "I'm sorry," I said. "I should never have let this process go this far. It was a terrible mistake. I am not qualified, Rob, and I just have to say no and get on with my life. Forgive me."

When the young man heard this, he went away sad, because he had great wealth . . .

The next day I began several days of intense meetings at Lenox with the chairman of our parent company and other senior leaders. I had to get my head back in the game. I had to move on. Rob called again and again that morning and was told I was busy. I called him back at the end of the day, and we talked. I explained as best I could why I couldn't do the job and asked him what World Vision would do now. Rob, who was quite shaken by my decision, said they would have to start all over again, because the board had felt convinced that the other candidates were not the right fit. (*How bad could they be?* I thought. *Worse than Mr. Fine China?*)

I came home from work that night, ready to collapse in emotional exhaustion, when Reneé announced that it was the opening night of our church missions conference and that I needed to get ready to go. I couldn't think of anywhere I wanted less to be at that moment than at a missions conference, I told her. She said that she and our children were going, and that it would be nice if their father came and set a good example for them. And so I dragged myself into the car.

At the service that night, I was distracted and paid little attention to the speaker. He had rambled on about the world and the great need—a good setup for asking us all for our money. But when he closed, he didn't ask for money. Instead he took a surprisingly different approach. He said, with some drama, that he believed God was speaking to someone there in the sanctuary that night—that God was, in fact, *calling* that person, not just to write a check, but to go and serve. He said that all around the world, children were hungry and suffering; they needed help. They had never heard the gospel, and the Lord needed people to step up and go to them. The speaker then said that while the music played, his closing prayer would be that God would touch this person's heart. I couldn't believe it. I felt as though I were the only person in the sanctuary that night. How could he have known? I kept trying to run away, only to find God there waiting—and asking, *Rich, are you willing to be open to My will for your life?*

That night, after we got home and the kids went to bed, Reneé and I sat alone in the kitchen—and I lost it. I just broke down sobbing. (I tend to do that a lot.) Two months of interviews, anxiety, and emotional and spiritual tension had taken their toll. But one thing came to me that night, with perfect clarity. The speaker had talked about children hurting around the world. I remember thinking, *What if there are children who will suffer somehow because I failed to obey God?* Hadn't I always taught my kids that actions had consequences? *What if my cowardice costs even one child somewhere in the world his or her life?* I couldn't live with that thought; I just couldn't, and so I broke down. All of my careful posturing and rationalizing about not being qualified collapsed into dust. God had broken me, and I knew I could no longer run from Him. Reneé hugged me, and we cried together. She had been the strong one through all of this. She had said from the beginning, "We need to be where

> *What if there are children who will suffer somehow because I failed to obey God? What if my cowardice costs even one child somewhere in the world his or her life?*

God wants us to be, and if that's at World Vision, we will just go." How many wives of corporate CEOs would say that? "Go ahead; sell my dream house; yank my five kids out of school; move us to Seattle, where we don't know a soul; and reduce our income by 75 percent because God is telling you to do it. No problem." But that was Reneé. She had dreamed of helping the poor since she was a little girl, and this seemed like God's way for us to do it. God had known all along that she was the woman I would need to be the man He wanted me to become.

The next day I called Rob back and told him I couldn't sleep or eat or live with myself. I think I lost ten pounds that month, and lots of sleep. I told him that my family and I would be praying over the next few days and asked him to lead the committee in the same kind of prayer at their upcoming meeting. I told him I really wanted them to pray—not just for five minutes, but deep, long, and heartfelt prayer—that God would give them (and me) clarity. This was too important to do without seeking God, too momentous for World Vision to make a mistake. We agreed to talk again a few days later, after the meeting. And we did. They prayed, I prayed, Reneé and the kids prayed, and our couples Bible study group prayed—*everybody* prayed. My ten-year-old son, Pete, with a child's faith, said he thought he should fast while he prayed, so he did. A few days later, after the committee met, Rob called again. He said that the board had also prayed fervently about their decision. They had prayed for me, for the other candidates, and for God's leading in their deliberations. Rob told me that after their time of prayer, the board felt more certain than ever that God was calling me to World Vision. Finally, with a sense of resignation and surrender, I said, "Okay, then let's do it, and if it's a terrible mistake, let's pray that God will slam the door on it."

He didn't.

In April, I officially accepted the board's invitation.

In May, I resigned as CEO of Lenox.

In June, I started my new job as World Vision's U.S. president.

In July, the moving van pulled up to our two-hundred-year-old fieldstone farmhouse.

And in August, I was in the jungles of Uganda, with Richard and his orphaned brothers. I wondered if Richard was that one child I had worried about in my kitchen that night so long ago, the one who might die if I disobeyed God. I think God was showing me that he was.

PART 2

THE HOLE GETS DEEPER

For I desire mercy, not sacrifice, and acknowledgment of God rather than burnt offerings.

—HOSEA 6:6

The first Reformation . . . was about creeds; this one's going to be about our deeds. The first one divided the church; this time it will unify the church.

—RICK WARREN

CHAPTER FOUR

THE TOWERING PILLARS OF COMPASSION AND JUSTICE

*Hell will be full of people who thought highly of the
Sermon on the Mount. You must do more than that.
You must obey it and take action.*

—JOHN MACARTHUR

*In the end, we will remember not the words of our enemies,
but the silence of our friends.*

—DR. MARTIN LUTHER KING JR.

Are you willing to be open to God's will for your life? That question, and the events that followed, led me on a new pathway of discovery. Just what *was* God's will for my life? What did He expect of me? What does He expect from any of us who want to be followers of Christ and bearers of the gospel? Those expectations are not mysterious or difficult to discern. They are, in fact, etched clearly in page after page of Scripture—a bright thread of God's compassion for people and His zeal for justice:

> He has showed you, O man, what is good. And what does the LORD require of you? To act justly and to love mercy and to walk humbly with your God. (Micah 6:8)

Christ's mission statement, declared in a Nazareth synagogue and recorded in Luke 4, was just the tip of the iceberg in understanding what was missing from my interpretation of the gospel and what it meant for me personally. The Luke passage was the culmination and fulfillment of more than twenty centuries of God speaking to the nation of Israel through Moses and the prophets. The great themes of reconciliation, compassion, and justice are woven deeply throughout both the Old and New Testaments. An exhaustive analysis of these themes is beyond the scope of this book. But there are two remarkable passages that provide us with great clarity about God's expectations for those who claim to follow Him. They are found in Isaiah 58 and Matthew 25.

ISAIAH 58

The following passage from Isaiah is almost breathtaking in its splendor, its vision of God's kingdom, and what that vision might look like manifested in the lives and communities of His people. Written in the seventh century BC, Isaiah's book was addressed to a people in captivity, a chastened people who had been brutally conquered by Assyria as God's punishment for centuries of unfaithfulness and idolatry under a succession of corrupt kings. They were a nation at the end of their rope, desperately trying to "get right with God." Yet God judged their attempts at holiness to be shallow and insincere. They were just going through the motions of faithfulness—by praying, fasting, holding religious observances and ceremonies, and so on. God first derided their hypocrisy and then cast a soaring vision of what true faithfulness would look like:

> Shout it aloud, do not hold back.
> Raise your voice like a trumpet.
> Declare to my people their rebellion
> and to the house of Jacob their sins.
> For day after day they seek me out;
> > they seem eager to know my ways,
> > as if they were a nation that does what is right
> > and has not forsaken the commands of its God.
> > They ask me for just decisions
> > and seem eager for God to come near them.
> "Why have we fasted," they say,

"and you have not seen it?
Why have we humbled ourselves,
    and you have not noticed?" (vv. 1–3)

God here acknowledged that the people *appeared* to be seeking His will and His presence. Their self-image was that of a nation "that does what is right and has not forsaken the commands of its God." They even "seem[ed] eager for God to come near them." In fact, they were actually a bit angry with God, who appeared to be ignoring their fasting, worship, and prayers. But God saw through their veneer of religiosity.

Yet on the day of your fasting, you do as you please
    and exploit all your workers.
Your fasting ends in quarreling and strife,
    and in striking each other with wicked fists.
    You cannot fast as you do today
    and expect your voice to be heard on high.
Is this the kind of fast I have chosen,
    only a day for a man to humble himself?
    Is it only for bowing one's head like a reed
    and for lying on sackcloth and ashes?
    Is that what you call a fast,
    a day acceptable to the LORD? (vv. 3–5)

Yes, God was wise to Israel's superficiality. On the surface, they may have looked godly. But they hadn't changed their underlying behavior. God is never satisfied with rituals and liturgies when the hearts of His people remain corrupt. So He suggested in this passage something that ought to stun our own beliefs about prayer—that because of their hypocrisy, He would not even listen to their prayers! We take it as foundational that God will always listen to our prayers, but this passage suggests that we should not expect God to listen to prayers offered by insincere hearts. So, if God is *not* pleased with man's prayers and veneration, what *does* please Him?

Is not this the kind of fasting I have chosen:
    to loose the chains of injustice

and untie the cords of the yoke,
to set the oppressed free
and break every yoke?
Is it not to share your food with the hungry
and to provide the poor wanderer with shelter—
when you see the naked, to clothe him,
and not to turn away from your own flesh and blood? (vv. 6–7)

These words describe a people and a society characterized by justice, fairness, and a concern for the poor. They portray not just a personal ethic but also a community ethic. The reference to "break[ing] every yoke" suggests that any system, law, or practice that is unjust must be broken—whether personal, social, political, or economic. This sounds a lot like what I described earlier as the "whole gospel," the good news inherent in a kingdom based on the character of God rather than of men. And for this kind of kingdom community, a people whose actions demonstrate this level of authentic personal and social change, God offers this amazing promise:

Then your light will break forth like the dawn,
    and your healing will quickly appear;
    then your righteousness will go before you,
    and the glory of the LORD will be your rear guard.
Then you will call, and the LORD will answer;
    you will cry for help, and he will say: Here am I.
If you do away with the yoke of oppression,
    with the pointing finger and malicious talk,
and if you spend yourselves in behalf of the hungry
    and satisfy the needs of the oppressed,
    then your light will rise in the darkness,
    and your night will become like the noonday.
The LORD will guide you always;
    he will satisfy your needs in a sun-scorched land
    and will strengthen your frame.
You will be like a well-watered garden,
    like a spring whose waters never fail. (vv. 8–11)

What a promise! These words require little explanation. God will delight in His people when they obey Him. When the hungry are fed, the poor are cared for, and justice is established, He will hear and answer His servants' prayers; He will guide them and protect them, and they will be a light to the world. This is a vision of God's people transforming God's world in God's way. There is no hole in this gospel. This is what Jesus meant when He prayed, "Thy will be done in earth, as it is in heaven." Charity, equity, and mercy are the marks of the kingdom of the Messiah, and Christ wanted it to begin *on earth*.

Later in Jesus' public ministry, even John the Baptist began to doubt that Jesus was actually the Messiah, so he sent some of his own followers to Jesus for reassurance. They said, "John the Baptist sent us to you to ask, 'Are you the one who was to come, or should we expect someone else?'" (Luke 7:20).

Jesus answered by listing the signs that heralded the coming of the good news (the Messiah): "Go back and report to John what you have seen and heard: The blind receive sight, the lame walk, those who have leprosy are cured, the deaf hear, the dead are raised, and the good news is preached to the poor" (v. 22). Jesus encouraged John by pointing to the *tangible* evidence of the coming of God's kingdom through Himself—the Messiah.

If we are to be part of this coming kingdom, God expects our lives— our churches and faith communities too—to be characterized by these authentic signs of our own transformation: compassion, mercy, justice, and love—demonstrated *tangibly*. Only then will our light break forth like the dawn, our healing quickly appear, and our cries for help be answered with a divine *Here am I.*

MATTHEW 25

Here we find another towering landmark that helps us understand the fullness of the gospel and just what God expects of His followers. This is a remarkable account of the future day of judgment, after the risen Christ has returned. The implications of this passage would have been as stunning in Matthew's day as they are to us today. Read through it carefully.

When the Son of Man comes in his glory, and all the angels with him, he will sit on his throne in heavenly glory. All the nations will be gathered before him, and he will separate the people one from another as a shepherd separates the sheep from the goats. He will put the sheep on his right and the goats on his left.

Then the King will say to those on his right, "Come, you who are blessed by my Father; take your inheritance, the kingdom prepared for you since the creation of the world. For I was hungry and you gave me something to eat, I was thirsty and you gave me something to drink, I was a stranger and you invited me in, I needed clothes and you clothed me, I was sick and you looked after me, I was in prison and you came to visit me."

Then the righteous will answer him, "Lord, when did we see you hungry and feed you, or thirsty and give you something to drink? When did we see you a stranger and invite you in, or needing clothes and clothe you? When did we see you sick or in prison and go to visit you?"

The King will reply, "I tell you the truth, whatever you did for one of the least of these brothers of mine, you did for me."

Then he will say to those on his left, "Depart from me, you who are cursed, into the eternal fire prepared for the devil and his angels. For I was hungry and you gave me nothing to eat, I was thirsty and you gave me nothing to drink, I was a stranger and you did not invite me in, I needed clothes and you did not clothe me, I was sick and in prison and you did not look after me."

They also will answer, "Lord, when did we see you hungry or thirsty or a stranger or needing clothes or sick or in prison, and did not help you?"

He will reply, "I tell you the truth, whatever you did not do for one of the least of these, you did not do for me."

Then they will go away to eternal punishment, but the righteous to eternal life. (vv. 31–46)

The big picture here is quite plain to see. This is a glimpse of the final judgment (see Daniel 7:13–14) at the end of history, when Christ will sit on His throne and judge humankind. The people gathered before Christ will be divided into two clear groups, the sheep and the goats. But what is perhaps most surprising is that the criterion for dividing the two groups is not that the sheep confessed faith in Christ while the goats did not, but rather that the sheep had acted in tangible and loving ways toward the poor, the sick, the imprisoned, and the vulnerable, while the goats did not. Those whose lives were characterized by acts of love done to "the least of these" were blessed and welcomed by Christ into His Father's kingdom.[1] Those who had failed to respond, whose faith found no expression in compassion to the needy, were banished into eternal fire.

Surely this is another one of those passages that would be easy to cut from our Bibles. We would much rather believe that the only things needed for our salvation are saying the right words and believing the right things—not living lives that are characterized by Christ's concern for the poor. Why is this passage so sobering for us to read in the twenty-first century? Might it be that it hits us very close to home? Let me take some liberties and paraphrase these verses for today's reader:

> For I was hungry, while you had all you needed. I was thirsty, but you drank bottled water. I was a stranger, and you wanted me deported. I needed clothes, but you needed *more* clothes. I was sick, and you pointed out the behaviors that led to my sickness. I was in prison, and you said I was getting what I deserved. (RESV—Richard E. Stearns Version)

If we are honest, our response to the poor might sometimes be better described by this irreverent version. Whatever the case, Christ's words in this passage cannot be dismissed out of hand. We have to face their implications no matter how disquieting. God has clear expectations for those who choose to follow Him.

But I want to be clear that this does not mean we are saved by piling up enough good works to satisfy God. No, it means that any authentic and genuine commitment to Christ will be accompanied by demonstrable evidence of a transformed life. In contemporary terms, those who talk the talk but do not walk the walk will be exposed as false. "We know that we have come to know him if we obey his commands. The man who says, 'I know him,' but does not do what he commands is a liar, and the truth is not in him" (1 John 2:3–4).

These verses from 1 John, like many of the others discussed in this section, suggest something quite disturbing: that many who profess to follow Christ will be found, in the end, to be false, deceiving even themselves. However, I don't want to also suggest that all true followers of Christ must forsake everything to bring comfort and justice to the poor. I only propose that a genuine concern for "the least of these" that finds tangible expression must be woven into the pattern of their lives and faith. That expression might involve small but regular gifts to compassion ministries, advocating on behalf of the poor to government representatives, or regular volunteering at a soup kitchen, the local nursing home, or the Ronald McDonald House (where my wife and daughters Sarah and Grace are tonight, as I write this). Even Jesus did not spend every waking hour helping the poor. He dined with the wealthy, celebrated at weddings and feasts, taught in the synagogue, and perhaps even did a bit of carpentry. Still, there is no question that His love for the poor found consistent and concrete expression in His life and ministry. The question for you and for me is this: will Christ find evidence of our genuine concern for His beloved poor when He looks at the fruit of our lives on that day? Further, what might He be calling you to do *today*? What new steps of faith might you take to demonstrate your own concern for "the least of these"?

One last startling aspect of this passage is the remarkable claim of our Lord that "whatever you did for one of the least of these brothers of mine, you did for me" (Matt. 25:40). Even the good sheep in this passage were surprised at this. What they had seen as simple human gestures of love to the needy turned out to be gestures to a "Christ" incognito. Mother Teresa once said that in the faces of the poor whom she served, she saw "Christ, in His most distressing disguise."

In summary, we see throughout both the Old and New Testaments the bright thread of God's concern for the poor and the marginalized. We see in Christ's dramatic announcement of His messianic identity and mission in Luke 4 that He came "to preach good news to the poor" (v. 18). We learn that Christ's criterion for determining the authenticity of someone's profession to follow Him is whether or not he or she tangibly cared for those in need. And now we are told that when we do care for them, we are actually caring for Christ Himself—His identity merged with the least and the last. There is no "whole gospel" without compassion and justice shown to the poor. It's that simple.

Now the question is, have we in the twenty-first century *missed* something so simple and profound?

A MOST DISTRESSING DISGUISE

We gathered together in a group of about sixty—me, my wife, and my daughter Hannah, along with a few World Vision Uganda staff and perhaps forty children of various ages. We were waiting for them to arrive, planning to greet them with songs and celebration. We had been told they would arrive that morning.

As the metal gates creaked open, our anticipation grew—they were here. The SUV slowly pulled in, inched its way toward us, and finally came to a stop. Then the doors opened, and two teenage boys tentatively stepped out to face the crowd. I could see both fear and confusion on their faces—they clearly weren't expecting this kind of welcome, not for two mass murderers.

I don't think I've ever been to a place as spiritually dark as Gulu, in northern Uganda. Gulu is the epicenter of more than twenty years of violent atrocities committed by the so-called Lord's Resistance Army and its leader, Joseph Kony, a monster who has declared himself to be the son of God. If Satan is alive and manifesting himself in our world, he is surely present in this cultish and brutal group whose trademark is the kidnapping of children who are subsequently forced at gunpoint to commit murder, rape, and even acts of cannibalism. During his reign of terror, it is believed that Kony has kidnapped more than thirty-eight thousand children, killing some and forcing the rest to become killers themselves by conscripting them into the LRA as child soldiers.[2] As a part of their brutal indoctrination, the children are often forced to hack their own brothers or sisters to death with a machete—because bullets are too precious to waste—and then to drink the blood of those they have killed. The girls, often just twelve or thirteen, are gang-raped and forced to become sex slaves and "wives" to the rebel commanders. As a result of the LRA's grisly raids over two decades, some 1.5 million people have been driven from their land and forced to live in camps for internally displaced persons[3] in and around Gulu. It was in this unlikely backdrop that I witnessed the awesome power of the gospel that has become so tame to us in America.

For more than a decade, World Vision's Children of War Center has worked to rehabilitate and restore the children who are rescued or manage to escape from the LRA rebels. These are children with unimaginable spiritual, psychological, and emotional wounds, kids who are typically feared as monsters and rejected by the very communities they once came from because of what they have been forced to do. Sometimes their own parents do not want them back; their childhoods have been stolen from them and their very souls desecrated by horror after horror. Intense spiritual and emotional counseling, forgiveness and reconciliation, and even job skills training have been provided to thousands of these damaged children. The two boys entering the compound that day had also been subjected to the depredations of their own captivity by the LRA. They, too, had been forced to kill and maim.

Their eyes were hollow and vacant—eyes that had seen unspeakable things. Their souls seemed dead. I could see no life in them. *Jesus in His most distressing disguise.* They had been captured by the Ugandan army, and now they were being brought to World Vision for help, for redemption, for healing. They had names, Michael and Joseph.[4] Michael's left arm was withered, the result of a gunshot wound sustained before he was fully grown, in some past firefight. The LRA warned their child soldiers that they would be murdered by their own people if they ever tried to go home. They were even told that if they were taken to the Children of War Center run by World Vision, they would be poisoned—or worse. That is why these boys were terrified that day, stepping out of the car.

The forty other "children of war"—damaged souls all—surrounded them and began singing and clapping joyfully. These songs of praise to God, anthems of healing and forgiveness, were more beautiful than any choir of angels. Michael and Joseph were dumbstruck at this welcome, so different from what they had expected. They began to see faces they knew, other kids who had escaped—who had, like them, also known the brutal hand of the LRA and had murdered at their command. Some spark of light began to return to their hollow eyes. Hesitant smiles slowly turned up the corners of their mouths, as high fives and hugs were offered by this one and that. Soon all fifty of us poured into the makeshift chapel of corrugated tin and rough wooden benches in the compound. A spontaneous worship service erupted as the songs of God's healing forgiveness and power were sung over and over again. *Welcome home, welcome home, Michael and Joseph. You are home now.* The good news—the glorious, life-transforming gospel—washed over Michael and Joseph, and in that moment the unthinkable possibility of forgiveness broke over them like a new dawn. They *could* be forgiven, restored, made whole again. This was almost impossible to believe, the "glad tidings" so overwhelmingly good.

> He has anointed me to preach good news to the poor. He has sent me to proclaim freedom for the prisoners and recovery of sight for the blind, to release the oppressed, to proclaim the year of the Lord's favor. (Luke 4:18–19)

Even a small match lit in a place of total darkness gives off a blinding light. So great had Michael and Joseph's darkness been that the light of the gospel, the whole gospel, was brilliant and blinding, shining with intensity, authority, and hope. Jesus, too, had been abducted. He, too, had been beaten and maimed. And He, like them, had faced unspeakable evil—and defeated it. Jesus had made forgiveness possible.

It was Easter week, and two days later I was asked to preach at the chapel service at the Children of War Center, to the forty child "soldiers" who had found the meaning of Easter in one of the darkest corners of the world. I decided to speak on the parable of the prodigal son, of the father embracing his estranged boy, forgiving every transgression unconditionally, slaying the fatted calf, celebrating the lost son being found—and restoring him to his place at home, *welcoming* him home. As I preached, I watched Michael and Joseph, now just two more faces in the choir, as they listened to the message with a new hope in their eyes and fervent praise on their lips. Prodigal sons too, they were home now, in the arms of their Father. They had experienced the good news, the *gospel*, and found in it their own redemption—just as I had.

> But we had to celebrate and be glad, because this brother of yours was dead and is alive again; he was lost and is found. (Luke 15:32)

CHAPTER FIVE

THE THREE GREATEST COMMANDMENTS

Live as if Christ died yesterday, rose this morning
and is coming back tomorrow.

—MARTIN LUTHER

If we have missed something in the full understanding of the gospel, we are not alone. Sometimes the most difficult thing for a person of faith to see is the big picture. The Bible is filled with passages, parables, and principles that can and do help us with the everyday, small things of life. We go to church each week and hear a sermon on just a few verses out of two thousand (or more) pages. We spend so much of our time, therefore, looking at individual "trees" that we can easily miss the "forest" that defines the big picture of our faith.

With the great advantage of hindsight, we can read the Old Testament accounts of the nation of Israel and understand why God called them a "stiff-necked" people (see, for example, Exodus 32:9; 33:3, 5; and Deuteronomy 9:13). How many times did they fail to "get it" and, instead, chose to behave in such a way that God's judgment was brought upon them? Time after time following the Exodus, the people disobeyed the plain teachings of God—they worshiped a golden calf at Sinai just after witnessing God's power in bringing the plagues upon Egypt and miraculously parting the Red Sea. During the period of the kings, leader after leader in both Israel and Judah disobeyed God and led the people to disobey as well. In fact, in Judges, 1 and 2 Kings, and 1 and 2 Chronicles, the phrase "did evil in the eyes of the Lord" is used fifty times[1] to describe the behavior of both the kings and their subjects, God's *chosen* people! Every time I read these passages, I am bewildered by how clueless the people of Israel and Judah seemed to be, even though God had chosen them, given them the prophets, and dwelled among them. How could they miss the big picture so badly?

Fast-forward to the New Testament. After more than two thousand years of prophecy, the long-awaited Messiah finally arrived in the person of Jesus. But not only did the very people who had waited so long for their Savior fail to recognize Him, but their leaders—the high priest, the Pharisees, and the Sanhedrin—even conspired to have Him executed because He challenged the prevailing religious system. In fact, Jesus' strongest denunciations were directed not at thieves, murderers, and adulterers, but at the faith leaders of the day, the very men who had studied the Scriptures most (in today's terms, the pastors and seminary professors). Yet in just twenty-one verses (Matt. 23:13–33) Jesus called them hypocrites seven times, blind guides twice, blind fools, sons of hell, whitewashed tombs, snakes, and a brood of vipers! How had these men, steeped in the Law and the history of Israel, gone so wide of the mark? It is shocking to me that their spiritual blindness was so profound that they could crucify their own Messiah.

THE "BIBLE FOR DUMMIES"

At that time Jesus said, "I praise you, Father, Lord of heaven and earth, because you have hidden these things from the wise and learned, and revealed them to little children." —Matthew 11:25

Through storytelling (parables), Jesus made God's truth much more accessible and understandable to the common person. He taught in a way that did not require sophisticated theological scholarship to decipher the meaning behind His words. The Sermon on the Mount, for example, is beautiful in its simplicity. But on one occasion, Jesus made it even simpler. He had just been peppered by the Sadducees with detailed questions on the Law. Now the Pharisees wanted their shot at Him, to see if they could trip Him up: "Hearing that Jesus had silenced the Sadducees, the Pharisees got together. One of them, an expert in the law, tested him with this question: 'Teacher, which is the greatest commandment in the Law?'"

In a sweeping simplification of thousands of years of Jewish teaching, Jesus summed up God's law in a way that anyone could understand. He replied, "'Love the Lord your God with all your heart and with all your soul and with all your mind.' This is the first and greatest commandment. And the second is like it: 'Love your neighbor as yourself.' All the Law and the Prophets hang on these two commandments" (Matt. 22:34–40).

> If we truly love God, we will express it by loving our neighbors, and when we truly love our neighbors, it expresses our love for God.

Love God. Love your neighbor. That's it. That's the "Bible for Dummies."[2] How much simpler this must have been to the common folk who were being manipulated by the complexity coming from their teachers and leaders. (Incidentally, listen to what Jesus had to say about these teachers: "They tie up heavy loads and put them on men's shoulders, but they themselves are not willing to lift a finger to move them . . . Woe to you, teachers of the law and Pharisees, you hypocrites! You shut the kingdom of heaven in men's faces. You yourselves do not enter, nor will you let those enter who are trying to" [Matt. 23:4, 13].) These two commandments are from the Old Testament (Lev. 19:18; Deut. 6:5). The first—to love God with all of our hearts, souls, and minds— means that we must love God with our *whole* being—totally and completely. It sits above the many detailed requirements of the Old Testament Law, because it recognizes that all forms of obedience to God must first and foremost flow out of our love for Him. Christ's castigation of the Pharisees condemned their legalism devoid of any love, mercy, or justice.

Quite intentionally, Jesus then linked the second greatest commandment to the first by saying, "And the second is like it . . ." In other words, loving our neighbor as ourselves *is like* loving God with all of our being. So then, Jesus equated loving our *neighbors* with loving *God*. If we truly love God, He was saying, we will express it by loving our neighbors, and when we truly love our neighbors, it expresses our love for God. The two loves are fully interconnected and intertwined.

This connection is exactly what we just saw in Matthew 25, where the evidences of true faith were acts of love *for others* that Christ viewed as acts of love *for Him*. It is also the core of Isaiah 58, where God equated true fasting (authentic worship) with feeding the hungry, clothing the naked, and bringing justice to the poor.

Notably, both of these "greatest commandments" involve expressing love—to God *and* to our neighbors. Love is preeminent, and "all the Law and the Prophets" hang on these two statements about it (Matt. 22:40). In 1 Corinthians 13, Paul echoed this theme in the most beautiful language: "If I speak in the tongues of men and of angels, but have not love, I am only a resounding gong or a clanging cymbal. If I have the gift of prophecy and can fathom all mysteries and all knowledge, and if I have a faith that can move mountains, but have not love, I am nothing. If I give all I possess to the poor and surrender my body to the flames, but have not love, I gain nothing" (vv. 1–3).

So what, then, is the third greatest commandment? Here, I take a bit of liberty, but as the last command given to us by Christ prior to His ascension, the Great Commission must surely carry a weight similar to the first two commandments. If the mission Jesus announced in the Nazareth synagogue in Luke 4 described a social revolution with a vision for a changed world, Jesus' Great Commission, then, challenged His followers to take this revolution to all the nations.

> Then the eleven disciples went to Galilee, to the mountain where Jesus had told them to go. When they saw him, they worshiped him; but some doubted. Then Jesus came to them and said, "All authority in heaven and on earth has been given to me. Therefore go and make disciples of all nations, baptizing them in the name of the Father and of the Son and of the Holy Spirit, and teaching them to obey everything I have commanded you. And surely I am with you always, to the very end of the age." (Matt. 28:16–20)

This was a brand-new command at the dawning of a totally new age, to take the whole gospel to the whole world. This command to "make disciples" would first entail announcing the good news that Messiah had come to reconcile man to God, once and for all, through Christ's atoning death and the forgiveness of sins—for *all*, Jew and Gentile. The call to go out—to take Christ's message into the world—is a bookend to the momentous announcement in Luke 4 that Christ came to preach the good news to the poor, restore sight to the blind, release the captives, and proclaim the year of the Lord's favor. But it is more than a call to proclaim; it is a call to make disciples. (Disciples are those who, because of their belief, live lives of obedience to "everything [Jesus] commanded" [v. 19].) The first two commandments, then, call believers to love God and then love their neighbors, and the third one calls them to go and disciple *new* believers who will do the same.

So, in its simplest form, here is the answer to the question, what does God expect?

- We are to *love God*.
- We are to *love our neighbors*.
- We are to *go and make disciples of others who will do the same*.

The spread of the "kingdom of God" was to be carried out on earth by His Church, men and women commanded by Christ, empowered by the Holy Spirit, and dedicated heart and soul to the task. Jesus' followers were not to sit idly and await His return; they were to strike out boldly as the advance guards in a revolution that will only be completed upon His return, when all things will be restored and His kingdom made complete. The same is true today. We are not to give up on the world, nor retreat from it—just the opposite. We are to reclaim and redeem the world for Christ's kingdom.

As the Father has sent me, I am sending you. —John 20:21

My colleague Sam Kamaleson, an Indian pastor and evangelist who served with World Vision for decades, helped me see the Great Commission in its most clear-cut terms. He said that the Lord's command to go out and make disciples is a direct invitation to join God in what He is doing—a call to action. Speaking to each of us, God is saying, *You, Me, let's go! We have work to do, and it's urgent! Join Me!* How amazing to see our participation in kingdom work in this way—as God's *partners*. And if we really *are* partners with Him, then it follows that we are not to stand by, "looking into the sky" (see Acts 1:11) and casually waiting for Christ's return. No, we're to go about the Master's business, carrying the good news through our words and deeds, thereby ushering in the kingdom of God. When Christ returns, it will be to complete the work that we, His followers, have begun in His name. He will then make whole that which we have accomplished only in part. N. T. Wright, in his wonderful book *Surprised by Hope*, described our role in God's plan this way:

> But what we can and must do in the present, if we are obedient to the gospel, if we are following Jesus, and if we are indwelt, energized, and directed by the Spirit, is to build *for* the kingdom. This brings us back to 1 Corinthians 15:58 once more: what you do in the Lord *is not in vain*. You are not oiling the wheels of a machine that's about to roll over a cliff. You are not restoring a great painting that's shortly going to be thrown on the fire. You are not planting roses in a garden that's about to be dug up for a building site. You are—strange though it may seem, almost as hard to believe as the resurrection itself—accomplishing something that will become in due course part of God's new world. Every act of love, gratitude, and kindness; every work of art or music inspired by the love of God and delight in the beauty of his creation; every minute spent teaching a severely handicapped child to read or to walk; every act of care and nurture, of comfort and support, for one's fellow human beings and for that matter one's fellow nonhuman creatures; and of course every prayer, all Spirit-led teaching, every deed that spreads the gospel, builds up the church, embraces and embodies holiness rather than corruption, and makes the name of Jesus honored in the world—all of this will find its way, through the resurrecting power of God, into the new creation that God will one day make. That is the logic of the mission of God.[3]

This "mission of God" is now our mission, and the "whole gospel," the good news, is born out of God's love for us and ours for Him. That love, when demonstrated to the world through acts of kindness, compassion, and justice, is revolutionary; and when we become the agents of it, we make credible the message of a Savior who transforms men and women for eternity.

The kingdom of heaven has been forcefully advancing, and forceful men lay hold of it. —Matthew 11:12

THE WHOLE GOSPEL IN ACTION

How, then, can they call on the one they have not believed in? And how can they believe in the one of whom they have not heard? And how can they hear without someone preaching to them? And how can they preach unless they are sent? As it is written, "How beautiful are the feet of those who bring good news!" —Romans 10:14–15

We had traveled for some hours up the Mekong River in a wooden boat. Our purpose was to visit the pastor of a small house church, a man named Roth Ourng. Pastor Ourng was a small man with a big smile. He eagerly bade us to climb the stairs to his small bamboo house on stilts. Pastor Ourng's day job was rice farming, but he also pastored a small church of eighty-three members that he had started a few years back. His congregation met in his tiny home each Sunday morning to worship.

As we sat with Pastor Ourng, we talked about his community, his congregation, and farming. He was eager to know about churches in the United States and whether we had Bible commentaries and study guides that helped us understand Scripture. His only book was a Bible in the Khmer language, a treasure to him. "But," he said, "this is a difficult book, and I would love to have other books to help me understand it." I realized that in comparison, I lived in a nation literally drowning in Christian books, commentaries, and resources.

Pastor Ourng showed us the handmade two-stringed musical instrument that served as his church's "orchestra." For a wedding or special celebration, he said, his church would send runners to two different churches, thirty miles in each direction, to borrow their guitars. Then the next day they would run them back. This made me think of my own church's million-dollar pipe organ.

After a while I asked him, "Pastor, living in a country that is more than 90 percent Buddhist, how did you come to be a Christian?" The story he told me was confirmation of the power of the whole gospel in action.

"Five years ago," he said, "World Vision came to our community and began to work. I was suspicious of these outsiders to our community and was convinced that they had their own hidden agenda. You see, in Cambodia, since the genocide by the Khmer Rouge, we are always distrustful of strangers. But these people from World Vision [also Cambodians] set up a TB clinic to care for those suffering from TB. They improved the schools our children attended, and they taught better agricultural methods to the farmers to improve our yields. But I was still suspicious and even angry, convinced that they were up to no good. *Why would these strangers help us?* I thought.

"One day I decided to confront them, and I went to the World Vision leader and demanded to know why they were here. His answer took me by surprise. He said, 'We are followers of Jesus Christ, and we are commanded to love our neighbors as ourselves. We are here to show you that God loves you.'

"I said in response, 'Who is this Jesus Christ that you talk about?'

"The man went and got me this Bible that you see here today and gave it to me. He told me that everything about Jesus was in this book. That night I went home and read the book of Genesis. I was truly amazed because in this Genesis I met the God I had wondered about all of my life. I met here the God who created heaven and earth, the Maker of the universe. The next morning I ran back and told him what I had read but said that I still did not know this Jesus he talks about. He told me he would take me to the city to meet with a Christian pastor that would explain these things to me. Some weeks later he took me and my friend to meet the pastor. He opened his Bible and read to us many passages about Jesus and explained the good news of salvation. At the end, he asked if we wanted to become disciples of Jesus and commit our lives to Him. We both said yes and that day committed to follow Christ as our Savior."

I was overwhelmed by this man's story. His encounter with Christ began with Christians who came to serve the poor—nursing the sick, educating the children, and helping increase food for the hungry. So compelling was this service that it provoked questions in the mind of a curious man: *Why are you here? Why are you helping us?* The answer to these questions was the *gospel*, the good news.

"Pastor, that is a wonderful story," I said. "Now, what about the eighty-three people who worship at your church; how did *they* come to follow Jesus?"

"I was so excited to learn about Jesus," he said, "that I had to share this good news with everyone I knew. These eighty-three, they are my little flock."

Wow. There, in a bamboo house in Cambodia, I heard echoes of the Great Commission: "Go and make disciples of all nations, baptizing them in the name of the Father and of the Son and of the Holy Spirit, and teaching them to obey everything I have commanded you" (Matt. 28:19–20). And I knew I had just witnessed the *whole* gospel—in action.

CHAPTER SIX

A HOLE IN ME

Two roads diverged in a wood, and I—I took the one less traveled by. And that has made all the difference.

—ROBERT FROST

I believe in Christianity as I believe that the sun has risen: not only because I see it, but because by it I see everything else.

—C. S. LEWIS

At the outset, I stated that I have struggled all my life with the implications of the gospel of Jesus Christ. I have wrestled and continue to wrestle with all of the issues raised in this book. What is my responsibility for the poor? How should I use my money? How do I deal with my own self-centeredness? What does God expect of me if I claim to follow Him? Can I call Him "Lord," even when I don't always do what He says? What right do I have even to write a book like this, challenging others in *their* Christian walk? I have no theological degree or training. I spent most of my adult life climbing the corporate ladder, not helping the needy. I feel a bit like Paul, who called himself the "chief" of sinners (1 Tim. 1:15 NKJV), giving advice to other sinners—like one blind beggar helping another blind beggar find food. And yet God uses broken and imperfect people to challenge and inspire others. He utilizes our mistakes and our victories to shine a light on the path, so that others might follow. The transforming power of the gospel in the life of each person is a miracle. What He has done in my life is a miracle too.

In the end, responding to the gospel is not something meant for nations or communities or even churches; it is meant for individuals—one person at a time. The three greatest commandments—to love God, love our neighbors, and make disciples in all nations—are the work of God's people, those who have first responded to the good news themselves. It takes transformed people to transform the world. But each of us must first have our own "Damascus Road" experience, our "Thomas moment," in which our doubts fall away and we drop to our knees and acknowledge *our* Lord and *our* God (see Acts 22:1–11 and John 20:24–28). Only then does the journey of faith truly begin.

DREAMING OF THE IVY LEAGUE

I can remember the night when I first understood that my parents could not help me. The memory still shines brightly. I was ten years old and lying in bed. The angry argument from the kitchen caused me to shrink beneath my covers. I felt safe as long as I hid there. My father had come home drunk yet again after several days of absence. I could not blame my mother for venting her anger and fear. Her world and her marriage were coming apart. The money had run out, the bank was about to foreclose on our house, and my father had again abandoned her and her two children for three days of drinking, escape, and presumably, other women.

At ten, a child does not understand these things. But he feels them. That night I felt unsafe, insecure, vulnerable, as if the floor beneath me was collapsing and I was starting to fall. No one could catch me. And that's when I understood. *They can't help me—not anymore.* It wasn't that my parents didn't love me, because they did. It was just that their lives, their problems, were so out of control that they could not even help themselves, let alone my sister and me. And so I understood that it was now up to me. I would have to be in charge of myself. If there was a way out of my situation, I would have to find it. And curiously, that realization gave me a sort of comfort. *I can do this.* Others might let me down, but I would never let myself down.

I began planning the things that would have to happen. First, I would have to survive my childhood—to be strong enough emotionally to weather my parents' separation, the bankruptcy, the eviction from our home, and the series of rented houses and apartments that would follow. I would have to live a life within the dysfunction of my home that would get me through it all intact. I remember thinking, *Eight years. That's how long I have to make it.* At eighteen I could be on my own. If I could just make it until then.

But then what? What would make my life turn out any better than my parents' had? School, I reasoned. Neither my mother nor my father had finished high school, my dad dropping out in the eighth grade. I had never seen either of them read a book. Yet how often had I heard people say that an education could be one's ticket to success? I knew then that *I* would have to get an education. None of these thoughts were crystal clear in my child's mind, but a plan began to take shape, and it developed year by year.

And that is why, at the age of thirteen, I typed letters to all eight Ivy League colleges, asking for their course catalogs. While other kids were presumably dreaming of becoming baseball players or firefighters, I was staying up at night and leafing through Princeton's and Cornell's course rosters, believing that maybe, someday . . .

I was never tempted by the alcohol and drugs that seemed to intrigue many of my classmates. Why would I touch the things that had devastated my father, as well as the rest of my family? I was on a mission and would not be distracted by such things.

After losing her marriage and her house, my mother rented a place and went to work at General Electric in a clerical job. Coupled with some erratic support from my father, this was enough to keep us in the same general neighborhood and school district for the next few years, which was a huge relief. At least that part of my life could remain intact while the rest of it unraveled.

My self-reliance grew through my teenage years. Perhaps even more than most teenagers, I became a know-it-all. I had gone through first Communion and confirmation in the Catholic Church, at the urging of my parents, but they themselves never darkened the church door. My father's previous two marriages and divorces had made both of my parents feel unwelcome and uncomfortable in the church. So, at age fifteen I announced abruptly that I would no longer go to mass either—that was for old ladies with rosaries, not budding intellectuals like me. The way I saw it, the Church was full of hypocrites and weak-minded people who needed a crutch— which I certainly did not. Besides, my new religion of self-reliance seemed to be working. I had a plan for my life, and I didn't need anyone else's help.

My sister, Karen, though, six years older, was a great encouragement. She, fighting the same odds as me, had gone to college and done well. She lived at home and managed to graduate from LeMoyne College in Syracuse with high honors, becoming a high school English teacher upon graduation. Even today she calls me her first student. Karen helped me keep my dreams alive and my homework done, and by my senior year I had managed to graduate at the top of my class. But the Ivy League seemed more and more out of reach. Could a kid from Syracuse, New York, who had never traveled to another state, really go off to Harvard or Princeton? Weren't these schools for the children of the wealthy? When I told my mother I planned to go to one of those schools, I remember her laughing. "That's nice," she said. "Who's going to pay for it? Not me, and certainly not your father!"

Perhaps *I* could. From the age of fourteen, I had worked odd jobs as a paper boy, as a grocery bagger, at the local movie theater, and even cleaning toilets in a nursing home (talk about starting at the bottom), saving every penny I could. But by age eighteen those savings amounted to just twelve hundred dollars, less than one semester of tuition at an Ivy League college.

Still, I applied to one of the Ivies—but just one: Cornell University, fifty miles from Syracuse. In the end, my dream was not big enough to imagine going farther, but Cornell, being so close, seemed possible. My best friend, Jon, had also chosen Cornell, which also made it seem doable. To my amazement (and my mother's) I was accepted and received a New York State Regents scholarship, a Cornell Engineering scholarship, and the largest student loan allowed. That September my father drove me the fifty miles to Ithaca and dropped me off. We stopped for breakfast at a diner along the way, and I remember him saying he was proud of me. He didn't come back again until I graduated four years later. But I was on the launchpad. So far, so good. I had made it.

A BLIND DATE—WITH GOD

Brothers, think of what you were when you were called. Not many of you were wise by human standards; not many were influential; not many were of noble birth. But God chose the foolish things of the world

*to shame the wise; God chose the weak things of the world to shame the
strong. He chose the lowly things of this world and the despised things—
and the things that are not—to nullify the things that are, so that no
one may boast before him.* —1 Corinthians 1:26–29

"God loves you and has a wonderful plan for your life." She smiled at me,
holding a small pamphlet in her hand as she read these words.

"You're kidding," I remember saying.

"No," she said, "I'm actually quite serious. May I continue?"

She was beautiful, blonde, nineteen, a freshman at Cornell, and we were
on a blind date. Six weeks later I would graduate and head off to my second
Ivy League school, the University of Pennsylvania's Wharton School of
Business, to pursue my MBA. I didn't know about God's plan for my life,
but my own plan was right on track.

My four years at Cornell had been amazing. They had fulfilled even
my loftiest expectations in enabling me to overcome my shaky childhood
to become whatever I wanted to be. Looking back, I don't know how I made
it financially through those four years. I did graduate with a mountain of
debts, but I had my "ticket." It was off to the Wharton School for me, and
then on to corporate America, the American Dream come true—*my* American Dream. I had majored in neurobiology, of all things. I loved the cer-
tainty and logic of the sciences. My personal religion of self-reliance resonated
well with social Darwinism—survival of the fittest. The strong prevail! I
was succeeding because I was tough, smart, and independent. And I had
done it, as Frank Sinatra once crooned, "my way."

So here I was, on a blind date arranged a couple of weeks earlier by
another freshman girl. She had been at my fraternity, talking about her
roommate, Reneé, the "Jesus freak." Apparently she thought that what her
roommate needed was a good dose of someone like me, a frat guy who was
anything *but* a Jesus freak. It seemed that I was always stumbling across these
Christians. The girl I dated in high school had come from the Christian
elite, with two grandfathers who were ministers and an uncle who sang
with the Billy Graham Crusade. She and I had argued about it on and off
for the two years we dated. But I was a hardened skeptic, and she ultimately
gave up on me. She gave me a book to read that she said would "explain it
all," but I didn't read it—not then.

Then I went on to Cornell, and on my first night I found myself standing at the end of my dorm hall, watching all the freshmen get drunk. Another freshman, Dave, was standing beside me. We were the only two not drinking. I knew why I wasn't, but I wanted to know why *he* wasn't, so I asked him.

"I'm a Christian," he said. "How about you?"

"My father is an alcoholic," I answered. So Dave and I became friends for the next four years. I don't know how many nights we sat up, arguing about whether Christ was God. I couldn't understand how my otherwise brilliant friend could believe that someone actually rose from the dead. To me, that was as ludicrous as the Easter bunny. I think I may have been the most frustrating part of Dave's four years at Cornell. I'm pretty sure he gave up on me too.

But now, here was *another* Christian. I had taken her to a movie, and afterward we had walked to a little coffee house on campus. (There were limitations when planning a date with a "Jesus freak.") We had made some small talk, but that had run out. It was in that awkward pause that she had reached into her purse for the pamphlet. It was Campus Crusade's *Four Spiritual Laws*, an evangelism tool. I had seen it before.

"God has a wonderful plan for your life," she said.

"You've got to be kidding." But she was quite serious. I told her to go ahead, take her best shot, and that I had heard it all before but would be happy to talk with her about it. So she took me through the whole deal, one page at a time, and then we started to discuss it. I gave her my "Easter bunny" line, which she didn't appreciate. But we ended up having a great conversation about God and truth and values. I hadn't had many talks with girls like that. Being twenty-two and *so* much older than she was, I asked what she wanted to do when she "grew up." She didn't appreciate that either but said that she knew exactly what she wanted to do—she had known since she was ten. She was going to become a lawyer and help the poor with their legal problems. That impressed me, and I thought it was nice.

"I'm going to become a CEO and make a lot of money," I said. (That *didn't* impress her.) Then I walked her home and went back to my own apartment, but I kept thinking about Reneé. She was different.

Improbably, we started seeing each other—often. "By accident" I would find her studying and would sit down beside her, pretending to study myself.

Soon I'd persuade her to take a break and get a cup of coffee. We'd go for walks outside as the days got sunny, and occasionally we'd drive to a nearby park. Springtime and romance are powerful companions, and within a few weeks we found ourselves falling in love, despite our clashing worldviews. Things would go along just fine until that awkward topic—God—came up. Whenever that happened, we would argue, tempers would flare, and feelings would be hurt. So we avoided talking about it as much as we could.

Tragically, just at the end of the school year, her father died suddenly of a heart attack, and she immediately flew back home to California. She had been very close to her dad and loved him deeply. His sudden death when she was only nineteen was devastating. It may have been that tragedy that ultimately drew us even closer. Our relationship took on a deeper and more personal complexion as I tried to walk with her through her loss. We wrote every day that summer, covering all kinds of issues and able to discuss matters of faith in a less threatening way than we had in person. At the end of the summer, I flew to California to spend some time with her before school resumed.

And then my American Dream, part 2, began as I enrolled at the Wharton School of Business in Philadelphia that fall, bankrolled by yet more scholarships and loans. Reneé and I maintained a long-distance relationship over the ensuing months, still writing and seeing each other every few weekends. But one weekend in November our repressed religious differences blew up. We had a terrible argument that led me to make some hurtful and foolish statements. "I will never, *ever* become a Christian," I told her, "and you had better accept that. It would take a walking-on-water, water-into-wine miracle for me to change my mind. I'm sick of arguing about it, so you have a choice to make: it's me or God." Even today I cringe at the arrogance of those words. But they were the inevitable ultimatum from one who had built his own religion around himself. What had begun as a way for a young boy to survive a rough childhood had flowered into a virulent religion of self, and now it was becoming self-destructive.

Reneé knew what she had to do. "You have made my choice an easy one," she said. "I never should have let this relationship develop. I knew in my heart it would not work. I could never marry someone who does not share my faith in Christ." And then it was over. With sadness and tears, we parted.

A HOLE IN MY WORLDVIEW

But the one who hears my words and does not put them into practice is like a man who built a house on the ground without a foundation. The moment the torrent struck that house, it collapsed and its destruction was complete. —Luke 6:49

It was an ordinary night, a couple of months later. I was on break, back in Syracuse, staying at my father's apartment for a few days. He still drank and had a succession of roommates—drinking buddies who sometimes shared his third-story walk-up. Most nights I would escape from that depressing scene by calling some friends and going out on the town. But on this particular night no one was around. I checked the TV listings and found nothing of interest there. I ended up rummaging through a box of books from college, stored in a closet.

That's when I pulled out *Basic Christianity*, by John R. W. Stott,[1] and thumbed it open. On the flyleaf I found a note from my high school girlfriend. "Richard," it said, "I hope you read this. It explains what I believe better than I can."

Huh, I thought. *I wonder what this guy has to say about the Easter bunny.*

Now, reading a book on theology on a Saturday night was, for me, a bit of a miracle. To this day I can't explain why I did it, but I started to read that book. Remarkably, I found that I couldn't put it down, and seven hours later, at four in the morning, I had finished it and sat trembling on my bed. What I had read had shaken me deeply. Somehow that night God had gotten hold of me, and the truth had come shattering into my life. My self-important, self-reliant, scientific worldview had been assaulted. I felt like a man at sea whose life raft had sunk, casting him into the waves with nothing left to hold onto.

I did not become a Christian that night. After so many years of skepticism, I would need much more intellectual "proof" before I could put my faith in anything other than myself. My years studying the sciences at Cornell had helped me build quite the rationalistic fortress against anything supernatural. But if I was honest with myself, despite the many courses that had taken me deeper and deeper into the inner workings of the natural world, a gnawing unease remained. I could give you a detailed explanation of photosynthesis, but still could not explain the beauty of a flower. I could tell you about phylogeny, ontogeny, and genetics, but I could not explain the miracle of a simple butterfly. I could read about the solar system, the life cycles of stars, and the big bang, but I could not explain how they had all come to be in the first place. There was a cavernous hole in my worldview that I had conveniently ignored.

Why are we here? Where did we come from? How do we explain the beauty and order and complexity we see all around us? Where do our notions of good and evil come from? What happens when we die? These are the questions that make even atheists and agnostics uncomfortable, because they have no real answers for them. That little book I found in my closet seemed to have the answers. The author had made a powerful, intellectually rigorous argument that the claims of Christianity were true—that Christ was a historical person who lived, died, and, yes, rose from the dead; that God was active in creation; and that it was possible to know Him. In this worldview, everything fit.

The next day, in a panic, I went out to a bookstore and looked for the religion section. I think I bought a dozen books on comparative religion, archaeology, theology, history, science, and Scripture. I voraciously read and studied anything I could get my hands on. A few days later I called Reneé in California. "Oh, it's you," she said. "I didn't expect to hear from you. Why are you calling?"

"I just wanted to tell you I've been reading up on the Easter bunny business, so the next time I see you, I'll have better arguments." She was not amused. "Seriously," I said (before she could hang up on me), "I started reading about all of this and wondered if you had any books you'd recommend."

"How about the Bible?" she answered. Amazingly, after five years in college, I didn't really know what the Bible even was. I recognized it was a religious book, but I knew almost nothing about what it said. Like many agnostics and atheists, I had rejected a book I had never read.

"Okay, where would I get one of those?"

She assured me that any bookstore would have one and that I should start reading the gospel of John first. So I bought myself a paperback Bible and added that to my reading list.

Over those next few months, I read more than fifty books. I felt like a private detective trying to unlock a mystery. For the first time in my life, I was actually searching for the truth instead of making up my own. Reneé and I would speak periodically, and I would pepper her with my new questions. She told me that her sorority sisters were praying for me, which made me mad. "I don't want your silly sorority sisters praying for me. I have to do this on my own!" (I even tried to be in charge of my own salvation!) But meanwhile, with every book I read, new questions were answered and puzzle pieces fell into place. I began to see the order and beauty and credibility of God's intricate truth.

Then, one ordinary day, I closed the last book, and I knew: it was true. Oh, there was still a leap of faith involved; there always is. But my investigation of the life of Christ and the compelling events surrounding that life had made the leap quite small. I was now convinced intellectually that the claims of Christianity were valid. They withstood the test of logic and historical analysis and did not require committing intellectual suicide to believe. Like the Cambodian pastor I would meet years later, I had found the God I always wondered about. It was this God who had created the incredible universe I had studied in my classes at Cornell. Inexplicably, God had become a man who lived and loved and died for me. More important, my sins of pride, arrogance, selfishness, and presumption could be forgiven.

But I also knew that I had a stark choice to make. I could accept the astonishing truth and commit my life to following Jesus Christ—or I could turn my back on God, walk away from something I knew to be true, and spend the rest of my life living a lie. There was no partial step I could take. Either Jesus would be the most important truth in my life, governing all that I would ever do, or I would go it alone, doing everything my way. He did say, "I am the way and the truth and the life. No one comes to the Father except through me" (John 14:6).

BETTING THE FARM

He is no fool who gives what he cannot keep to gain what he cannot lose.
—Jim Elliot

The thing about truth that is most annoying is that it is *true*, making anything that contradicts it *false*. Christ is either God incarnate, risen from the dead, or He is not. There is no halfway position here. If He is not, then His teachings hold no more authority than those of Confucius, Dr. Phil, or Oprah. We can take them or leave them. But if Christ is God, it changes everything—there is nothing more important, more authoritative, or more central to the human race, to the way we live our lives, and to our very understanding of the world. Christ is an all-or-nothing proposition, and one way or another, every one of us has already made a choice about Him. We have either committed our lives to Him wholeheartedly, or we have not.

> Christ is an all-or-nothing proposition, and one way or another, every one of us has already made a choice about Him. We have either committed our lives to Him wholeheartedly, or we have not.

Maybe you have rejected Christ outright, as I did for so many years. You've decided that you have a better answer to those troubling questions about why we are here and where we are going. Or perhaps you affirm the importance of Christ in the same way that you would your political party or favorite sports team. He occupies one room in the "house" of your life, but He's not the foundation upon which the whole house stands.

Or maybe you're someone who hides behind the veil of agnosticism, saying, "I'm not really sure." You've simply postponed the decision, deciding to not decide—which is itself a decision. Or perhaps you've shaped God to conform to your own values, making Him a "rubber stamp" for whatever you think is best for you.

For me, the decision to choose Christ was not a small one. I knew what it meant. In this kind of faith commitment, nothing is held back, no price is too high to pay, the farm is bet, and the deed is signed over. If Christ is Lord, then nothing He asked us to do is optional. His teachings become the operating system of our lives. So central was this truth that every action, every decision, every aspect of my life would now have to be defined by Him.

And so that day, in my room and by myself, I did what "doubting Thomas" had done so many centuries before. I fell to my knees and said, "My Lord and my God." I asked to be forgiven for my arrogance and unbelief, and I committed my life from that day forward to the service of Christ. There was no choir of angels, no dramatic epiphany, but I knew my life had changed forever. The gospel, the good news of God, had entered my life with power, and nothing since has ever been the same. The hole in me had been filled.

POSTSCRIPT

Reneé and I started dating again as we celebrated my new faith, and we began to redefine our relationship with Christ at the center. I had been quite deliberate about making sure I did not become a Christian for the wrong reason: to reconcile with her. I had to make my decision based on whether Christianity was true. Still, I am convinced that her courageous decision to walk away from the man she loved because she loved God even more played a role in my own coming to faith. God honored her decision to choose Him and ultimately gave her the desire of her heart. We both had a sense that God had done something miraculous and sacred in our relationship. The love that we now shared seemed so much deeper and more vivid than what we had experienced before. It was not just emotional and sentimental anymore; it now had a spiritual dimension—like a circle that had become a sphere, or a black-and-white photo that suddenly gained full color. We got engaged about seven months after I accepted Christ and were married immediately after we both finished school in June 1975. Ours was a love story for which God Himself provided the happy ending.

"WHY DO YOU CALL ME, 'LORD, LORD'?"

And so began my own walk of faith, with a decision—and a commitment—to literally change everything in my life based on a radically altered worldview. I had crossed over from unbelief to belief, but this was just the first step. The real journey of faith requires that our choices, our actions, and everything else in our lives be surrendered to God's will rather than our own. For the Christian, it is a lifelong process. Belief—that is, faith—is just the beginning. Yes, we must *believe* that Christ loves *us*, but Christ also calls us to *demonstrate* His love to others through the good things that we do, what the Bible calls "works." Faith without works is no faith at all. But authentic faith, rooted in the heart of God, is expressed in deeds done to ease the pain of others; it is imbued with personal sacrifice, and it comes with a cost.

Jesus understood that not everyone who called Him "Lord" would truly surrender their lives in sacrificial service, and He reserved some of His strongest words for those who professed to be His followers but whose lives showed no evidence of their faith. Surely this is one of the hardest things ever said by Jesus to those who claimed to follow Him: "Why do you call me, 'Lord, Lord,' and do not do what I say?" (Luke 6:46). Each time I read these words, I tremble.

He could not have been any more direct. Jesus was telling not only His hearers but all who would someday read His words that if we dare to call Him Lord, then He expects us to do what He says. In other words, once we *believe* that Jesus is Lord, then our lives must change; we must *do* as He commanded.

Just before asking this demanding question, Jesus used a metaphor of a tree bearing fruit to teach His followers, then and now, how to recognize the *true* servant of God: "No good tree bears bad fruit," He said, "nor does a bad tree bear good fruit. Each tree is recognized by its own fruit" (vv. 43–44). His true disciple, then, like the good tree, will bear good fruit. It follows that one who does *not* bear good fruit is not Christ's disciple at all. This is not an argument that salvation comes through works, but rather an assertion that one who has committed his life to Jesus will bear quality fruit as evidence of the lordship of Christ. These good works are not superficial but are instead the natural fruits of those who have truly embraced and internalized the radical message of the Sermon on the Mount, immediately preceding Jesus' question in Luke 6. What Jesus was calling for was nothing less than a repudiation of the status quo, far beyond doing a few good deeds. His followers were to love their neighbors *and* their enemies, turn the other cheek, give to the poor, avoid judging others, forgive those who have wronged them, and store up their treasure in heaven, using their money to further the kingdom of God. Those who could legitimately call Jesus "Lord" were to be willing to let the Holy Spirit change everything, from the inside out. The same is true today.

In the parallel passage, found in Matthew 7, Jesus got more explicit about the non–fruit-bearing trees, that is, the people who call Him "Lord" but do not do His will:

Every tree that does not bear good fruit is cut down and thrown into the fire. Thus, by their fruit you will recognize them. Not everyone who says to me, "Lord, Lord," will enter the kingdom of heaven, but only he who does the will of my Father who is in heaven. Many will say to me on that day, "Lord, Lord, did we not prophesy in your name, and in your name drive out demons and perform many miracles?" Then I will tell them plainly, "I never knew you. Away from me, you evildoers!" (Matt. 7:19–23)

Does this harsh warning cause you to tremble as it does me? It should. It is the same message we heard in Matthew 25, when the sheep were separated from the goats based on their response to the poor and the sick. Is it possible that many who today profess to be Christians will one day be told, "I never knew you; go away, evildoers!"? Evidently. Jesus was clearly saying that only those of us who do His Father's will can enter the kingdom of heaven.

But is this just one short passage that, perhaps, we could disregard if it doesn't suit us? Is it without support elsewhere in Scripture? Unfortunately, if we want to cut verses like this out of our Bibles, we have a lot more cutting to do.

In the book of James, we find another direct correlation between our faith and our works. The apostle put it pretty succinctly: "Do not merely listen to the word, and so deceive yourselves. *Do what it says*" (James 1:22, emphasis added). James then went on to put a bit more flesh on the bones of this blunt demand:

What good is it, my brothers, if a man claims to have faith but has no deeds? Can such faith save him? Suppose a brother or sister is without clothes and daily food. If one of you says to him, "Go, I wish you well; keep warm and well fed," but does nothing about his physical needs, what good is it? In the same way, faith by itself, if it is not accompanied by action, is dead.

But someone will say, "You have faith; I have deeds." Show me your faith without deeds, and I will show you my faith by what I do.

You believe that there is one God. Good! Even the demons believe that—and shudder. (2:14–19)

Here James stated in black and white that belief is not enough. It must be accompanied by faith *demonstrated by actions*. My former pastor and good friend Gary Gulbranson once said, "It's not what you believe that counts; it's what you believe enough to do." I think James would have liked Gary's understanding of the gospel in action.

Let's look at what the apostle John had to say: "We know that we have come to know him if we obey his commands. The man who says, 'I know him,' but does not do what he commands is a liar, and the truth is not in him. But if anyone obeys his word, God's love is truly made complete in him. This is how we know we are in him: Whoever claims to live in him must walk as Jesus did" (1 John 2:3–6). Read that again and let it sink in. Our obedience is the way we determine whether or not we really know God.

> It's not what you believe that counts; it's what you believe enough to do.

If we claim to know Christ but do not do what He commands, John said that we are liars!

And just one chapter later John got even more specific about what obedience might look like, linking it with how we use our *wealth*:

This is how we know what love is: Jesus Christ laid down his life for us. And we ought to lay down our lives for our brothers. If anyone has material possessions and sees his brother in need but has no pity on him, how can the love of God be in him? Dear children, *let us not love with words or tongue but with actions and in truth*. This then is how we know that we belong to the truth, and how we set our hearts at rest in his presence whenever our hearts condemn us. (3:16–20; emphasis added)

The conclusion is inescapable. Jesus asks much more of us than just believing the right things.

Think for a moment of your life as a house with many rooms. Your faith cannot be just one more room in the house, equal with your job, your marriage, your political affiliation, or your hobbies. No, your faith must be like the very air you breathe, in *every* room of the house. It must permeate not just your "Sunday worship," or even your vocation and your behavior at home, but also your dealings with *everyone* around you—including the poor. That's how deep the commitment must be.

So what does God expect of you, then? Everything.

CHAPTER SEVEN

The Stick in Your Hand

A holy life will produce the deepest impression.
Lighthouses blow no horns; they only shine.

—D. L. MOODY

If God only used perfect people, nothing would get done.
God will use anybody if you're available.

—RICK WARREN

My conversion to Christianity that day in a college dorm and my subsequent commitment to God became the compass that guided me through the next two decades of my life, my marriage, and my career. Those who knew me saw that I had changed. In fact, fraternity brothers scoffed, saying that it wouldn't last six months, but it did. Yet while some changes happened right away, others took years. Becoming a follower of Christ is a lifelong process of growing, learning, and changing. It is also a process of surrender. For me, because of my years of determined independence, that surrender has been a continuing battle for control.

A fitting metaphor for the Christian walk is that of enlisting in the army. Upon enlistment, the soldier immediately surrenders control of his or her life. Where the enlistee lives, when he or she moves, what clothing will be worn, how that enlistee will behave, and what he or she will do— *all* of these things are given over to the commanding officers to decide. Becoming a Christian requires a similar surrender—except that no one is *ever* drafted; it's always voluntary, and it takes longer to realize than a four-year enlistment. The truth is that surrender is not an easy thing to do. But without that surrender a soldier is not useful to the army, and a Christian is not useful to God.

Earlier I mentioned that one of the most powerful reasons we don't totally surrender our lives to Christ is that we don't want to sacrifice the things we possess; they have begun to possess us. These things can include our jobs, our material assets, our money, our communities, and our friends— even our families. We cling to them, often out of a desire for security, comfort, and happiness, even though we know in our hearts that we can only find real happiness by serving the Lord. Consequently, our things become idols. In fact, *anything* we put ahead of God in our lives becomes an idol. Jonah learned that lesson the hard way. God can't give you the blessings He has for you until you first put down the other things you are clutching in your hands.

> God can't give you the blessings He has for you until you first put down the other things you are clutching in your hands.

When God told Jonah to go to Nineveh to preach to the pagans, Jonah bolted and got on the first ship out of town. No way was he going *there*. It was the land of his greatest enemies. Of course, when the ship was beset by a terrible storm, the crew threw Jonah overboard, believing that he was the cause of God's wrath. Jonah then ended up being swallowed by a great fish.

In the "belly of the whale," Jonah cried out to God, knowing he had disobeyed Him. I found these words from his prayer to be particularly relevant to my own struggle to obey God's call to World Vision: "Those who cling to worthless idols forfeit the grace that could be theirs" (Jonah 2:8). Jonah's "clinging to idols" also drove home something Reneé had said over and over: "If we turn our backs on God's will for our lives, what makes us think we'll be better off? Maybe God is saving us from something we can't know—one of our kids getting into trouble, losing your job, a terrible accident, or worse."

If you study the book of Jonah, you *have* to conclude that clinging to one's "worthless idols" is the *real* risk. (Duh!) Obeying God is the *only* safe thing.

Another excuse we often use quite effectively to avoid serving God is that we don't have the right skills or abilities. We bow to feelings of inferiority, which tell us again and again that God can't use someone like us. *I'm not spiritual enough. I don't have the right education. I'm not smart.* Or, *I don't have enough money to be of any use to God*, the little voices whisper. And when we listen, we miss the whole point of 2 Corinthians 12:9. We *think* God prefers to use the strong and the capable, but He said, "My grace is sufficient for you, for my power is made perfect *in weakness*" (emphasis added). And it's true. Look at the great stories of the Bible. In most cases, God chose those deemed to be weak and imperfect by the world to do great things. Many of them were quite reluctant to serve.

Take Moses, the stutterer. He was the biological son of slaves, a murderer, and a runaway adopted prince with a price on his head. Yet God dramatically appeared to him in a bush that burned but was not consumed. Shouldn't that have given him the courage and boldness to serve?

Apparently not. Listen to the dialogue between God and Moses:

> "The cry of the Israelites has reached me, and I have seen the way the Egyptians are oppressing them. So now, go. I am sending you to Pharaoh to bring my people the Israelites out of Egypt."
>
> But Moses said to God, "Who am I, that I should go to Pharaoh and bring the Israelites out of Egypt?"
>
> And God said, "I will be with you. And this will be the sign to you that it is I who have sent you: When you have brought the people out of Egypt, you will worship God on this mountain."
>
> Moses said to God, "Suppose I go to the Israelites and say to them, 'The God of your fathers has sent me to you,' and they ask me, 'What is his name?' Then what shall I tell them?"
>
> God said to Moses, "I am who I am. This is what you are to say to the Israelites: 'I AM has sent me to you.'" (Ex. 3:9–14)

But Moses insisted upon whining to God. He didn't want to go where God was sending him. He didn't want to leave his *comfort zone*. Just a few verses later . . .

> "What if they do not believe me or listen to me and say, 'The LORD did not appear to you'?"

> Then the LORD said to him, "What is that in your hand?"
> "A staff," he replied.
> The LORD said, "Throw it on the ground." (Ex. 4:1–3)

You know the story. When Moses threw that staff down, God performed a miracle: He turned it into a snake. Note that God did not review Moses' qualifications for the job at hand; He only wanted his obedience. God would do the rest. He would, in fact, bring Pharaoh to his knees, using that very staff—a mere stick of wood—to demonstrate Moses' authority. Surely *this* would give Moses the confidence to obey, right?

Not!

> Moses said to the LORD, "O Lord, I have never been eloquent, neither in the past nor since you have spoken to your servant. I am slow of speech and tongue."
> The LORD said to him, "Who gave man his mouth? Who makes him deaf or mute? Who gives him sight or makes him blind? Is it not I, the LORD? Now go; I will help you speak and will teach you what to say."
> But Moses said, "O Lord, please send someone else to do it."
> Then the LORD's anger burned against Moses. (vv. 10–14)

I took comfort in my own misery that Moses had been just as pathetic as I was.

We know that Moses did finally obey and confront Pharaoh, using his staff to perform miracle after miracle. God then enabled Moses to successfully lead the people of Israel out of Egypt. Moses' staff parted the Red Sea and brought manna from heaven, sustaining the Israelites in the wilderness for the next forty years. The point? God didn't need great courage and skill from Moses; He could have used *just* a stick to save the nation of Israel. But He chose to use Moses—and his stick. All He required was for Moses to be available and obedient.

> "God does not call the equipped; He equips the called."

Someone once said, "God does not call the equipped; He equips the called." Saying that we are not clever enough, good enough, or talented enough to serve God is just making excuses. All of us have something God can use, even if it's only a stick. The question is whether we will offer whatever stick we have to His service.

Before this whole World Vision thing happened in my life, I thought that being "called" by God was a rare thing and maybe didn't even happen so much anymore. It was easy to see God calling people in the Bible. Moses got a burning bush—hard to write that off as a coincidence. Each disciple was called personally by Jesus. Paul had his Damascus Road encounter. And Jacob wrestled with God. But the events surrounding my own call to World Vision changed the way I think about calling. Bill Hybels—then a member of World Vision U.S.'s board as well as the presidential search committee—encouraged me during the process by saying that every follower of Christ was made for a purpose and that our most important task is to discern what that purpose is. When we find it, he said, we are in "the zone" with God, just like an athlete during his or her best-ever performance. Bill also said that God does nothing by happenstance. He doesn't wake up one day and say, "I need to find someone to run World Vision; I wonder who I can find?" No, God is a God of order. He created us all for a purpose and envisioned our lives at the very beginning of time itself. He gave us each a unique personality and a set of aptitudes and placed us each in a particular family. Day by day, He brings key people into our lives and provides life experiences that shape us. God does all of this with His purpose in mind, tailored to the individual—you and me.

In the Academy Award–winning movie *Chariots of Fire*, which tells the story of Olympic medalist Eric Liddell, there is a scene in which Eric's sister, Jennie, criticizes him for being sidetracked by running, when he should be on the mission field. I will never forget Liddell's response. In essence, he said, "I believe God made me for a purpose, but he also made me fast. And when I run I feel his pleasure."[1] Eric Liddell was in "the zone" with God, that place where his giftedness, his circumstances, and God's plan for his life had all come together. He had found his calling, and he used it as a witness to the world. First, he made headlines in newspapers globally when he dropped out of one of the events because he refused to run on a Sunday. Then, as a further witness, when he went on to win the gold medal in his other event, he publicly gave the glory to God.

Discerning our unique calling is not always a simple thing. We need to be quiet enough to hear God's still, small voice. We must also faithfully read the Scriptures, pray diligently, follow the Lord's teachings, listen to wise friends who know us, and consistently make ourselves available to serve. Finally, we have to remain open to God's possibilities, always willing to take the outrageous risk and do the unpredictable thing.

Often we are too busy pursuing our careers to discern our calling. I was. But there is a vast difference between *career* and *calling*. Read what Pastor John Ortberg had to say about it:

> American society does not talk much about calling anymore. It is more likely to think in terms of career. Yet, for many people a career becomes the altar on which they sacrifice their lives.
>
> A calling, which is something I do for God, is replaced by a career, which threatens to become my god. A career is something I choose for myself; a calling is something I receive. A career is something I do for myself; a calling is something I do for God. A career promises status, money or power; a calling generally promises difficulty and even some suffering—and the opportunity to be used by God. A career is about upward mobility; a calling generally leads to downward mobility.[2]

The demands of my career and the busyness of raising five kids had made it difficult for me to hear God's call. I had come perilously close to walking away from it. But God kept pursuing me, opening door after door and bidding me to walk through them. Finally, I did.

SCARED STIFF . . .

I still remember that first day in my new office at World Vision. I had taken the plunge, but I was still terrified. I drove in early, actually hoping I wouldn't see anyone as I rode the elevator to my new life. I was certain I looked like a deer in the headlights. I slipped into my office, closed the door, and cried out to God in prayer. "I showed up, Lord. I'm here. It took every ounce of my courage just to be here. But I can't do this job. I feel helpless for the first time in my life. I don't even know what to do next. It's up to You now. You got me into this, and You'll have to do the rest. Help me." And He did. For perhaps the first time in my life, God had me right where He wanted me, helpless and relying completely on Him.

> Mother Teresa once said, "I am a little pencil in the hand of a writing God who is sending a love letter to the world." She had it right. We're not authors, any of us. We are just the "pencils." Once we understand that, we might actually become useful to God.

Mother Teresa once said, "I am a little pencil in the hand of a writing God who is sending a love letter to the world."[3] She had it right. We're not authors, any of us. We are just the "pencils." Once we understand that, we might actually become useful to God.

Are you willing to be open to God's will for your life? That was the question that once rocked my world, the one that changed everything for me. To answer it I had to let go of the things in my life that possessed me and stop hiding behind the fallacy that God could not use me. I had to pursue my calling, not my career, and I had to throw my "stick" on the ground, offering it to God in service. God wants each of us to surrender our lives to Him completely, to follow Him, to obey His commands, and to show His love to others. But before we can demonstrate that love and offer the gospel to the rest of the world, we have to fill the hole in our own gospel.

Why did God make me? To love, serve, and obey Him. Very simple, yet extremely profound. If we all woke up every morning asking, "How can I love, serve, and obey God today?" it might change everything—it might even change the world.

PART 3

A HOLE IN
THE WORLD

The poverty of our century is unlike that of any other.
It is not, as poverty was before, the result of natural scarcity,
but of a set of priorities imposed upon the rest of the world by
the rich. Consequently, the modern poor are not pitied . . .
but written off as trash.
The twentieth-century consumer economy has produced the first
culture for which a beggar is a reminder of nothing.

—JOHN BERGER

We know that the whole creation has been groaning as in the pains
of childbirth right up to the present time.

—ROMANS 8:22

CHAPTER EIGHT

THE GREATEST CHALLENGE OF THE NEW MILLENNIUM

Our desire is not that others might be relieved while you are hard pressed, but that there might be equality. At the present time your plenty will supply what they need, so that in turn their plenty will supply what you need. Then there will be equality, as it is written: "He who gathered much did not have too much, and he who gathered little did not have too little."

—2 CORINTHIANS 8:13–15

More and more I come to value charity and love of one's fellow being above everything else . . . All our lauded technological progress—our very civilization—is like the axe in the hand of the pathological criminal.

—ALBERT EINSTEIN

A few years back I had the opportunity to spend some time with former president Jimmy Carter. World Vision was collaborating with Habitat for Humanity on one of their massive "blitz build" projects in the Philippines, and I was assigned to work on the same house as President Carter. (At the time, he was approaching eighty, and I was amazed at how long he was willing to work in the hot sun, doing hard manual labor.) As we worked, he shared that he had just been asked to prepare a speech that would answer the question, what is the greatest challenge facing humankind in the twenty-first century? It was 1999, and the world was focused on the beginning of the new millennium. I was quite surprised at the former president's conclusion.

He believed that the greatest problem of our time was *the growing gap between the richest and poorest people on earth.*

Just three years later President Carter was awarded the Nobel Peace Prize for the accomplishments of his postpresidency years, fighting poverty and disease and promoting democracy, and in his acceptance speech he echoed the comments he made to me on the Habitat building site:

> At the beginning of this new millennium I was asked to discuss, here in Oslo, the greatest challenge that the world faces. Among all the possible choices, I decided that the most serious and universal problem is the growing chasm between the richest and poorest people on earth. Citizens of the ten wealthiest countries are now seventy-five times richer than those who live in the ten poorest ones, and the separation is increasing every year, not only between nations but also within them. The results of this disparity are root causes of most of the world's unresolved problems, including starvation, illiteracy, environmental degradation, violent conflict, and unnecessary illnesses that range from Guinea worm to HIV/AIDS.[1]

Here was a man who had seen and done it all. He had been president of the United States, had traveled to almost two hundred countries, and had met most of the world's heads of state. He was certainly qualified to speak to this question. But what is most astounding is not what he chose as the greatest challenge facing the world but rather what he did *not* choose. Though his speech was given just a year after the terrorist attacks of 9/11, he did not address global terrorism or religious extremism. He did not speak about climate change, globalization, nuclear tension, HIV and AIDS, political corruption, or ethnic and religious tensions. Neither did he mention hunger, illiteracy, or disease. Instead, he saw "the growing chasm between the richest and poorest people on earth" as a root cause of many of these other problems. It is also of note that he did not cite poverty itself as the most challenging problem facing the world but instead the *disparity* between the rich and the poor. If we were all rich, or at least comfortable, then this would not be a problem. Conversely, if we were all poor, no one would be in a position to help another. But when some of the world is rich and the rest of the world is poor, it indeed creates a moral and practical dilemma.

I recently traveled with my wife to Cape Town, South Africa, one of the most beautiful and breathtaking cities in the world. We went there to see World Vision projects and to visit Fish Hoek Baptist Church, to learn about their remarkable AIDS ministry. We also built in a couple of days to do some sightseeing—but found it difficult to enjoy it. Cape Town is one of those few places in the world where the worst imaginable poverty and the most opulent wealth live together, sometimes just fifty yards apart. In the shadows of the luxury homes, high-rise hotels, wineries, and upscale shopping malls lie acre upon acre of run-down shantytowns reeling with hunger, poverty, crime, disease, and despair, and populated by hundreds of thousands of broken-down human beings. The "haves" live in gated communities adorned with security cameras. The "have-nots" peer from their tin huts as Mercedes and BMWs from another world pass them by. For me it was a microcosm of the "chasm" President Carter had described. How can the rich and the middle class live like this, I wondered, forced to see the stark contrast between themselves and the desperately poor *every single day*?

They do exactly what you and I do: they ignore them. The only difference is that it is easier for us to ignore the world's poorest because they are "over there."

President Carter ended his speech on a note of pessimism, doubting that the chasm of which he spoke could ever be bridged: "But tragically, in the industrialized world there is a terrible absence of understanding or concern about those who are enduring lives of despair and hopelessness. We have not yet made the commitment to share with others an appreciable part of our excessive wealth. This is a potentially rewarding burden that we should all be willing to assume."[2]

WHO IS MY NEIGHBOR?

Transport of the mails, transport of the human voice, transport of flickering pictures—in this century as in others our highest accomplishments still have the single aim of bringing men together.
—Antoine de Saint-Exupéry

If the second greatest commandment tells us to love our neighbors as ourselves, then the crucial next question is, who is my neighbor? In the world of haves and have-nots, are we to view poverty-stricken people ten thousand miles away as our neighbors?

That same question—who is my neighbor?—was at the core of the well-known parable of the Good Samaritan (Luke 10:25–37). An "expert in the law" sought to understand the limits of his responsibility with regard to Christ's command to love his "neighbors." Jesus answered by telling the now-familiar story of a man beaten by robbers and left lying at the side of the road. First a priest and then a Levite (the religious leaders of their day) walking the same road passed by on the other side, ignoring the man's distress. Then a Samaritan—a theological and racial half-breed despised by the Jews—saw the man and immediately came to his aid.

At the end of the parable, Jesus turned the question around and asked His questioner, "Which of these three do you think was a neighbor to the man who fell into the hands of robbers?" (v. 36).

The man, who could not even bring himself to say the word *Samaritan*, answered, "The one who had mercy on him" (v. 37).

Jesus rewarded the man's correct response with just four words that surely stand among the greatest moral teachings in all of history: "Go and do likewise" (v. 37).

For most of the past two thousand years, "loving our neighbors as ourselves" has meant exactly that—loving our *immediate* neighbors, those people whom we encounter daily in *our* communities. For the most part, it has been impossible to "love" people hundreds or thousands of miles away from us, and only in the last century or so have we been able to even have an awareness of their needs. That one's "neighbors" might include those living on another continent was ludicrous until recent times. In fact, the great disparity between rich and poor nations, described by President Carter, largely didn't even exist before 1800. According to Jeffrey D. Sachs, in 1820 the difference in per capita income between the wealthiest region of the world and the poorest was perhaps four to one.[3] Compare that to the seventy-five to one cited by President Carter in 2002. Prior to 1800, disease and inadequate health care were facts of life that affected all people. Lack of clean water and sanitation would have been virtually universal. Droughts, crop failures, famines, and epidemics would have periodically devastated almost all countries. Illiteracy was common everywhere. It was the legacy of colonialism combined with the advances of the Industrial

Revolution that ultimately resulted in the rapid development of some economies over others. This effected the imbalance we see today. Even as economic disparities between nations widened in the nineteenth century and into the twentieth, the notion that the wealthy (or middle class) of one nation had a responsibility to the poor of another nation was not commonly accepted. Perhaps the exception to this was the thousands of missionaries who traveled to other nations to reach out to their neighbors. Their heroic efforts in the cause of Christ must not be overlooked, as they of necessity tackled the issues of poverty, justice, sickness, and education that they encountered. But for the general public, three major impediments stood in the way of anyone wanting to love their distant neighbors, even into the mid-twentieth century: *awareness*, *access*, and *ability*.

AWARENESS

Before one can be held accountable for helping someone in need, there must first be an awareness of the need. Before 1900, there were no mass international communication vehicles available. The telegraph was in use, but not on a widespread basis, and the telephone was still a curiosity. Radio broadcasts and even ownership of radios were not common in the United States until the 1920s, and television did not become a mass medium until the 1940s and '50s. As a result, the only international information regularly available to the public was through newspapers, most of which devoted little space to what we today call "humanitarian concerns." Even after World War II, broad-scale media as we know it was limited. Only 3.6 million TV sets had been sold in the United States by 1949, and most of those received only one or two channels.[4]

Bob Pierce, the founder of World Vision, returned from Korea in 1950 with 16-millimeter films that visually documented the suffering of children and the human devastation of the war. It is hard for us today to imagine the shocking impact these films must have had on those who viewed them as Pierce went across the United States, from church to church, with his projector. Never had vivid images such as these been brought across the ocean into the small towns of America. It should not surprise us that viewers responded with the avalanche of donations that enabled the fledgling World Vision to bring desperately needed help to these children.

Today we live in a media-saturated, Internet-connected, cell phone–equipped world in which everything that happens anywhere is instantly available everywhere. We are assaulted by images and stories of human tragedy and suffering, 24/7. International aid organizations broadcast their messages constantly via the Internet and other media outlets, providing convenient "on-ramps" for those who want to help but don't know how. Lack of awareness is no longer an issue. And yet only about 4 percent of all U.S. charitable giving goes to international causes of any kind.[5] We have become detached and indifferent toward the constant and repeated images of poverty and adversity that bombard us. In fact, our apathy has even earned its own term: *compassion fatigue*.[6] But we *cannot* claim that we don't know our distant neighbor is in need—not anymore, not today.

ACCESS

If lack of *awareness* was a problem prior to World War II, then lack of *access* to suffering populations would have been equally daunting. Prior to 1940, international travel was extremely uncommon for Americans, and air travel was not considered accessible to the public. Records indicate that just 42,570 American passengers flew internationally in 1930, most of them presumably to European destinations.[7] Almost no one would have been able to travel to Africa to either see firsthand the suffering of those lacking food, water, sanitation, and health care or to actually do something about it. By 1949, the number of international passengers was up to about one and a half million, yet still a small fraction of the U.S. population.[8] Compare these numbers to the 2005 statistic: more than 150 million American passengers flew internationally.[9] Today, not only can we be on the other side of the planet in fewer than twenty-four hours, but tens of millions of

Americans fly internationally. We now have the opportunity not only to see those in extreme poverty but also to help them.

ABILITY

Even after our *awareness* of and *access* to the poorest of the poor internationally became less restricted, our *ability* to provide effective assistance remained limited for a time. It is true that even before World War II, health advances in the developed world had greatly outstripped those available in third-world countries. Vaccines for diseases such as smallpox and typhoid were already available, and basic knowledge of first aid, nutrition, the spread of infectious diseases, and safe childbirth provided the ability to help underdeveloped communities. However, only in the last fifty years has our understanding of the complex relationship between poverty, health, culture, and economics made it possible to implement effective and sustainable strategies to address poverty.

Today we have sophisticated and field-tested interventions to deal with myriad community health issues, including malaria, polio, tuberculosis, pneumonia, HIV and AIDS, prenatal and postnatal care, nutrition, vitamin deficiencies, tropical diseases, parasites, and the major childhood diseases. Multilateral institutions such as the World Health Organization and U.S. agencies such as the Centers for Disease Control and the National Institutes of Health now have decades of experience in dealing with these and other global health issues. New technologies abound for developing safe water sources through improved methods of aquifer location and borehole drilling, water purification, and rainwater catchment. These alone can cut child mortality in half almost overnight in water-poor communities. The so-called green revolution in agriculture that began in the 1950s has led to vastly improved crop yields, allowing much larger populations to be fed per hectare of arable land. And since the '70s, the entire field of microfinance, which addresses poverty at the level of individual and community economics, has emerged. We have further identified sociological links between poverty and things such as gender roles and cultural practices. At the same time, hundreds of reputable and professional humanitarian organizations operating on the ground offer simple opportunities for any American to get involved. In short, for the first time in the history of the human race, we have the awareness, the access, *and* the ability to reach out to our most desperate neighbors around the world. The programs, tools, and technologies to virtually eliminate the most extreme kinds of poverty and suffering in our world are now available. This is truly good news for the poor—or is it?

Not really, because we are not doing our part.

Here is the bottom line: if we are aware of the suffering of our distant neighbors—and we are—if we have access to these neighbors, either personally or through aid organizations and charities—and we do—and if we have the ability to make a difference through programs and technologies that work—which is also the case—then we should no more turn our backs on these neighbors of ours than the priest and the Levite should have walked by the bleeding man.

Listen to the words of a modern-day prophet, and let them challenge you:

> Fifteen thousand Africans are dying each day of preventable, treatable diseases—AIDS, malaria, TB—for lack of drugs that we take for granted.
>
> This statistic alone makes a fool of the idea many of us hold on to very tightly: the idea of equality. What is happening to Africa mocks our pieties, doubts our concern and questions our commitment to the whole concept. Because if we're honest, there's no way we could conclude that such mass death day after day would ever be allowed to happen anywhere else. Certainly not North America or Europe, or Japan. An entire continent bursting into flames? Deep down, if we really accept that their lives—African lives—are equal to ours, we would all be doing more to put the fire out. It's an uncomfortable truth.

This is a prophetic voice, one of both passion and vision. I wish I could say that it belongs to one of the great Church leaders of our day, one who is leading the Church of Jesus Christ to the front lines of the battle against poverty and injustice in our world. But, no, this voice that should shake our churches to the core with its high call to moral responsibility is the voice of a rock star—one who may have done more to advance the cause of the poor in the last twenty-five years than anyone alive. His name is Bono, and he passionately answers the question, who is my neighbor? Then he bids us, as Jesus did, to go out and love them "as ourselves." His impassioned plea gives voice to the moral responsibilities inherent between those who suffer needlessly and those who have the power to intervene.

Listen again to Bono's call to our generation to make our mark on history:

> We can be the generation that no longer accepts that an accident of latitude determines whether a child lives or dies—but *will* we be that generation? Will we in the West realize our potential or will we sleep in the comfort of our affluence with apathy and indifference murmuring softly in our ears? Fifteen thousand people dying needlessly every day from AIDS, TB, and malaria. Mothers, fathers, teachers, farmers, nurses, mechanics, children. This is Africa's crisis. That it's not on the nightly news, that we do not treat this as an emergency—that's *our* crisis.
>
> Future generations flipping through these pages will know whether we answered the key question. The evidence will be the world around them. History will be our judge, but what's written is up to us. We can't say our generation didn't know how to do it. We can't say our generation couldn't afford it. And we can't say our generation didn't have reason to do it. It's up to us.[10]

President Carter identified a hole in our society, defined by poverty, human suffering, and inequality. He sees a world unraveling at an alarming rate as the rich get richer and the poor get poorer, creating greater and greater social and international disparity and isolation. Bono sees a hole too—in our morality. He sees the world's poor, beaten and bloody, lying at the wayside, while the majority of us pass by without stopping. Either way you look at it, there is a *hole* that needs to be repaired—and it's getting deeper.

CHAPTER NINE

ONE HUNDRED CRASHING JETLINERS

Facts are stubborn things.

—JOHN ADAMS

The truth does not change according to our ability to stomach it.

—FLANNERY O'CONNOR

Let the little children come to me, and do not hinder them, for the kingdom of God belongs to such as these.

—MARK 10:14

Whenever a major jetliner crashes anywhere in the world, it inevitably sets off a worldwide media frenzy covering every aspect of the tragedy. I want you to imagine for a moment that you woke up this morning to the following headline: "One Hundred Jetliners Crash, Killing 26,500." Think of the pandemonium this would create across the world as heads of state, parliaments, and congresses convened to grapple with the nature and causes of this tragedy. Think about the avalanche of media coverage that it would ignite around the globe as reporters shared the shocking news and tried to communicate its implications for the world. Air travel would no doubt grind to a halt as governments shut down the airlines and panicked air travelers canceled their trips. The National Transportation Safety Board and perhaps the FBI, CIA, and local law enforcement agencies and their international equivalents would mobilize investigations and dedicate whatever manpower was required to understand what happened and to prevent it from happening again.

Now imagine that the very next day, one hundred more planes crashed—and one hundred more the next, and the next, and the next. It is unimaginable that something this terrible could ever happen.

But it did—and it does.

It happened today, and it happened yesterday. It will happen again tomorrow. But there was no media coverage. No heads of state, parliaments, or congresses stopped what they were doing to address the crisis, and no investigations were launched. Yet more than 26,500 children died yesterday of preventable causes related to their poverty,[1] and it will happen again today and tomorrow and the day after that. Almost 10 million children will be dead in the course of a year. So why does the crash of a single plane dominate the front pages of newspapers across the world while the equivalent of one hundred planes filled with children crashing daily never reaches our ears? And even though we now have the *awareness*, the *access*, and the *ability* to stop it, why have we chosen not to? Perhaps one reason is that these kids who are dying are not our kids; they're somebody else's.

SOMEBODY ELSE'S KIDS

A few years ago the book *Compassion Fatigue* by journalist Susan Moeller was published.

In it she quoted a shocking statement that she found often repeated in newsrooms around the country. "In the news business, one dead fireman in Brooklyn is worth five English bobbies, who are worth fifty Arabs, who are worth five hundred Africans."[2] What a terrible equation—terrible, but accurate. If we are honest with ourselves, we must admit that we simply have less empathy for people of other cultures living in faraway countries than we do for Americans. Our compassion for others seems to be directly correlated to whether people are close to us socially, emotionally, culturally, ethnically, economically, and geographically. But *why* do we distinguish the value of one human life from another? Why is it so easy to shut out the cries of these dying foreign children from our ears? In some ways, the reasons are obvious.

Let me give you a couple of illustrations. If you heard on the radio that thousands of children die each year in car accidents, it would likely strike you as sad, but I doubt you would become very emotional. If instead you learned that your neighbor's child just died in a car crash, it would hit much closer to home, and your emotional response would be much deeper. You would immediately want to respond—to comfort your neighbors and to come alongside them in their grief, helping in any way you could. But what if you learned that your *own* child had been killed? You would be devastated at the deepest possible level. It would be a life-shattering and profoundly personal tragedy for you, one that would forever after redefine you. For some reason we are wired in such a way that we can become almost indifferent to tragedies that are far away from us emotionally, socially, or geographically, but when the same tragedy happens to us or someone close to us, everything changes.

Let me use a different example. If you read in the newspaper about hundreds of children dying of malnutrition in a famine in Africa, you might pause for a moment of genuine sadness—but wouldn't you finally turn the page, read the sports section, check the TV listings, and go about your daily routine? But imagine for a moment that you somehow discovered one of these starving African children dying on your front doorstep the very next morning as you left for church. Would you not stop everything, pick up the child, and rush her to the emergency room, offering to pay whatever it might cost to save her life? You would almost certainly respond with urgency as one human being to another, and that faraway famine you had read about the night before would very suddenly become intensely personal. You see, our problem is that the plight of suffering children in a far-off land simply hasn't gotten *personal* for us. We may hear about them with sorrow, but we haven't really been able to look at them as if they were our own children. If we could, then we would surely grieve more deeply in our spirits. We would weep for their parents, and we would respond with far greater urgency.

How might God think about this issue? Does He look at the suffering of a child in Cambodia or Malawi with a certain sense of emotional distance? Does God have different levels of compassion for children based on their geographic location, their nationality, their race—or their parents' income level? Does He forget about their pain because He is preoccupied with other things? Does He turn the offending page to read the sports section—or is His heart broken because each child is precious to Him? God surely grieves and weeps, because every one of these children is *His* child—not somebody else's.

I have to confess to you that I, too, struggle to mourn over these kids as if they were my own. Becoming the president of World Vision didn't turn me into Teresa of Calcutta. It is altogether possible for me to do my job at World Vision with a sense of emotional detachment. I can sit in meetings all day, review financial statements, attend chapel at eleven o'clock on Wednesdays, and even write a book about the poor, without my heart burning every moment with sadness. Like most Americans, I can get easily distracted by the details of my own life and family. We have a nice home, live in a pleasant neighborhood, and go to a beautiful church. We make trips to the mall, go out to the movies, and take family vacations—often with little thought for the tragic lives of children thousands of miles away. But then I get on a plane, and twenty-four hours later I find myself in the home of a grieving mother dying of AIDS and leaving her five children orphans. Or I see a baby slowly starving to death, a child with one leg because of a landmine accident, or a little girl who was rescued from prostitution. And all of a sudden it becomes very personal again. Somebody else's kids just became very important to me because now I know their names, I have looked into their eyes, and I have cried with their parents. I come back home angry at myself, incensed by my own apathy, with a fresh resolve and a renewed passion to crusade on behalf of these kids, to fight for them with every breath in my body. The meetings are no longer routine, and the balance sheets are no longer just numbers; they are now life-and-death issues. They're *urgent. We've got to do something! We've got to help!* But then, a few weeks later, the fire dies down again, the images in my head fade, I drift back inside my safe and protected world, and they're somebody else's kids again—not mine.

I mentioned earlier the prayer of World Vision's founder, Bob Pierce: "Let my heart be broken by the things that break the heart of God." As I have tried to walk in some of his footsteps these past ten years, I have gained new insight into his prayer. While it was a prayer he hoped everyone would pray, it was even more personal for him. You see, I believe that even Bob Pierce struggled to sustain the level of brokenheartedness and caring required to press ahead year after year in this work of loving the poor. His prayer was a crying out to God, that God would break his heart yet again and again, because if He didn't, Bob knew that he could not love somebody else's kids the way God did. No man or woman can unless God breaks that individual's heart. Only then can he or she—or *we*—care as God cares and love as He loves. That's why we must pray constantly that God will soften our hearts so we see the world the way He sees it.

AN ATHEIST HOLDS US ACCOUNTABLE

The worst sin towards our fellow creatures is not to hate them, but to be indifferent to them; that's the essence of inhumanity. —George Bernard Shaw

Several years ago some of the writings of Peter Singer, Ira W. DeCamp professor of bioethics at Princeton University, came to my attention. Singer, who admits to being an atheist, has been extremely controversial because of his views on animal rights, abortion, euthanasia, and numerous other matters of ethics. Many of his positions would be downright repugnant to most Christians. But I found his writing on our moral responsibility to care about other people's kids, even when they are far away, so compelling. He illustrated the principle in his own version of the parable of the good Samaritan:

> The path from the library at my university to the Humanities lecture theater passes a shallow ornamental pond. Suppose that on my way to give a lecture I notice that a small child has fallen in and is in danger of drowning. Would anyone deny that I ought to wade in and pull the child out? This will mean getting my clothes muddy, and either canceling my lecture or delaying it until I can find something dry to change into; but compared with the avoidable death of a child this is insignificant. A plausible principle that would support the judgment that I ought to pull the child out is this: if it is in our power to prevent something very bad from happening, without thereby sacrificing anything of comparable moral significance, we ought to do it. This principle seems uncontroversial.[3]

You can see how similar Singer's parable is to the story Jesus told. And Singer went on to suggest that failing to save a child one has the power to save (a sin of omission) has significant moral consequences:

Nevertheless, [this principle] is deceptive. If it were seriously acted upon, our lives and our world would be fundamentally changed. For the principle applies, not just to rare situations in which one can save a child from a pond, but to the everyday situation in which we can assist those living in absolute poverty. Not to help would be wrong, whether or not it is intrinsically equivalent to killing.[4]

In a related article he went on to explain:

For the principle takes, firstly, no account of proximity or distance. It makes no moral difference whether the person I can help is a neighbor's child ten yards from me or a Bengali whose name I shall never know, ten thousand miles away . . . Unfortunately, for those who like to keep their moral responsibilities limited, instant communication and swift transportation have changed the situation. From the moral point of view, the development of the world into a "global village" has made an important, though still unrecognized difference to our moral situation . . . There would seem, therefore, to be no possible justification for discriminating on geographic grounds.[5]

The argument I have made for acting to save somebody else's child on the basis of Scripture and Christian compassion, Singer has made on the basis of ethics and moral equivalence. Yet on the question of who is my neighbor, Singer is advocating the same radical thought that Jesus did: that is, to walk by on the other side of the road is wrong—for a Christian or an atheist.

One Such Child

And if anyone gives even a cup of cold water to one of these little ones because he is my disciple, I tell you the truth, he will certainly not lose his reward. —Matthew 10:42

A few years back I had my own encounter with somebody else's child. I was in Gujarat, India, about six months after the massive 2001 earthquake. We were leaving the last village at the end of the final day of a ten-day, multicountry trip. I was exhausted and looking forward to getting back to the hotel and then back home the next morning. But something happened. As our car began to pull away, and a throng of people crowded around to wave good-bye, a desperate woman rushed up to my window with a little boy in her arms. She held him out to me with a pleading look in her eyes that said, *Please help me! Please help my little boy.* To my absolute horror, I then saw that her little boy had no feet. His legs had both been amputated below the knee. And then, just as quickly, she was gone, our car was on the road, and we were headed back to the hotel.

Gradually I put her haunting face out of my mind. I was tired. World Vision had helped so many thousands in Gujarat in the months after the earthquake; we couldn't be expected to help *every* child. That last boy was not my responsibility, I reasoned, and so I tried to forget what I had seen as I flew home the next morning.

Over the next few days, my body readjusted from jet lag, and I returned to the daily demands at my office, but I could not get the disturbing image of this mother and child—someone *else's* child—out of my mind. It nagged at me and challenged me. Was I just a hypocrite, always talking about the importance of helping every child but not practicing what I preached?

One night at dinner I told my own kids about what I had seen and how it was troubling me. "Can't you do something, Dad?" they asked. That very night I sent an e-mail to our team in India, describing the boy and asking if they could find him, one child in the midst of a billion people. I didn't know his name, and I could not remember even the name of the village where I had seen him. But two weeks later I received an e-mail with a photo of six-year-old Vikas and the story of what had happened to him. During the earthquake, his house had collapsed on him, crushing both of his legs and injuring his mother. With no immediate medical care, by the time help finally arrived, days later, amputation was his only option. To save his life, a relief medical team from Korea amputated both of his legs. Unable to walk, Vikas now could only crawl on all fours or be carried everywhere by his mother or father. So when I arrived in his village that day, a desperate mother waited for her moment and rushed to my departing car, hoping against all hope that maybe this man from America could help.

Believing that He could help—isn't that what grieving parents did when Jesus passed through their village? Like the father who approached

Jesus, knelt before Him, and said, "Lord, have mercy on my son"? (Matthew 17:15).

I asked our team in India whether we could help him. The answer came back that he would need another surgery and then prosthetic limbs. It would cost three hundred dollars; would the U.S. office authorize the expenditure? they asked.

"No," I replied. "World Vision would not pay for this; Rich Stearns will pay for this." You see, this was personal. Arguably, in my role at World Vision, I was already doing more than most people can do to help children in need. But God wanted more than my institutional programs and strategic responses; He wanted it to be as personal for me as it always is for Him. Children are not statistics to God. And so I sent the money.

Four months later, over the Christmas holiday, I was muttering under my breath; someone had sent me a large e-mail file that was taking far too long to download on my home computer. Finally, I opened the file with irritation and saw that it was a photograph—of Vikas, holding his mother's hand and standing on his new legs. I wept as I stared into the eyes of somebody else's child, a little boy I had never actually met but whose predicament had become so very personal to me.

Today, his picture hangs in my office in Seattle to remind me that every child is precious.

CHAPTER TEN

WHAT'S WRONG WITH THIS PICTURE?

There are three kinds of lies: lies, damned lies, and statistics.

—BENJAMIN DISRAELI

*There will always be poor people in the land. Therefore
I command you to be openhanded toward your brothers
and toward the poor and needy in your land.*

—DEUTERONOMY 15:11

I have a love/hate relationship with statistics. On the one hand they are a priceless tool that helps us understand the dimensions of the problems affecting the human race. With statistics, we can diagnose and prioritize these problems according to their severity and extent. We can also better target our efforts and allocate our manpower and resources as we attempt to tackle the greatest causes of human suffering and depredation in our world. (Should we not strive to treat the disease that kills a million children before the disease that kills one thousand?) Essentially, statistics aid us in finding both cause and cure.

But they can also numb our sensibilities. You have already heard perhaps the most shocking statistic of all: that 26,575 children die each day of largely preventable causes related to their poverty. But that very statistic, so critical to our understanding of the extent and urgency of the plight of the world's children, also begins to obscure the humanity, the dignity, and

114

the worth of each of those children. It takes away their names and their stories, homogenizes their personalities, and cheapens the value of each individual child, created in the very image of God. Statistics can become just another way to look away from the faces of the poor, just one more way to walk by on the other side of the road. In fact, behavioral studies seem to prove this.

In 2006, researcher Paul Slovic at the University of Oregon and colleagues Deborah Small of the Wharton School and George Lowenstein of Carnegie Mellon University performed a simple behavioral experiment.[1] A test group of ordinary people was divided into three subgroups. The first read the story and saw a photo of a poor, starving seven-year-old African girl named Rokia. The second group was given a statistical portrait of seventeen million Africans in four countries who were desperately hungry because of crop failures and food shortages. They were told about yet another four million who were homeless. In other words, group two read about hunger and suffering on a massive scale. The third group was given the story about the little girl Rokia but was also given the statistical information given to group two. Finally, participants in all three groups were asked to donate money to relieve the suffering. Amazingly, the group that heard only Rokia's story gave the most money. The group that was given the statistics about twenty-one million suffering people gave the least, and the group that received both pieces of information was only slightly more generous than the statistics-only group.[2] The story of one child was more compelling than the suffering of millions.

Wow! Do you see the disturbing significance of this? Human beings, when enabled to depersonalize a large group of people, respond to them with far less compassion. So the very statistics that should mobilize us to urgent action actually do just the opposite; they seem to excuse our inaction. We can perhaps extrapolate this finding to help us understand the existence of other appalling realities in our world. If we are able to objectify whole classes of people so that we don't think of them as persons equal with us, the unthinkable becomes possible. Was it not this flaw in our human character that allowed the Holocaust and the Rwanda genocide to occur? Might this explain how Christian people not only tolerated but promoted and sustained slavery for so many centuries? Did this type of depersonalization permit people—many of whom claimed to follow Christ—to perpetuate and uphold apartheid in South Africa and racial segregation in the United States?

As followers of Christ, we must become acutely aware of the darkness and hardness of the human heart. God is certainly aware. He spoke of it when He said of His people, "I will remove from them their heart of stone and give them a heart of flesh" (Ezek. 11:19). It is our "stony hearts" that are the root cause not only of apathy toward our fellow man but even of hatred, murder, and genocide. Divided between the things of God and the things of the world, our "hearts of stone" are incapable of loving the poor unless God changes them to hearts of "flesh." Should this not cause us to plead with God daily, as Bob Pierce did, for our hearts to "be broken by the things that break the heart of God"?

And so it is with some trepidation that I now try to describe to you, with statistics, the poverty of our world. Yet, before I can begin to convey the scope of it, I have to first challenge some of your attitudes about the word itself.

POVERTY IS A FOUR-LETTER WORD

Christianity is flourishing wonderfully among the poor and persecuted while it atrophies among the rich and secure. —Philip Jenkins

Defend the cause of the weak and fatherless;
*   maintain the rights of the poor and oppressed.*
Rescue the weak and needy;
*   deliver them from the hand of the wicked.* —Psalm 82:3–4

I don't like the word *poverty*. It is one of those loaded words that carries with it a great deal of baggage and stigma. It sounds like a disease or a bad character trait that some people have and others don't. It's also a word that divides the world into two unequal groups, the poor and the rest of us, as though somehow we are different. Each of us brings different associations to the word *poverty* based on our past understandings and misunderstandings. In America, which has prided itself as being a "land of opportunity," it is not uncommon for us to make value judgments about those who are poor. If they are poor in America, we reason, it must be because they don't work as hard as the rest of us or have made bad choices. We may think that the poor are lazy or stupid, even if we wouldn't say it aloud. When we think about the poor in places such as Africa or Southeast Asia, we may bring other stereotypes into play, perhaps racial or cultural. We may shake our heads at why this nationality or that race just can't seem to get their act together. We wonder why their governments are so ineffective, their leaders so incompetent or corrupt, and their economic development so weak. Or we may look at them paternalistically, feeling sorry for them as a parent would a helpless child. All of these biases are patronizing at best and prejudiced at worst; they lessen the human dignity of people created in God's image. If we are to see the poor as God sees them, we first have to repent of our judgmental attitudes and feelings of superiority. I had to do it myself.

Having overcome my own dysfunctional upbringing and financial handicaps, I had managed to graduate from two Ivy League schools and become a corporate CEO. I fell quite easily into the bias that poverty was somehow a choice one made—that if you were poor, you probably deserved it. In truth, my hard work as a young man produced results largely because my circumstances were favorable. Though I grew up with challenges, the opportunities I had made it quite possible to overcome those obstacles. I lived in a country that embraced basic freedoms and protected individual rights and the rule of law. I attended good public schools and had access to libraries that I did not have to pay for. I did not suffer from hunger, contaminated water, or lack of basic health care. I was vaccinated against devastating childhood diseases. I had more than three thousand colleges and universities from which to choose, and scholarships and loans were available to make attendance possible, even for someone with no money. I entered an economy that was strong and growing, with opportunities for me to put my education and God-given abilities to work productively. Best of all, I found that diligence and hard work were almost always rewarded.

But what if I had been born in Sudan or Bangladesh? Would those same things have played out?

I must say a few words here about poverty in the United States. The advantages I listed that contributed to my own story of success and development were not and are not available to all Americans. When I grew up in the 1950s and '60s, African-American children were often segregated into different and inferior schools, and prevented from going on to higher education. They found that even in America they suffered from severe limitations on their choices.

Though I grew up in the lower middle class, I was not poor, and I lived in a safe neighborhood with good schools and low crime rates. Then and now, though, the children of the poor in America live in communities that often expose them to very destructive forces; crime, gangs, violence, rape, drugs, domestic abuse, economic deprivation, and prostitution are just a few. A child living in a slum, who has never met his father and whose mother is a crack addict, does not start with the same choices I had. And while poverty in America is not usually characterized by bad water, famine, and epidemics, it replaces those destructive elements with others that are equally powerful: discrimination, intimidation, alienation, and exploitation. The result is the same as it is in Sudan—hopelessness. Poverty in America is just as real as poverty in Africa, and it is just as damaging to the human spirit. At its root it has the same causes: a defacing of the human spirit and, effectively, a lack of real choices.

What I have discovered in my travels to more than forty countries with World Vision is that almost all poverty is fundamentally the result of a lack of options. It is not that the poor are lazier, less intelligent, or unwilling to make efforts to change their condition. Rather, it is that they are trapped by circumstances beyond their power to change. Robert Chambers, a British researcher, has said somewhat indelicately, "People so close to the edge cannot afford laziness or stupidity. They have to work and work hard, whenever and however they can. Many of the lazy and stupid poor are dead." I have found that the poorer people are, the harder they work, usually. In fact, their daily labor is more strenuous than most of us could tolerate. It is their circumstances that conspire to prevent their hard work from bearing fruit.

Several years ago I attended the Clinton Global Initiative, the former president's annual gathering of some of the most powerful people on earth from government, business, and the nonprofit sector, focusing on tackling the problems of global poverty, disease, and climate change. President Clinton spoke to the issue of poverty by asking the one thousand leaders present to think about what circumstances in our lives had brought us to this very evening, where we were gathered based on our positions and our success in various fields. He then postulated that two things were at play: first, that during our lives we had all been presented with opportunities of one kind or another, and second, that we had worked hard to capitalize on those opportunities and that our hard work had paid off. He said that each of us had seen a direct correlation between how hard we worked and the results we achieved. "Now," he said, "I want you to imagine what would have happened in your lives if there had been no connection whatsoever between how hard you worked and the results you got, because that is exactly the situation faced by the more than one billion people who live on less than a dollar a day. The connection between how hard they work and the result they will get has been broken."

President Clinton's observation is profound. For most of the poorest people in the world, their hard work doesn't matter. They are trapped within social, cultural, political, and economic systems that do not reward their labor. The result of this entrenched futility is devastating to the human spirit. A person, no matter how gifted or determined, cannot escape the trap in which he finds himself. He has lost the one thing that every person needs to thrive: hope—hope that he will somehow overcome his circumstances, that tomorrow can be better than today, and that his children might someday have a better life than his. Such people discover that they are in an economic and social prison from which there is no escape—unless something happens to change their circumstances and to restore the link between their effort and their reward.

Even in Jesus' time it was common to believe that the poor, the sick, and the disabled were unworthy or were even being punished by God for their sins. This is why the Pharisees and Sadducees were so shocked that Jesus would actually touch a leper, heal the blind and lame, and associate so consistently with the underclass. These people were thought to be unclean and undeserving. But this was never the view of the Old Testament prophets, who railed tirelessly against God's people for not showing compassion to the poor and, worse, for exploiting them. Indeed, the prophet Ezekiel wrote that Sodom's cardinal sin was wealth-induced arrogance and unconcern for the poor, not the sexual immorality that we more commonly associate with its violent destruction: "Now this was the sin of your sister

Sodom: She and her daughters were arrogant, overfed and unconcerned; they did not help the poor and needy" (Ezek. 16:49).

It is crystal clear from Scripture that God loves the poor while hating their poverty, the man-made actions that contribute to it, and the apathy of the "well off" who allow it to persist. Perhaps this was why the poor figured so centrally into Christ's incarnation and ministry. His identification with the poor was and is startling. In His new, upside-down kingdom—the kingdom of God—the poor are placed at the top of the status pyramid.

> *For you know the grace of our Lord Jesus Christ, that though he was rich, yet for your sakes he became poor, so that you through his poverty might become rich.* —2 Corinthians 8:9

Bringing It Home

Think about your own life. How successful would you or your family have been if you had lived in a place where there was no clean water and one-quarter of all children died before their fifth birthday? Imagine growing up constantly weak and malnourished, to the point where both your body and your mind became stunted. What if there had been no health care system, and therefore an abscessed tooth or an ear infection was a death sentence? What if you had lived where you couldn't go to school because you had to fetch water six hours a day—or where there was no school? Or worse, think about what might have happened to you if rebel armies had sacked your community, killed your parents, and driven you hundreds of miles from your home to live in a refugee camp.

These are the daily realities of the world's poor. No matter how hard they work, how gifted and talented they are, or how big their dreams, the poor have few choices and even fewer opportunities to fulfill their God-given potential. These precious human beings created in God's image have been left behind and cast on the garbage dump of history by circumstances they cannot change. We must never say it is their fault. How dare we?

The Dimensions of Human Suffering

> *One death is a tragedy; a million is a statistic.* —Josef Stalin

Let's begin with the biggest statistic of all: there are, today, 6.7 billion people living on earth. Now, most of us are not that great with statistics or understanding what makes a particular number significant. So let me give you a mental picture: if we all joined hands and formed a human chain, we would circle the globe about 250 times. The population of the world is about twenty-two times as great as that of the United States. Said differently, Americans comprise only about 4.5 percent of the world. Most people are surprised at how small the United States is compared to the rest of the world.

To better understand the makeup of the human race, imagine that all 6.7 billion people on earth could be represented by a single "global village" of just 100 people. If we picture this, then we can more easily comprehend the different proportions we find across the world in terms of race, ethnicity, and gender. Here's a snapshot of what that global village would look like.

Out of 100 people:

60 would be Asian
14 would be African
12 would be European
 8 would be Latin American
 5 would be American or Canadian
 1 would be from the South Pacific
51 would be male; 49 would be female
82 would be non-white; 18 white
67 would be non-Christian; 33 would be Christian[3]

We might summarize this by saying we live in a world that is non-American, non-white, and non-Christian.

But now, let's take the 6.7 billion people and divide them a different way, into the haves and the have-nots. There are many ways to define the "have-nots," but for simplicity, we will define them by income. The average income in America is $38,611 per person or about $105 per day.[4] Compare that to the shocking daily reality of almost half the people on earth.

Less than $2 a day	2.6 billion people	(40 percent of the world's people)
Less than $1 a day	1.0 billion people	(15 percent of the world's people)[5]
$105 a day (U.S.A.)	0.3 billion people	(4.5 percent of the world's people)

One dollar a day versus more than a *hundred* dollars a day—that is the disparity between the average American and the bottom billion people on the planet. Here are a few other facts that illustrate this chasm:

- Today's 1,125 billionaires hold more wealth than the wealth of half of the world's adult population.[6]
- The wealthiest 7 people on earth control more wealth than the combined GDP (Gross Domestic Product) of the 41 most heavily indebted (poor) nations.[7]
- The poorest 40 percent of the world's population accounts for just 5 percent of global income. The richest 20 percent accounts for three-quarters of the world's income.[8]
- The top 20 percent of the world's population consumes 86 percent of the world's goods.[9]

You get the idea; the discrepancy between the wealthiest and poorest people on earth is vast. But as President Carter stated in Oslo, this growing chasm between the rich and the poor did not always exist; in fact, it is a relatively recent phenomenon. In 1820, the gap between the richest and poorest countries was about four to one.[10] In 1913, it was eleven to one, and in 1950, it was thirty-five to one. And, as President Carter stated, by 2002, the gap was seventy-five to one.[11]

The apostle Paul spoke to this same issue of disparity in 2 Corinthians, when he urged the wealthier Corinthian church to make a relief offering to the Christians in Jerusalem, who were in dire economic circumstances. "Our desire is not that others might be relieved while you are hard pressed," he wrote, "but that there might be equality. At the present time your plenty will supply what they need, so that in turn their plenty will supply what you need. Then there will be equality, as it is written: 'He who gathered much did not have too much, and he who gathered little did not have too little'" (8:13–15).

The Bible is clear from the Old Testament through the New that God's people always had a responsibility to see that everyone in their society was cared for at a basic-needs level. Ruth was able to glean wheat from Boaz's field because God had instructed those who controlled the land to not harvest everything, so that there would be food left for the poor: "When you reap the harvest of your land, do not reap to the very edges of your field or gather the gleanings of your harvest. Leave them for the poor and the alien" (Lev. 23:22). A modern-day version of this might read: "If your job produces a decent income for you, do not spend it all on yourself. Make some of it available to the poor and the less fortunate, that they, too, might live a decent life." For Christians, this is a justice issue or, stated more bluntly, a moral issue in which those of us who have plenty seem willing to allow others to have nothing.

I have developed a mental picture that helps me see my own sin of injustice more clearly. I imagine that I am on a deserted island with just nine other people trying to survive. Then I imagine that God gives me a huge gift-wrapped package filled with all the food I could possibly ever need. Finally, I ask myself whether God would expect me to hoard it all for myself or to share it. I also try to think how the other people on the island would view me if I kept it all for myself. That helps me sharpen the focus on what God expects of us with regard to the poor, since He has given so many of us more than we need.

Here I want to make a key point: it is not our fault that people are poor, but it *is* our responsibility to do something about it.[12] God says that we are guilty if we allow people to remain deprived when we have the means to help them. It is our moral duty to help our neighbors in need. We cannot look at their situation and simply say, "Not my problem." Neither can we sit smugly in our comfortable bubbles and claim no responsibility for the disadvantaged in our world. God did not leave us that option.

Going back to 2 Corinthians, Paul continued to build his argument that the wealthy church had a duty in Christ to help the desperately poor churches in Jerusalem with perhaps the most eloquent statement in Scripture about giving:

> Remember this: Whoever sows sparingly will also reap sparingly, and whoever sows generously will also reap generously. Each man should give what he has decided in his heart to give, not reluctantly or under compulsion, for God loves a cheerful giver. And God is able to make all grace abound to you, so that in all things at all times, having all that you need, you will abound in every good work. As it is written: "He has scattered abroad his gifts to the poor; his righteousness endures forever." Now he who supplies seed to the sower and bread for food will also supply and increase your store of seed and will enlarge the harvest of your righteousness. You will be made rich in every way so that you can be generous on every occasion, and through us your generosity will result in thanksgiving to God.
>
> This service that you perform is not only supplying the needs of God's people but is also overflowing in many expressions of thanks to God. Because of the service by which you have proved yourselves, men will praise God for the obedience that accompanies your confession of the gospel of Christ, and for your generosity in sharing with them and with everyone else. And in their prayers for you their hearts will go out to you, because of the surpassing grace God has given you. Thanks be to God for his indescribable gift! (9:6–15)

Can you see here God's way of dealing with disparity? "He has scattered abroad his gifts to the poor." In other words, He has given them to you and me to steward and to distribute so that the poor will not be without. Take note also that the result of this generosity of Christians toward the poor is that "men will praise God for the obedience that accompanies your confession of the *gospel* of Christ."

There's that "whole" gospel again that is so attractive to people, giving evidence to the world of the coming kingdom of God.

CHAPTER ELEVEN

CAUGHT IN THE WEB

Although the world is full of suffering,
it is also full of the overcoming of it.

—HELEN KELLER

We are continually faced with a series of great opportunities
brilliantly disguised as insoluble problems.

—JOHN W. GARDNER

So now we need to dig a little deeper to better understand the impact of poverty on human beings. Statistics, again, can help us understand the dimensions of this "condition" in much the same way that numerical values from a blood test can tell a doctor why we are feeling sick. Blood counts—statistics, really—provide clues and insights to your doctor that can then lead to a diagnosis and a course of treatment. Likewise, we need to look at the clues where poverty is concerned, because how we perceive it and what we believe are its causes will ultimately determine what actions we take to address it.

But poverty is extremely complex. Picture the poor caught in a spider-web of interwoven causes that trap them hopelessly while the marauding spiders of hunger, war, disease, ignorance, injustice, natural disasters, and exploitation prey upon them unrestrained. While there are solutions to poverty—ways to free them from the web—there are no simple solutions.

The most common view held by Americans is that poverty is *the absence of things.* If only the poor had *things* like nutritious food, medicines, better houses, clean water wells, adequate clothing, agricultural tools, and seeds, they would no longer be poor. This is why we throw a dollar in the panhandler's cup, give our old clothes to Goodwill, and take short-term missions trips to other countries to dig irrigation channels, teach English, or build schools. But this kind of charity, while it has its place, can backfire on naive "good Samaritans" who discover that those who receive their gifts are soon back asking for more of them. They saw an easy way to have their needs met and became dependent on the givers for their livelihoods. While providing things like these in urgent situations is sometimes necessary, it neither addresses the underlying stubbornness of poverty, nor is it sustainable; it just creates a dependency. Frankly, giving things to the poor does much more to make the giver feel good than it does to fundamentally address and improve the condition of those in need.

> Frankly, giving things to the poor does much more to make the giver feel good than it does to fundamentally address and improve the condition of those in need.

Another view is that the poor just need more knowledge, that if they had the right education and job skills, they'd no longer be poor. But while it's true that often they do need skills and education, this view fails to take into account the impact of the *systems* within which the poor are embedded. A farmer may learn improved farming methods, but if government land-use restrictions prevent him from owning arable land, he is stymied. If a person receives training that qualifies her for a job but she lives in a broken economy with 70 percent employment, the training is useless. Children may now have schools, but they cannot attend if they have to spend all of their time fetching water or working in the fields. Certain cultures often forbid girls to get an education or women to own assets, severely limiting their potential to better their situations. And government health systems can be so inadequate that even trained doctors and nurses cannot successfully treat patients for lack of money, supplies, beds, and clinics.

When talking about poverty's root causes, it's important to realize that *injustice* is often the "cause behind the cause." In other words, if people lack food, health care, or education; are vulnerable to disease; and have no access to land or financial capital, it is frequently because they have been exploited or manipulated by unjust people and structures—man's inhumanity to man. Widows have their land confiscated by bullying male relatives; girls are raped or forced into prostitution; money lenders prey upon children through bonded labor; corrupt governments embezzle the money meant to build schools and clinics. The age-old problem of the powerful exploiting the powerless is a virulent disease in our world today. But in the book of Amos, God condemned such exploitation of the poor: "You trample on the poor and force him to give you grain . . . For I know how many are your offenses and how great your sins. You oppress the righteous and take bribes and you deprive the poor of justice in the courts" (5:11–12).

And listen to how He feels when those same oppressors claim to be religious:

I hate, I despise your religious feasts;
    I cannot stand your assemblies.
Even though you bring me burnt offerings and grain offerings,
    I will not accept them.
Though you bring choice fellowship offerings,
    I will have no regard for them.
Away with the noise of your songs!
    I will not listen to the music of your harps.
But let justice roll on like a river,
    righteousness like a never-failing stream! (vv. 21–24, emphasis added)

Martin Luther King Jr. frequently quoted this last verse in his quest for racial equality and civil rights for the millions of African-Americans who were deprived of justice in our own country. Like Dr. King, those who see how these unjust systems trap the poor often become crusaders for social justice, criticizing cultural practices, governments, and corporations; writing letters of protest to elected officials; and even marching in the streets.

Yet while it is true that systems that oppress the poor must be challenged to achieve any lasting escape from poverty, even righting all of the systemic wrongs in a community does not automatically liberate the poor from their shackles. There are other, more subtle factors at play. After decades of entrenched material poverty, many communities suffer from a poverty of spirit as well. They have lost faith in themselves and given up after too many heartbreaks and disappointments. My World Vision colleague Jayakumar Christian calls this the "marred identity" of the poor.[1] After a lifetime of exclusion, exploitation, suffering, and want, they no longer see themselves as people created in God's image with creativity, potential, and worth. They have lost the last thing that can be taken from them—hope.

Finally, many Christians believe poverty to be the result of sinfulness and therefore see evangelism as the best, and sometimes only, medicine. They reason that if only the poor were reconciled to God through Jesus Christ and their spiritual darkness lifted, then their lives would begin to change. Poverty indeed can have profound spiritual dimensions, and reconciliation through Christ is a powerful salve in the lives of the rich or poor. But salvation of the soul, as crucial as it may be for fullness of life both in the here and now and in eternity, does not by itself put food on the table, bring water out of the ground, or save a child from malaria. Many of the world's poorest people are Christians, and their unwavering faith in the midst of suffering has taught me much.

Perhaps the greatest mistake commonly made by those who strive to help the poor is the failure to see the assets and strengths that are always present in people and their communities no matter how poor they are. Seeing their glasses as half full rather than half empty can completely change our approach to helping.

PAYING IT FORWARD

A few years ago, on a trip to Zambia, I was introduced to a man named Rodrick who was about thirty. Rodrick's story was heartbreaking. After serving in the Zambian military, he hoped to return home to his wife, Beatrice, but was instead falsely accused of plotting against the government and thrown into prison. Beatrice gave birth to their son, John, while Rodrick was imprisoned. After several years Rodrick was cleared and released, only to come home to a wife and child living in poverty. The next few years were grim as they had more children and struggled to support them. They tragically lost one child to cerebral malaria. Meanwhile, they literally had nothing—no income, no food, no health care, and no opportunities. But Rodrick and Beatrice were hardworking and clever. The one possession they had was a small hair dryer, so they started a haircutting business to earn a few dollars. World Vision staff, impressed by their initiative, looked past Beatrice and Rodrick's poverty and saw instead their assets. They were industrious and entrepreneurial, willing to work hard. So instead of giving them food and other *things*, World Vision gave them a small loan for an idea they had. Their idea? They would buy bolts of cloth and tie-dye them in hopes of selling the cloth to women who made their families' clothing. I have to admit I was skeptical. How in the world would this couple ever sell enough cloth to make a living? I had spent a career in consumer product marketing and knew a bad idea when I saw one. This idea seemed like a loser to me in a place where there seemed to be no market at all for tie-dyed cloth. Even after they presented me with a beautiful bolt of fabric to take home to my wife, I only felt pity for them, knowing their business would likely fail.

In 2008, I returned to Zambia and had an opportunity to see Rodrick and Beatrice again. It had been four years since they started their little enterprise. I was stunned. Their tie-dye business has succeeded. With the money they saved, they paid back their loan and then started a small storefront to sell food, diapers, and other sundries. One store had turned into two, and they hired their first employee. Rodrick then was able to get connected to the electric grid, and he started a welding business. Once on the grid, Rodrick began charging car batteries overnight for a fee. (These batteries are often used for home electricity by people who can't afford to be on the grid.) Next door he built a Cel-Tel station, where those with cell phones can buy their minutes. He then built a long building out of scrap lumber and tin; filled it with benches; bought a TV, DVD player, and satellite dish; and opened the first movie theater in his community. Not only did he show movies, but he also received all of the professional soccer matches, which the men of the community gladly paid to see. When I visited, he was showing—I kid you not—*The JESUS Film* in the middle of the day to about ten customers.

During my visit, Rodrick took me to a concrete slab with a roof over it that he had just built. The next week, he said, a pool table would arrive, and the first community pool hall would open—a good thing, he explained, because it helped keep the younger men occupied and out of trouble. The young men in his community looked up to Rodrick.

In all, Rodrick and Beatrice, a couple I had pitied just four years earlier, now had eleven different businesses! When I first met them, I had seen only their deficits, not their assets—a mistake I will never make again.

I wanted to test Rodrick's values, so I asked him a question. "Rodrick," I said, "you are now a rich man. What are you going to do with all of your newfound wealth?" Rodrick thought for a moment, and then told me that he had been teaching a Sunday school class at his church for many of the orphans in his community. There are forty-one in his class, and he has committed to visiting each one at his or her home twice a month. Then he said, "God has been good to us, and with His continued blessings I hope to build a school for the orphans. Pray that He will allow me to do this." Rodrick was paying it forward. He rather reminded me of Jimmy Stewart in the classic Christmas movie *It's a Wonderful Life*. His solid example and caring spirit were changing the lives of others. In fact, the whole community seemed more alive than it had four years before. With Rodrick and Beatrice as role models, others had begun to believe that it was possible to succeed, and they were following their leaders' example. One couple's lives and faith were lifting and inspiring an entire community—unleashing the potential that had been there all along.

There is no space here to do justice to all of the various theories on why people are poor and how they can move toward wholeness, but it is important for you to understand that poverty is highly complex and that there are no simple and quick fixes. And when we prescribe one particular "pill" because we see just one particular symptom, the poor never seem to get well. In fact, they find themselves gulping down handfuls of pills prescribed by too many would-be doctors with too little real understanding of their lives. The poor are not lab rats on whom we can experiment with our pet theories; they are human beings with rich cultural and personal stories of their own. They have hopes and dreams, tragedies and triumphs in their lives. They need us to love them first and then listen to them. They need us to see their assets and their God-given abilities. Mother Teresa once said, "When we see [those in poverty] as God sees them, we will glimpse His image in their faces—*Christ in His most distressing disguise.*"

Once we understand all of these factors—a deficit of things, a lack of education and knowledge, unjust systems, marred identity, and even spiritual darkness—to be strands in the web that traps the poor, we must next turn our attention to the "spiders"—hunger, disease, exploitation, armed conflict, and a host of others—that scutter across that web to feast on their prey. I call them the "horsemen of the apocalypse."

CHAPTER TWELVE

THE HORSEMEN OF THE APOCALYPSE

Woe to those who make unjust laws,
to those who issue oppressive decrees,
to deprive the poor of their rights
and withhold justice from the oppressed of my people,
making widows their prey
and robbing the fatherless.

—ISAIAH 10:1–2

I WAS HUNGRY . . .

He who is dying of hunger must be fed rather than taught.

—SAINT THOMAS AQUINAS

I looked, and there before me was a black horse! Its rider
was holding a pair of scales in his hand. Then I heard . . . a voice . . .
saying, "A quart of wheat for a day's wages, and three
quarts of barley for a day's wages."

—REVELATION 6:5–6

Perhaps the quintessential image in our minds when we think of the poor is that of an emaciated child. Undoubtedly that picture has been seared into our minds over decades by the many appeals from aid agencies and the newscasts that seem to cover the poor only when there are graphic visuals and dire emergencies to report. No one who was an adult during the 1984–85 Ethiopia famine will forget the vivid images of death that sent shock waves around the world and resulted in unprecedented media attention, giving, and the involvement of hundreds of celebrities. The unfortunate thing about most of the imagery of starvation is that it has caused most of us to think of poverty one-dimensionally. In essence: for many Americans, hunger equals poverty. Yet poverty, as I have stated, is a complex condition caused by a web of interwoven factors. Hunger is but one symptom of this underlying condition. But hunger is surely one of the worst of the "horsemen of the apocalypse" that ravage the poor.

In 2008, I was reading an editorial in the *New York Times* about the world's food crisis, caused by spiraling food prices. Listen to the heartbreaking newspaper story of those in Haiti, just a few hundred miles from Miami:

> In Haiti, where three-quarters of the population earns less than $2 a day and one in five children is chronically malnourished, the one business booming amid all the gloom is the selling of patties made of mud, oil and sugar, typically consumed only by the most destitute. "It's salty and it has butter and you don't know you're eating dirt," said Olwich Louis Jeune, 24, who has taken to eating them more often in recent months. "It makes your stomach quiet down."
>
> Meanwhile, most of the poorest of the poor suffer silently, too weak for activism or too busy raising the next generation of hungry. In the sprawling slum of Haiti's Cité Soleil, Placide Simone, 29, offered one of her five offspring to a stranger. "Take one," she said, cradling a listless baby and motioning toward four rail-thin toddlers, none of whom had eaten that day. "You pick. Just feed them."[1]

Can you imagine your children so hungry that you offer to give them to strangers—just so they will live? Unthinkable. Most of us have never been truly hungry. Oh, we say things like, "I'm *starving*," or "I'm *famished*," but few of us have gone even one day without food. So it is very difficult to understand what hunger really means for the poor. Its cascading impact goes far beyond just the pangs and physical discomfort that accompany it. Hunger also affects the human spirit. Perhaps most destructive of all is the desperation felt by parents who know that there will be no food today, and likely none tomorrow, to satisfy their hungry children. This horror gnaws at the heart, perhaps even more than it gnaws at the stomach, and it colors every other aspect of life. Each day becomes a struggle to survive. Everything else must be pushed aside: productive work; education; family and community projects; even social interactions, celebrations, and play—all tabled in favor of the quest for food.

Imagine for a moment that beginning tomorrow there would be no more food available—no supermarkets selling groceries, and no money to buy them if they did. Everything would change. You would not wake up, get dressed, and head off to work or school. You would awake to the knowledge that every hour of your day must be obsessively devoted to the search for sustenance. No more social gatherings with friends or times of merriment. No more planning for the weekend or the week to come. Life as we know it would cease. This is the reality for the chronically hungry, but it gets worse.

> One out of four children in developing countries is underweight, and some 350 to 400 million children are hungry. Worse, it is estimated that a child dies every five seconds from hunger-related causes.

Malnutrition compromises the human body in shocking ways. The body, in an attempt to conserve energy, compensates by slowing down physical and mental processes. A hungry mind cannot focus. A starving person does not have the strength to labor. And a child who hungers loses the ability to learn and even the desire to play. Undernourished women are more likely to die in childbirth or have underweight children that are malnourished from birth. Mothers who survive the birthing process often fail to produce enough milk to sustain their infants for more than three to six months. Malnutrition in children stunts brain development and can leave children mentally impaired for life, producing a whole generation of adults with compromised mental abilities. It stunts physical growth as well and impairs the body's immune system, making children and adults alike more vulnerable to the legion of diseases usually present among the poor: malaria, measles, worms and other parasites, tuberculosis, cholera, yellow fever, dengue fever, diarrhea, and dysentery. Vitamin and mineral deficiencies (B_{12}, iron, iodine, vitamin A, and other critical nutrients) harm young bodies in myriad ways, diminishing every facet of a child's potential.

Sadly, one out of four[2] children in developing countries is underweight, and some 350 to 400 million children are hungry.[3] Worse, it is estimated that a child dies every five seconds from hunger-related causes.[4] Remember those one hundred crashing jetliners? Hunger is one of the airports from which they take off.

In numbers, chronic hunger/malnutrition is one of the fiercest apocalyptic horsemen that ravage the poor. Almost one in seven worldwide, 854 million people, do not have enough food to sustain them.[5] This makes hunger/malnutrition the number one risk to health globally, greater than AIDS, malaria, and tuberculosis combined.[6] About 25,000 people die each day of hunger or related causes—9 million people per year.[7]

HUNGER AT A GLANCE

- Roughly 1 of 4 children in developing countries is underweight.
- Some 350 to 400 million children are hungry.
- About 1 in 7 worldwide—854 million people—do not have enough food to sustain them.
- Approximately 25,000 people die each day of hunger or its related causes—about 9 million people per year.

The world can and does produce enough food to feed all of its 6.7 billion inhabitants. The problem is that both the food and the capacity to produce it are unequally distributed. Actually, the underlying causes of food shortages are many. Climate, drought, and natural disasters are major contributors to both chronic and short-term food shortages. War, displacement of people, and political corruption are other major contributors. Additional causes include a lack of technical expertise and agricultural infrastructure in poor countries where the need is greatest. The cycle is vicious—the poor are hungry, and their hunger keeps them poor.

I WAS THIRSTY . . .

Water is life, and because we have no water, life is miserable.
—a voice from Kenya[8]

Most of you began this morning with a hot, clean shower. You brushed your teeth, filled a glass with water, and took a few vitamins. (The older I get, the more pills I seem to take.) Perhaps you brewed a cup of coffee or drank a glass of juice with breakfast. And each day you run your washing machines and dishwashers and take your toilets for granted. You probably have one, two, or even three bathrooms in your home. You may also have a sprinkler system to water your lawn and garden. Your refrigerator is filled with cold drinks, bottled water, and maybe even ice-cold water dispensed from its door. If you have children, they probably haven't spent even one hour of their lives fetching water for the family to drink or to bathe with. And I'll wager that neither you nor your children have ever had a sick day due to unclean water—unless you have traveled to *another* country and picked up one of many waterborne bacteria or parasites.

So now, as you did with hunger, I want you to imagine for a moment that when you wake up tomorrow, all of the water-related fixtures and appliances have been removed from your home. The sinks, toilets, bathtubs, and showers are gone. Dishwasher, washing machine, garden hoses, sprinklers—all gone. Let's say, though, that everything else about your home remains the same. Still, how would your life change with just this one difference?

Well, think about it. You would wake up wanting to use the toilet, take your hot shower, brush your teeth, swallow those vitamins, and fix breakfast—but you can't. What would you do? At first, you would be irritated by the minor inconvenience of having no showers, toilets, dishwasher, or washing machine—until it started to dawn on you that this is far more serious—a threat, actually, to your health, your family, even your survival. Finding a way to get water would begin to consume your life. Without food you can live sometimes for weeks, but without water? Life as you know it would be transformed—and not in a good way.

Where I live, we are fortunate to have a wonderful lake just about two miles away, so if I knew I was going to be without water, I could begin to plan ahead to organize some water fetching. On foot, it would take about two hours round-trip to go fetch water to use for drinking and some rudimentary bathing, but thirty gallons of water weighs about 250 pounds. I checked my water bill and learned that my family uses about three hundred gallons a day. That would weigh more than a ton and would require fifty round-trips to the lake each day, so my family might have to reduce their water consumption a bit. Reducing to thirty gallons would be a 90 percent reduction, but carrying thirty gallons of water two miles would still take about five or six trips a day, carrying fifty pounds each time, consuming about ten hours of hard labor. If you think it's inconvenient to go to the gym to work out every morning, try lugging fifty pounds of water back to your house so you can brush your teeth and have a sponge bath—then try making that trip five times. Now, if you had to work this routine into your schedule every day and still get everyone off to work or school on time, you would have to begin your treks in the wee hours of the morning. Washing your clothes and dishes, let alone your own body, would become an overwhelming task.

Last year my wife, Reneé, was asked to speak to a group on the topic of clean water. Because she has not had the opportunity to visit as many World Vision water projects in the field as I have, she felt she needed to get a little firsthand experience. She decided to go through a whole day without turning on the water in our house. While going without a shower, not brushing her teeth, and forsaking her morning coffee were daunting enough, she was determined to carry it a bit further, so she set off with her Rubbermaid bucket toward that lake two miles away. She then dipped it into the lake and started home, carrying perhaps just three or four gallons in her bucket.

By the time she got home, she was exhausted and less than a gallon of water was left in her bucket, as much of it had sloshed out along the way. It had been a terrible experience—made worse by the fact that a neighbor driving by saw her schlepping the bucket and asked if she had started a cleaning business! Reneé found the whole experience quite challenging, and she was able to speak to her audience a few days later with the passion that only comes from experience.

Now, this little imaginary dilemma I took you through earlier may sound a bit amusing as you think about how absolutely dependent you and your family are on water, but let me add a more sinister dimension. Imagine that the water you fetched from the lake was teeming with deadly bacteria, parasites, and waterborne diseases—that are literally killing you. This is the grim reality for about 1.2 billion people in our world today.[9] As many as 5 million people die every year of water-related illnesses.[10] A child dies every fifteen seconds of a waterborne disease.[11] This creates a no-win situation for millions of parents in our world today—they can watch helplessly as their children die for lack of water, or they can watch them die from diarrhea, because the only water they have is tainted.

Tragically, living without water has even more dimensions. Thousands of hours are lost seeking and hauling water, especially by women. These are hours that could be spent earning an income or contributing to the well-being of the family and community. This same task affects children too: millions of them are unable to attend school because of the hours they spend fetching water. And because of the unsafe quality of their water, many who can go to school are chronically sick and struggle with learning. Some waterborne parasites—Guinea worm, for example—can even result in crippling, and bacterial diseases such as trachoma can cause blindness.

> As many as five million people die every year of water-related illnesses. This creates a no-win situation for millions of parents in our world today—they can watch helplessly as their children die for lack of water, or they can watch them die from diarrhea, because the only water they have is tainted.

Despite the risks, women and children in developing countries invest two hundred million hours a day fetching water.[12] That's equal to a full-time workforce of twenty-five million people fetching water eight hours a day, seven days a week! The men, as unremittingly ill as their wives and children, become less productive in their work, often reducing the agricultural output and food supply of the whole community. Those whose immune systems have been weakened by AIDS or tuberculosis are further ravaged by waterborne illnesses, and it is estimated that as many as one-half of the world's hospital beds are occupied by people with a water-related illness.[13]

A few years ago I was traveling in West Africa with Steve Hilton, head of the Conrad N. Hilton Foundation, one of our most faithful partners in bringing clean water to the poor. We visited a village in Northern Ghana called Gbum Gbum (pronounced *boom boom*). As we gathered around the borehole well that World Vision had drilled several years earlier right next to the school, the school's headmaster told us that before the borehole he had just forty students. Now more than four hundred children attended the school! The difference? Before the water came to Gbum Gbum, the women and children had to spend about five hours each day fetching water from a waterhole several kilometers away. They would rise early, before dawn, making several trips throughout the day; they had no time or energy for school. Another man told me that before the well, children and adults alike were riddled with Guinea worm disease (dracunculiasis) caused by parasitic nematodes found in contaminated water. These worms grow inside the body, sometimes up to three feet in length, and then when full-grown, burrow out through the skin, causing crippling pain and infection. Now the Guinea worms were gone.

As Steve and I continued our walk through the village, we met several dozen women working with great effort to make something called shea butter, an ingredient used in skin lotions and cosmetics, from a locally grown plant. To my amazement, they were selling this shea butter for a profit. In fact, I was told that it was even being bought by Bath and Body Works—in the United States! The only thing these women had needed to create this business was time and clean water, both of which were now available.

We also talked with some of the men in the community who told us that since they now had more water for irrigation, they also had improved crop yields. Then one man said something that caused them all to laugh. Our guide, who translated for us, told us that the men also felt that the women now "smelled better," since they no longer had to fetch water all day in the hot sun. Water had transformed Gbum Gbum in every way imaginable.

I can imagine my own life without many of the so-called necessities that I have. You can take away my car and I would find a way to compensate by using public transportation or carpooling with a friend. You could take away my computer and my Internet access, my television, stereo, and radio, and I could still have a full and prosperous life. You could reduce the size of my house and my income by half, and even take away my education and I could survive and perhaps even thrive. But if you take away water and sanitation, you take away my health and that of my children. If you take away my health, you have taken away my energy and my industry. If you take away my energy and ability to support my family, you have taken away my dignity; and if you take away my dignity, you have taken away hope—for the future, for my children, for a better life. This is the harsh reality of the more than one billion people in the world who live without access to clean, safe water.

In Africa they don't say that water is *important* to their lives; they say that water is *life*. It is absolutely the foundation upon which civilization and human life is built, and the best news is that we have the knowledge and the technology to provide it. All we lack is the will.

I WAS SICK . . .

I looked, and there before me was a pale horse! Its rider was named Death . . . [He was] given power over a fourth of the earth to kill by . . . plague, and by the wild beasts of the earth. —Revelation 6:8

If poverty is a web of interwoven causes that trap the poor, then surely disease is one of the most vicious spiders patrolling that web—and one of the fiercest of the horsemen. Just two statistics sum up the ravages of disease on the poor: child mortality rates and life expectancy. In the United States and Europe, only about 2 out of every 1,000 children die before their fifth birthday.[14] In Africa, on the other hand, 165 (16.5 percent) of each 1,000 are dead by age five. And in Sierra Leone, the worst country in the world for child mortality, 28.2 percent of all children are dead by age five.[15] But as Bono said, "We can be the generation that no longer accepts that an accident of latitude determines whether a child lives or dies."[16]

What about the average life *expectancy* for a child born today? In the United States, it is seventy-eight.[17] But for Sub-Saharan Africa, it is just forty-seven,[18] and for the worst countries, especially those impacted by HIV/ AIDS, life expectancy is between thirty-five and forty.[19] This means that in much of Africa a teenager is already what we would call "middle-aged."

Raising five children, I have often marveled at the sheer number of times Reneé and I (mostly Reneé) had to take our kids to see a doctor. When they were small, sometimes there would be a trip to the doctor every week for one thing or another—ear infections, fevers, colds, broken arms, rashes, cuts, coughs, dental work, and, of course, inoculations and regular health checkups. We were regular customers at the pharmacy, buying whatever combination of medications the doctor prescribed. As many young parents will attest, sometimes our kids' illnesses and accidents produced anxious moments fraught with worry over whether our child would be okay and if the doctor would be able to see him or her right away. There were many times, even, when we called the doctor in the middle of the night for help. I struggle to imagine what would have happened to our children if there had been no doctor to call, no medicines to give.

Awhile back, Reneé traveled to Niger, by some standards considered the poorest country in the world. She was there at a time of severe famine that had followed on the heels of both a drought and a massive plague of locusts, both of which had destroyed the crops—some countries never get a break. Once there, she went to a remote area where Doctors Without Borders had set up a clinic and feeding station to deal with masses of people migrating to find food and help. As she talked to some of the young mothers who had walked for miles and miles with their emaciated infants, she tried to understand their tragic stories.

One seventeen-year-old mother, Saa Mamane, had brought her infant son, Sahabi Ibrahim, to see the doctors. He had then been put in the tent with the sickest children. Feeding tubes were taped to his little nose, and a nurse desperately tried to find a vein to insert an IV. Her baby cried, but with no tears. He'd been vomiting for days and was severely dehydrated. When Reneé asked this mother why she hadn't come for help sooner, she said that it was much too far to walk with a sick baby, and that until two days earlier, she didn't have the fifty cents required to come by car.

This is the disparity in access to health care that exists in our world. The wealthiest countries, where just one-fifth of the world's population lives, spend 90 percent of the world's health care dollars, allowing the remaining four-fifths of the planet to spend only 10 percent of the money. In the United States, we spend about $3,170 per person on health care each year. In much of Africa and Southeast Asia, the comparable figure is $36, an eighty-eight-fold difference.[20]

In chapter 9, I wrote that almost ten million children will be dead in the course of a year. These deaths, all occurring before the child reaches the age of five, are caused by the following health predators:

% of Under 5 Child Deaths[21]	
Birth complications	21%
Pneumonia	19%
Diarrheal diseases	17%
Neonatal (infant) illnesses	15%
Malaria	8%
Measles	4%
AIDS	3%
Injuries	3%
All other	10%

I can't emphasize enough that the conditions in which the poor live produce a kind of "perfect storm" for the spread of disease. Health experts believe that undernutrition is a contributing factor in half of these deaths, with unsafe drinking water being a second leading contributor. Living in close quarters with farm animals, coupled with poor sanitation practices to deal with human waste, expose the poor to additional hosts of bacteria. Lack of knowledge concerning basic medical concepts, such as how diseases are spread, safe childbirth, infant care, and how to treat a wound, also takes a heavy toll. Add to this list the absence of effective health care providers and infrastructure and you begin to understand the staggering death toll in poor communities. An abscessed tooth or an infected cut can become a death sentence. A slight complication in childbirth can take the lives of both mother and child. A fall or accident that breaks a bone becomes permanently crippling. The list of diseases that prey on the poor runs into the thousands, but three of the most horrific warrant further understanding and explanation: malaria, tuberculosis, and AIDS.

MALARIA

Malaria is one of the world's deadliest diseases. Even though it has been largely eradicated in the developed world (in the United States it was wiped out by 1950 through widespread spraying of DDT in swamps and in homes), it is deadlier than ever in poor countries. According to the World

Health Organization, there are more than 500 million clinical cases of malaria each year, resulting in 1.5 to 2.7 million deaths.[22] A 2007 cover article in *National Geographic* featured the extent to which malaria has plagued the human race over the centuries:

> Few civilizations, in all of history, have escaped the disease. Some Egyptian mummies have signs of malaria. Hippocrates documented the distinct stages of the illness; Alexander the Great likely died of it, leading to the unraveling of the Greek Empire. Malaria may have stopped the armies of both Attila the Hun and Genghis Khan.
>
> At least four popes died of it. It may have killed Dante, the Italian poet. George Washington suffered from malaria, as did Abraham Lincoln and Ulysses S. Grant. In the late 1800s, malaria was so bad in Washington, D.C., that one prominent physician lobbied—unsuccessfully—to erect a gigantic wire screen around the city. A million Union Army casualties in the U.S. Civil War are attributed to malaria, and in the Pacific theater of World War II casualties from the disease exceeded those from combat. Some scientists believe that one out of every two people who have ever lived have died of malaria.[23]

Despite the scope of malaria's impact on the world today and on human history, most of us know nothing about it. The one-celled parasites that transmit the disease, known as *plasmodia*, are carried by mosquitoes of the genus *Anopheles*. Just one drop of water the size of the period at the end of this sentence can contain as many as fifty *thousand* plasmodia[24]—yet it takes just one to kill a person. That's because once in the body, a single plasmodium can multiply into the billions. These "storm troopers" invade the blood stream, entering and destroying red blood cells. The body's temperature then rises sharply in an attempt to "cook" the parasites to death, and the victim suffers headaches, muscle pain, and extreme cycles of fever and chills. In the worst cases, the parasites manage to invade the brain—cerebral malaria—causing it to swell and pushing the

> Some scientists believe that one out of every two people who have ever lived have died of malaria.

victim into a coma. As brain cells die, the body begins to shut down. Once too many blood cells have been destroyed, the blood supply to vital organs is disrupted, the lungs can no longer get enough oxygen, and the heart struggles to pump. The weakest and most vulnerable victims, usually children, succumb, as their little bodies can no longer fight the disease. This spiral of events results in one child dying of malaria every thirty seconds.[25] Those who survive their bout with malaria may suffer brain damage and diminished capacity and will most likely have recurring episodes of the disease several times a year if they live in a malarial region.

But loss of life and wellness are not the only impacts of this disease. Because so many people become sick with malaria (one of every thirteen people in the world every year), the loss of productivity is debilitating. In high-incidence countries it is estimated to cause a 1.3 percent deficit in economic growth (GDP) due to lost hours and impaired abilities.[26] Students who survive the disease lose many days of school, and when they return, their ability to learn is often reduced. Because malaria is endemic in the poorest countries, it, too, acts as a horseman of the apocalypse that disproportionately hurts the poor, who can neither escape it nor afford to be treated for it.

But malaria need not reap so grim a toll. Medicines are available that, when administered on a timely basis, can stop the progression of the disease and save lives. Spraying insecticides in mosquito breeding areas and inside houses can reduce the likelihood of being bitten. Perhaps one of the most effective interventions is the use of insecticide-treated bed nets, especially for the most vulnerable, children and pregnant women. At a cost of about ten dollars, these simple nets provide personal protection that can greatly reduce risk. If malaria were taking more than a million lives in the United States, you can be sure that every possible resource would be deployed to stop it and that all of the major drug companies would be working on vaccines.

Thankfully, the Bill and Melinda Gates Foundation has reignited efforts not just to control malaria but to eradicate it. They are pouring hundreds of millions of dollars into research on both treatments and the development of a vaccine. In October 2007, Melinda Gates addressed a large gathering in Seattle on the issue of malaria and made this bold statement:

> The first reason to work to eradicate malaria is an ethical reason—the simple human cost. Every life has equal worth. Sickness and death in

Africa are just as awful as sickness and death in America. In Africa and other areas of the developing world, malaria keeps adults from going to work, students from going to school, and children from growing up. Any goal short of eradicating malaria is accepting malaria; it's making peace with malaria; it's rich countries saying: "We don't need to eradicate malaria around the world as long as we've eliminated malaria in our own countries." That's just unacceptable.[27]

TUBERCULOSIS

Last summer my son Pete had to go in for his obligatory precollege physical, as he was going off to Wheaton College just a month later. Pete is an athlete and is as healthy as a horse, so you can imagine our shock when we were told by the doctor that Pete had tested positive for tuberculosis (TB). In fact, the doctors were just as surprised as we were, since positive TB tests in Bellevue, Washington, are quite rare. Concerned about how a suburban teenager could have come into contact with the disease and about a possible outbreak in Bellevue, they started to ask him questions to determine where he might have come into contact with it. "Have you traveled outside of the United States?" they asked. Pete said that, yes, he had gone to India with his parents four months earlier and had been visiting AIDS patients. Prior to that he had gone to Mexico with his youth group to build houses, and he had spent time volunteering in homeless shelters in both Seattle and San Francisco. "Oh," the doctor said knowingly, "that explains it." You see, Pete had been with the poor, and that's where tuberculosis is typically found. But because he is fortunate enough to live in the United States, he finished his nine months of intensive antibiotic treatments to prevent the bacillus from becoming active. Still, he will test positive for TB for the rest of his life.

Pete's diagnosis should not have surprised us, because it is estimated that one-third of the world's population is infected with the TB bacillus![28] Yes, you heard me correctly, a third of the world—two billion people. Fortunately, only 5 to 10 percent of them will develop full-blown TB during their lifetimes, but that's still one to two hundred *million* cases. And for people who are HIV-positive with an already weakened immune system, TB is their leading cause of death.

TB is caused by a bacterium that usually attacks the lungs but can also assault other parts of the body (kidney, spine, brain, etc.). If not treated, it is often fatal. TB is highly contagious and is spread through the air from one individual to another. About nine million new cases are reported annually (83 percent of them in Africa, Southeast Asia, and the Western Pacific regions[29]), and it causes almost two million deaths.[30] TB was once the leading cause of death in the United States.

> It is estimated that one-third of the world's population is infected with the TB bacillus! Yes, you heard me correctly, a third of the world— two billion people.

Tuberculosis is treatable through a regimen of drug combination therapy that must be administered consistently for months. However, due in part to the difficulty of monitoring the compliance of patients undergoing the regimen, drug-resistant strains have developed that are stubbornly hard to control. Here again is a disease that lives primarily among the poor. Weakened immune systems due to poor nutrition, contaminated drinking water, and the spread of HIV, combined with overcrowding and the absence of health care, compose an open invitation to diseases such as tuberculosis to invade the lives of the destitute.

HIV AND AIDS

As I have said, my own journey with World Vision began at ground zero in Uganda's AIDS pandemic, with three orphaned boys. That I could have been so unaware of something that causes human suffering on such an unimaginable scale makes me feel ashamed even now. That experience was the one event that finally shook me out of the numbing apathy that had prevented me for so long from seeing the world as God might see it. And it may even now be the reason I am writing this book—that others might see what God allowed me to see: the things that break His heart.

We have all seen movie thrillers about a so-called doomsday virus that has been unleashed on an unsuspecting world, wreaking havoc on the human race and changing the course of history. Usually, a small group of stalwart heroes is racing against the clock to save the world from certain annihilation. In this drama, the powers that be seem clueless about the impending doom unfolding right in front of their eyes, and the unsuspecting public goes about their daily lives, blissfully unaware of the coming catastrophe. Unless our heroes are successful at sounding the alarm and defeating their malignant enemy, all will be lost. We know the plotline well.

HIV is just that kind of threat to the human race, in that it has profound implications for our world. If one of those movie producers tries to invent another diabolical "doomsday virus," he will be hard-pressed to come up with something more frightening than HIV.

Consider these facts. A person who becomes infected with HIV today may have no symptoms of the disease whatsoever for three to five years or even longer as the virus establishes itself in his body and begins to attack his immune system. Every sexual encounter that person has during those next three to five years potentially infects each sex partner. Then each newly infected person is also asymptomatic for three to five years and potentially passes the virus on to all of his or her sexual partners, and so on and so on. I once asked a man if he knew how he had been infected. He said, "It is an age-old story: I slept with a woman who had slept with a man who had slept with a woman who had slept with a man . . ." Because HIV is spread primarily through sexual activity, it carries a strong stigma; there are taboos in most cultures that prevent even discussing it. Those who carry the disease often choose to remain anonymous lest they become branded, refusing even to be tested and thereby rejecting the very medical help that might ease the pain. The result is that the disease spreads with stealth from man to woman, husband to wife, and even mother to children through childbirth and breast-feeding. And worst of all, this doomsday virus is fatal—and there is no cure![31]

HIV now infects 33 million people,[32] 70 percent of them living in Africa,[33] and it has taken more than 25 million lives since 1981.[34] There are now three nations in sub-Saharan Africa where more than 20 percent of adults are HIV-positive and ten nations where more than 10 percent are infected. In Swaziland, nearly one in three adults is infected with HIV![35] But the disease is not limited to Africa. India ranks number two in the world for HIV infections,[36] Ukraine has the fastest-growing prevalence,[37] and the disease is spreading like wildfire in Latin America and the

Caribbean. The United States alone has more than 1 million cases.[38] Every day more than 6,800 new people are infected and more than 5,700 die from the disease; that equals 2.5 million new infections per year and 2 million deaths.[39] Put another way, each *week* AIDS takes more than ten times as many lives as the United States lost in the first *five years* of the war in Iraq.

> AIDS has now left 15 million children behind as orphans. In Africa they say that when it comes to HIV, everyone is either *infected* or *affected*—no one escapes completely.

But I'm not done. Perhaps the most disturbing fact of all is that AIDS has now left 15 million children behind as orphans.[40,] [41] Again, this is a number that is incomprehensible. Picture a chain of children holding hands and stretching out across America. This chain, starting in New York, would stretch all the way to Seattle, back to Philadelphia, back to San Francisco, then east to Washington DC, back again to Los Angeles, and finally to about Kansas City—more than five and a half times across the United States! Do you now see why I have called HIV a "doomsday virus"? These are the grim statistics of AIDS, but they do not tell the story of the men, women, and children whose lives have been destroyed. In Africa they say that when it comes to HIV, everyone is either *infected* or *affected*—no one escapes completely.

If we think of AIDS only as a medical crisis with a medical solution, we misunderstand it. AIDS is a sociological tsunami that is eviscerating much of Africa. Typically, the husband who brings it home to his wife becomes sick and dies an agonizing death in front of his own children, leaving the already poor family without a breadwinner. A courageous widow carries on, struggling to raise and support her children alone, usually through backbreaking labor in the fields. Soon though, she, too, becomes sick and too weak to carry on, and her children become her caregivers, bathing her, feeding her, and even changing her soiled bedclothes as she becomes too feeble to move. And then the children are alone. The lucky ones have an aunt or a grandmother to take them in. Grandparents in Africa have become the amazing heroes of the AIDS pandemic as they have risen up to care for their grandchildren and great-grandchildren by the millions. Desperately poor themselves, and in their old age, when others should be caring for them, they soldier on, sometimes caring for twelve or even more children. But when the grandmothers or aunts succumb to disease or old age, the children are orphaned once again, consequently becoming child-headed households, like the boys I met in Uganda. These children are the lost generation of AIDS, vulnerable to dangers of all kinds—starvation, sickness, dropping out of school, child labor, rape, early marriage, prostitution, crime, and drugs. There are no safety nets for most of these kids as they fall through the cracks and are eventually infected by HIV themselves, becoming the "echo boom" of the pandemic. Families are destroyed and whole communities are devastated as AIDS kills the most productive layer of African society—the mothers and fathers, the teachers and farmers, even the health care workers and government officials—causing whole economies to stagger and fall.

> AIDS is a sociological tsunami that is eviscerating much of Africa.

Several years ago I had an audience with the president of Malawi, Bakili Maluzi. We talked of the challenge that AIDS presented to his country and some of the things World Vision was doing to fight the disease and help Malawian communities affected by it. Just before our time was finished, he asked me a question. "Mr. Stearns," he began, "does World Vision have ideas about how we can replace the teachers, the farmers, the nurses that Malawi is losing to this disease?"

"Mr. President," I said, "there is only one way that I know to replace a teacher, a farmer, or a nurse: you must start with a child and carefully nurture and teach them until they become what God has gifted them to be. I'm afraid World Vision knows no secret shortcuts for that."

"I suspected as much," President Maluzi replied, "but do you now see the challenge I face in Malawi? We are losing our most productive people, and they cannot be replaced." And his reality is being faced by much of Africa today. If you really want to paint a doomsday picture for this pandemic, ask an economist what will happen if India, China, or Russia reaches an infection rate comparable to Africa's and its economy starts to falter, triggering a global economic domino effect—and a downward spiral of failed economies, ruined states, and political chaos.

These are the brutal facts of the AIDS pandemic, the doomsday virus that I sometimes call the greatest humanitarian crisis of all time. But once again I want to stress that there is reason for hope. The battle against AIDS, like that against malaria and tuberculosis, is a winnable war—*if* we are willing to take up the fight. Uganda's incidence of HIV infections in 1991 was 21 percent.[42] Then Uganda's president, Yoweri Museveni, declared war on AIDS as a threat to Uganda's future and security. He called on every sector of Ugandan society—schools, churches, the media, businesses, and the health care system—to join the battle and invited international governments and aid agencies to help. Education was central to his campaign, and he and his wife even went door-to-door offering AIDS tests. Billboards were visible everywhere, calling people to abstinence, faithfulness to one partner, and safer sexual choices as part of one's *patriotic* duty. The result was astounding. The incidence of HIV infections fell from 21 percent to about 6 percent between 1991 and 2000[43] as people changed their sexual behaviors. According to Harvard researcher Dr. Ted Green, Uganda's success was the equivalent of a "social" vaccine with an 80-percent effectiveness rate.[44] And all of this occurred before antiretroviral drugs were readily available to treat those already infected. Other countries have also made strong progress. Between 2001 and 2005, prevalence rates fell in Botswana from 38.8 to 24.1 percent, in Zimbabwe from 33.7 to 20.1 percent, and in Kenya from 15 to 6.7 percent.[45]

Three diseases alone—malaria, TB, and AIDS—result in more than five million deaths per year and half a billion new infections, virtually all in the world's poorest countries. The poor are routinely exposed to situations and conditions that attack their health—disease, malnutrition, parasites, and bad water. Poor health, in turn, saps their energy, limits their capacity, and kills their children. They live in places where doctors and medicines are largely unavailable, and even if such health care were available, they lack the money to pay for it. In short, poverty leads to poor health, which in turn leads to greater poverty—one more strand in the web that traps the poor.

And there are many, many spiders . . .

CHAPTER THIRTEEN

SPIDERS, SPIDERS, AND MORE SPIDERS

Injustice anywhere is a threat to justice everywhere.
—MARTIN LUTHER KING JR.

"He defended the cause of the poor and needy,
and so all went well.
Is that not what it means to know me?"
declares the LORD.
—JEREMIAH 22:16

I WAS NAKED, A STRANGER, IN PRISON . . .

I realize as I write this that my descriptions of the legion of things that prey so heartlessly upon "the least of these" in our world must be overwhelming to someone reading about them for the first time. I am trying to walk a fine line between providing you the knowledge so important to understanding the plight of the poor and driving you away—engulfing you with a sense of hopelessness. Please hold tightly to three things as you continue to read:

- Every one of these hurting people is created in God's image and loved by Him.
- Every one of these challenges has a solution.
- Every one of us can make a difference.

Bob Pierce once said, "Don't fail to do something just because you can't do everything." These are wise words to anyone overwhelmed with the magnitude of human suffering in our world. We are not asked to help all of them at once, just one at a time.

While this cataloging of the challenges facing the poor cannot be complete in only a few chapters of a book, you need to be aware of the most dangerous spiders on the web. I will not do them justice but will at least attempt to mention them to round out your understanding.

NO MONEY, NO CLOTHES

It's not about charity. It's about justice. —Bono

He who is kind to the poor lends to the LORD, and he will reward him for what he has done. —Proverbs 19:17

In Matthew 25, as Jesus was listing those He considered "the least of these," He specifically mentioned the "naked" (vv. 36, 40, 43, 45 NKJV). I want to expand this idea to speak to the whole issue of *economic well-being*. In Jesus' time, the "naked" were those so poor that they literally lacked clothes to wear. While that may seem impossible today, I have personally met hundreds of people in my travels who own only the clothes on their backs. They have no closets. A few years ago I spent some time with one of these people, a courageous grandmother in her seventies, named Finedia, in Zambia. All of her children and grandchildren had died of AIDS—two whole generations—and she was left to care for her one great-grandchild, Maggie, who was seven. They lived in an abandoned shack with a dirt floor and a collapsing roof. Neither owned shoes, and the tattered dresses they wore were the only clothes they had.[1]

> Don't fail to do something just because you can't do everything.

People like Finedia, who are economically poor, essentially have no money with which to buy anything, whether clothes, food, school supplies, or medicines. That's because they have no jobs—and there are no jobs to be had. Many underdeveloped countries have unemployment rates as high as 75 percent. The result is that people literally live off the land, eking out a livelihood by growing their own food and raising a few animals. If they end up with more food than they need, they may be able to sell off a few chickens or bags of corn in local markets, but even this is unreliable.

Many of these people are endowed with creativity and initiative, and they have great ideas for businesses and income generation—Rodrick, for example, the clever entrepreneur I described earlier. But because they require an investment of money, sometimes as little as fifty dollars, they cannot bring their ideas to fruition. Truly, the hopes of millions of the hardworking poor to earn a living are thwarted for lack of a few dollars—to buy a swatch of fabric, a couple of breeding chickens, or a litter of pigs. Historically, banks and financial institutions have been unwilling to lend to the poor since they have no collateral. They consider them bad credit risks.

Muhammad Yunus, who won the Nobel Peace Prize in 2007 for his revolutionary dedication to becoming a "banker to the poor," has worked his entire life to create the emerging microfinance industry, based on the belief that providing loans and financial services to the poor will allow them to work their way out of poverty. Yunus and the thousands that followed him have proven this to be true, and it has become one of the most effective weapons we have in the war against poverty.

While microfinance can take many forms, typically loan groups of six or twelve people are formed in a community comprised of neighbors who know and are willing to vouch for one another. Each member develops a plan to create a livelihood relying on his or her own talents, networks, and access to resources, estimating the amount of money needed to launch or capitalize the businesses. In this model, the microfinance institution (often operated by a nonprofit, such as Opportunity International, World Vision, or CARE) then makes a loan to the loan group, who then lends to the individual. The idea is that if the individual fails to pay back the loan, the group is responsible for repaying it. This results in considerable peer pressure and accountability, but it also promotes mutual support and cooperation among group members. More important, this approach recognizes and leverages the talents and capabilities of the poor. Best of all, when loan recipients successfully start their businesses, repay their loans, and create income that can support their families, they feel the sense of self-worth and human dignity that we all seek as they literally lift themselves out of poverty. And receiving a "hand up" instead of a handout makes a huge difference, not just in terms of self-esteem, but in sustainability as well. The old adage is true: "If you give a man a fish, he'll eat for a day, but if you teach a man to fish, he'll eat for a lifetime." Listen to what happened to one woman when she was taught to "fish."

"NOT BAD FOR A WOMAN"

I met this remarkable woman named Lida Sargsyan a few years ago in Armenia, a country still recovering economically from years under Soviet rule. I was there to visit some of the clients who had received microloans through World Vision's separate microloan institution. Lida was one of the "stars." A talented seamstress, she had approached World Vision several years earlier for a loan of a few hundred dollars to buy a sewing machine. She repaid that loan quickly and took additional loans to buy more equipment and supplies, each time a bit larger and each time paying them back with interest. She was building and growing an apparel business specializing in tailored suits for men, women, and children.

As we walked into her factory, I was astonished to find large sewing and cutting machines, a warehouse full of supplies, a shipping room filled with orders soon to be shipped, and forty employees! She was virtually bursting with pride as she showed me what she had been able to create with her own talents—and a few strategic loans from World Vision.

We ended the tour in her office, where she pulled out printed proofs of her fall catalog. In it were photographs of all of her new styles and products for the coming season. This catalog would be distributed not only throughout Armenia but also in several neighboring countries—she had gone international. The point is, years earlier, World Vision could have simply given her handouts to address her poverty, but instead we chose to believe in her—and to give her a hand up. As a result, she and forty others were drawing paychecks to support their families.

As I was leaving, I told her that while I had been the CEO of two American companies, I had rarely met anyone as talented as her in business. Obviously delighted, she smiled at me and said, "Not too bad for a woman, eh?"

No, what she had achieved would not be too bad for a Wharton MBA!

ILLITERACY

I am illiterate. I am like a blind person. —an illiterate mother in Pakistan[2]

As I shared in an earlier chapter, my own ticket to prosperity was education. Even though neither of my parents finished high school, I was able to attend some of the best universities, because in America, it's possible to do so. The education I received had leveled the playing field and allowed me to pursue a productive career. The same thing can be true for the poor in developing countries; an education can greatly enhance their ability to prosper and make a contribution to their community and their nation. That link between education and success is something we understand well in wealthier nations, so we invest billions of dollars to make a good education available to as many people as possible. But education is expensive, and poorer countries simply don't have the financial wherewithal to provide a high-quality education for all children. For comparison, the United States spends about $1,780 per capita on primary and secondary education; Uganda spends just $5 per capita.[3]

Today one in six adults in the world is illiterate, and two-thirds of them are women.[4] And the picture for the world's future adults doesn't look any better. There are 115 million children who do not attend primary school. In Africa, only 59 percent attend school at all, and only one in three will complete primary school. The reasons children do not attend school are many. For some, their families need them to work—fetching water, farming, or even working in bonded labor[5] to pay off a debt. UNICEF estimates that, in the least-developed countries, 29 percent of the world's children aged five to fourteen are engaged in child labor.[6] Others may have to stay at home to care for a sick parent, particularly in regions where AIDS is rampant. Girls are often thought to not need an education and are kept home to do domestic work. And poor governments do not always provide schools in every district or may face a serious shortage of teachers. (I have been to communities in high-HIV areas where so many teachers have died, they cannot find replacements.) Education is foundational to the development of a child, his or her community, and the entire nation, and no long-term escape from poverty is possible without the methodical and routine education of children—both boys and girls.

GENDER

Thank heaven for little girls, for little girls get bigger every day! . . .
They grow up in the most delightful way! —Maurice Chevalier

If only it were so.

The lyrics to Maurice Chevalier's most enduring song describe an idyllic view of little girls and the women they become. There is much in our Western art and literature that romanticizes girls and women and the role they play in our culture. But, sadly, in our world today, being female often means being sentenced to a life of poverty, abuse, exploitation, and deprivation.

> There is a saying in many parts of Africa: "If you educate a man, you simply educate an individual, but if you educate a woman, you educate a nation."

Compared to her male counterpart, a girl growing up in the developing world is more likely to die before her fifth birthday and less likely to go to school, since girls are often forced to work rather than attend school. (As proof, two-thirds of the world's eight hundred million illiterate are women.[7] In Niger, only 15 percent of the women can read.[8]) She is also less apt to receive adequate food, health care, and economic opportunities, but more apt to be forced to marry before age sixteen *and* to be the victim of sexual and domestic abuse. Some two million children, mostly girls as young as five years old, are part of the growing commercial sex trade around the world.[9]

Five hundred thousand women die every year from complications in childbirth; that's one woman every minute.[10] Girl babies are even killed in countries where males are considered more valuable. Those who survive are denied property rights and inheritance in many countries. In fact, women own less than 1 percent of the world's property.[11] They also work two-thirds of all the world's labor hours, but earn just 10 percent of the world's wages.[12]

So, as you can see, though Chevalier may have thanked heaven for little girls, being female in much of our world is anything but heavenly. So, in my opinion, the single most significant thing that can be done to cure extreme poverty is this: *protect, educate, and nurture girls and women and provide them with equal rights and opportunities—educationally, economically, and socially.*

According to former UN secretary-general Kofi Annan, "No tool for development is more effective than the empowerment of women."[13] This one thing can do more to address extreme poverty than food, shelter, health care, economic development, or increased foreign assistance.

There is a saying in many parts of Africa: "If you educate a man, you simply educate an individual, but if you educate a woman, you educate a nation." When a girl is educated, her income potential increases, maternal and infant mortality are reduced, children are more likely to be immunized, the birth rate decreases, and the percentage of HIV infections (especially in Africa) is lowered. An educated girl is more likely to acquire skills to improve the economic stability of her family, and she is also more apt to ensure that her daughters receive an education too. Educating girls pays dividend after dividend to the whole community.

REFUGEES AND WAR

Addressing global poverty would certainly be simpler and more straightforward if it were not exacerbated by wars, civil strife, and other forms of violence. Since the end of World War II, there have been some 250 major wars fought, killing about 23 million people and creating tens of millions of refugees and displaced people driven from their homes. Ninety percent of these casualties have been civilian, and three out of four have been women or children. Today there are 42 different conflicts being waged across the world. The twentieth century was the bloodiest in human history, and its war casualties were three times greater than those of the previous five hundred years combined.[14] The ongoing war in the Democratic Republic of Congo has taken more than five million lives, with more than forty-five thousand people dying each month.[15]

When we think of war, we tend to think only of the fighting, without regard to the social, economic, and emotional consequences. War disrupts food production as farmers are driven from their land. This results in prolonged periods of hunger and even famine. Markets and economies are also upset, making it impossible for the working poor to earn a living. Schools are closed, and children go uneducated, or worse, are conscripted as soldiers. Health care delivery is interrupted too, leading to additional casualties. Women and girls are raped routinely by invading armies, accelerating the spread of AIDS. War changes everything.

There are now 9.9 million refugees (people driven to another country) in the world and 23.7 million people who are internally displaced (driven from their homes within their country). That's a total of about 34 million people who have lost everything because of war and conflict.[16] Again, these statistics are numbing. Try to imagine that yesterday you and your family were violently driven from your home with only the few possessions that you could carry. Then imagine being forced into massive refugee camps with no sanitation, health care, or schools, living in makeshift tents or shelters, and you will get a glimpse of the horrors facing the war-displaced poor. I have visited camps in Uganda where some of these folks had lived for more than twenty years. Many have seen their children and grandchildren born there.

The other dimension of war and conflict is the economic cost. Here comes a very big number: $1.2 *trillion*![17] (If you do the math, you'll find that means twelve hundred *billion*—in digits, $1,200,000,000,000.) That is how much the governments of the world are spending on their militaries. The United States accounts for almost half of this figure and spends more than the next forty-six nations combined. To put this number in perspective, compare it to the total global humanitarian assistance from rich nations to assist the poor: $104 billion.[18] In other words, the world spends twelve times more per year on militaries and defense than it does for development assistance for the poorest of the poor. (No wonder Jesus said, in Matthew 5:9, "Blessed are the peacemakers.") By one estimate, just an additional $65 billion per year would be enough to lift the one billion people who live on less than a dollar a day out of their extreme poverty.[19] That would only require diverting 5 percent of global military spending toward helping those struggling to survive in our world.

A SMILE WITHOUT LIPS

In the midst of war, true evil abounds; unspeakable atrocities are committed; brutality is endemic. War is never benign. But war is more than just an impersonal term that we can brush aside at will. It has a face—and it is human. One human face of war, whom I will never forget, is that of a woman named Margaret, who was caught in the violence of Northern Uganda's war against the rebel Lord's Resistance Army. One day Margaret, six months pregnant, was working in her garden with several other women when rebels—a group of child soldiers led by an adult LRA commander—emerged from the bush. They had come to steal food and other supplies. But stealing was not enough, and they attacked the women, literally hacking Margaret's friends to death with machetes while she watched. But as they approached Margaret to do the same, the commander noticed that she was pregnant. Believing it would bring bad luck to murder a pregnant woman, he instructed his child soldiers to not kill her. Instead, he gave the order to cut off her ears, nose, and lips and leave her to die; that way, he reasoned, her subsequent death would not be on their hands. So they carried out the unthinkable and left Margaret maimed and bleeding to death.

But Margaret was found and rushed to a hospital for treatment. Remarkably, she survived and three months later gave birth to a son, James. She and James were then brought to World Vision's Children of War Center, where she received trauma counseling, support, and, later, skills training as a seamstress. Margaret, traumatized and permanently disfigured, was trying to rebuild her life and be a mother to her child. This is where I met her, perhaps a year after her ordeal.

To our American sensibilities, Margaret's story seems beyond comprehension. There is nothing in our frame of reference that allows us to understand such brutality. What happened next can only be understood through the miracle of God's love—as a demonstration of the incredible power of the gospel to redeem even the darkest kinds of evil.

One day, months after her son's birth, Margaret saw the commander who had given the order to maim her, arriving at the same rehabilitation center. He had been captured and had also been sent for counseling and rehabilitation. I cannot imagine the emotions this must have triggered in Margaret. In great distress, she frantically told one of her counselors that she had to leave immediately, that she could not be near him, and that she wanted to kill him. In response, the man was moved to a different rehab center several kilometers away. But Margaret's anxiety remained.

World Vision counselors began working with this man. At first, he denied that he had committed the atrocities. They worked, too, with Margaret, trying to lessen her anxiety and exploring the possibility of forgiveness. After weeks had passed, the man confessed to his involvement in Margaret's attack, even as she worked through her own fears and anger. Finally, a meeting was arranged. The man asked Margaret to forgive him. And Margaret, reaching deeply into the source of all forgiveness—Jesus Christ—forgave. Here again was the power of the gospel to redeem and restore, and to meet evil and turn it back. On the wall of the Children of War Center are photographs of that day—Margaret and this man who had mutilated her.

He is holding little James in his arms as she stands next to them—smiling without lips.

CHAPTER FOURTEEN

FINALLY, THE GOOD NEWS

*"Sometimes I would like to ask God why He allows poverty,
suffering, and injustice when He could do something about it."
"Well, why don't you ask Him?"
"Because I'm afraid He would ask me the same question."*

—ANONYMOUS

Bad news goes about in clogs, good news in stockinged feet.

—WELSH PROVERB

*"In this world you will have trouble. But take heart!
I have overcome the world."*

—JOHN 16:33

I had to tell you the bad news before ending with the good news. We must not, as Christians, stick our heads in the sand and pretend that the world is doing just fine because we are. We must not avert our eyes, like the priest and the Levite, walking by those suffering on the other side of the road—our neighbors. We must face the brutal facts about poverty and injustice—only then can we take the first steps to respond. But the magnitude of the problems facing the poor can be overwhelming and can drive us away. That is why it is so critical to remember the three principles I stated earlier:

- Every one of these hurting people is created in God's image and loved by Him.

- Every one of these challenges has a solution.
- Every one of us can make a difference.

SEEING STARFISH

There is an oft-told parable I have always liked that will help you wrap your mind around the daunting statistics of poverty. It is about just one man—and a million starfish.

> One early morning, after a fierce storm had hit the coast, I strolled to the beach for my morning walk. Horrified, I saw that tens of thousands of starfish had been washed up on the beach by the winds and waves. I was saddened by the realization that all of them would die, stranded on the shore, away from the life-giving water. Despairing that there was nothing I could do, I sat down on the sand and put my head in my hands.
>
> But then I heard a sound, and I lifted my eyes. There, in the distance, I saw a man bending down and then standing up, bending down and standing up. Curious, I rose and walked toward him. I saw that he was picking up the starfish, one at a time, and throwing them back into the sea.
>
> "What are you doing?" I yelled.
>
> "Saving the starfish," he replied.
>
> "But don't you see, man, that there are tens of *thousands* of them?" I asked, incredulous. "Nothing you can do will make a difference."
>
> He did not answer me but instead bent down, picked up another starfish, and cast it back into the water. Then he smiled, looked me in the eye, and said, "It made a difference to that one!"[1]

These last few chapters, which exposed the raw, unvarnished reality of human suffering, may have been difficult for you to read. They may even have had the numbing effect on your senses that I warned you about. But let me ask you, what did you see in those narratives and statistics that described the plight of the poor? Did you see just a beach littered with bodies, or did you see each unique starfish—a precious part of God's creation—lying there, with a better life just waiting to be lived? The truth in this familiar story is important: we must never see poverty or justice as "issues" that need solutions; rather we must see the human beings at the heart of those issues as *people* who need and deserve our love and respect. I believe that we really can alter the world, but we can only do it one person at a time. And when enough people choose to do this, even a crisis on a global scale can change.

In fact, there is some good news for us to celebrate. Things are actually much better for many of the world's poor today in comparison to thirty or forty years ago. Efforts by humanitarian aid organizations, governments, church groups, businesses, and the United Nations have resulted in slow but steady and encouraging progress on many fronts. This is a race that we can win—indeed, that we *are* winning—but it is a marathon, not a sprint.

Consider just a few of the accomplishments that have occurred over the past few decades:

- Life expectancy in developing nations increased from 46 years in 1960 to 66.1 in 2005.[2]
- The under-five child mortality rate has been cut in half since 1970.[3]
- Preventable child deaths have fallen 50 percent since 1960 from more than 20 million per year to fewer than 10 million.[4]
- The percentage of the world's people classified as hungry has been reduced from 33 to 18 percent over the past forty years.[5]
- The percentage of people with access to clean water in developing countries went from 35 percent in 1975 to 80 percent in 2007.[6]
- Polio has been almost eradicated from the globe.
- Adult literacy has risen from 43 to 77 percent since 1970.[7]

Another encouraging development was the adoption of the Millennium Development Goals by the General Assembly of the United Nations in 2000. These eight ambitious goals to greatly reduce extreme poverty in our world were adopted and embraced by the nations of the world with tangible and measurable metrics to be achieved by 2015.

The Millennium Development Goals – Adopted September 8, 2000
By 2015 we resolve to:

1) Eradicate extreme hunger and poverty
2) Achieve universal primary education

3) Promote gender equality and empower women
4) Reduce child mortality
5) Improve maternal health
6) Combat HIV/AIDS, malaria and other diseases
7) Ensure environmental sustainability
8) Develop a global partnership for development[8]

At the halfway point, in 2007, progress had been made on many fronts but was lagging in others. Still, the overall effect of these clear goals has been to focus the world on specific actions and achievements that will change the equation for billions still living in poverty.

It is possible to change the world's realities, and that is exactly what God has challenged us to do. This is what it means to be "salt and light" in a dark and bleak world (see Matthew 5:13–14). It's what the Great Commission was all about. With some two billion Christians in the world, almost one-third of the population, changing the world by addressing poverty and injustice does not seem by any means beyond our grasp. But we must remember, too, Paul's reminder in Ephesians, that "our struggle is not against flesh and blood, but against the rulers, against the authorities, against the powers of this dark world and against the spiritual forces of evil in the heavenly realms" (6:12). Sometimes I will say to my friends, "If you don't believe Satan is real, come with me to Africa, or Asia, or, for that matter, anywhere the poor are marginalized and exploited. Then you will see the face of evil alive and active in our world." Margaret's story of dismemberment is surely proof that spiritual evil is real.

So, in addition to mustering the moral and political will to rise to these challenges, we must also go forth armed with the spiritual power of prayer. And prayer is not the domain of the United Nations or of the governments of the world. Only the faith community can draw upon the power of God through prayer. Perhaps after reading so many pages of heartache and suffering, the notion of prayer as a weapon against the pain of the world seems naive. Maybe you don't believe God answers such prayers.

Read on.

PRAYER AT 14,000 FEET, IN THE ANDES

Pray, but when you pray, move to your feet. —African proverb

A few years ago my wife and I traveled to Peru. We were there with a film crew, trying to capture some before-and-after stories that would appear on one of our World Vision TV specials. We wanted to show our viewers the difference in the lives of the poor after World Vision had worked in their communities for several years, proving to them that we *can* have a transforming effect in people's lives and literally restore hope to their part of the world.

On one particular day we were traveling high up in the Andes Mountains to film one of the "before" stories. It was there that God taught me something about the people behind the statistics—because it was there that I met a woman I will never forget. Her name was Octaviana. These are the field notes I wrote as I returned home a few days later:

Today our travel took us two hours from Cuzco, high up in the Andes to a mountain community called Callqui Central. Our vehicle left the main road and began the arduous ascent up a winding and treacherous dirt road to an elevation of 14,000 feet—almost the equivalent of Mt. Rainier's summit near where I live in Washington State. On this gloriously clear and sunny day, the views of the surrounding peaks and valleys were spectacular. This was literally a natural paradise . . . Shangri-La in this mountain range, second only to the Himalayas in their grandeur. Adding to this natural beauty were the occasional adobe brick houses with sheep, llamas, and alpacas grazing on the slopes . . . and the remarkable people—native Peruvian Indians adorned in festive colors with brightly woven shawls and skirts with their distinctively colorful hats. Children waved eagerly at the rare sight of a vehicle passing through. Most women carried infants slung over their backs.

In the United States, this would be priceless land, dotted with resort hotels, ski lodges, and condominiums. But here the natural majesty was a deceptive veil hiding the suffering and poverty of these beautiful people.

We stopped in front of a small adobe structure and were greeted by a remarkable woman, Octaviana, and her three children—Rosamaria (9), Justo (6), and Francisco (4). This was an exciting day for them because of our visit.

We entered this small, one-room structure with walls and floor of dirt. We sat and let Octaviana tell us her story. She was widowed just nine months earlier. Her husband succumbed to respiratory problems and suspected tuberculosis, leaving Octaviana and the children alone to fend for themselves in this harsh mountain environment. She wept in despair as she described the loss of the man who was her provider, her husband, her children's father and her friend. She spoke of her loneliness and her fear, with no one but her and the children to carry on the strenuous work of raising sheep, growing crops, and the daily struggle just to survive.

In this "paradise" we had found pain and suffering. No heat, no lights, contaminated water, and little food. The entire family was sick with parasites and respiratory disease. The children had to stop attending school to help with the heavy workload, and on top of it all, Octaviana was struggling to pay a three-hundred-dollar debt her husband had incurred buying his livestock. Worst of all, her only source of income, her small flock of sheep, were dying of some disease. She could no longer sell them at the market; she could only bury them.

Octaviana's story, sadly, was not unique. Each of the families in this region had their own tale of sadness, sickness, and death. These magically beautiful people in this breathtaking setting suffered deeply and anonymously. How rarely do we pause to remember the poor, to consider their suffering? Some, like Octaviana, are eight thousand miles away, and even more remote from us culturally. Some are just a few miles away, yet their pain is real whether we know of it or not. They suffer alone, with no one to hear their cry.

I asked her what she prayed for, because I could tell she was a woman of deep faith. She said that she prayed to God that He would not forget her and her three children on that remote mountain—that He would help her carry this burden and that He would send help. And as I held her hand and prayed for her, God revealed to me a profound truth—that I was the answer to Octaviana's prayer. Eight thousand miles from my home in Seattle, 14,000 feet up in the Andes Mountains, she had cried out to God for help, and He had sent me. God had sent me to help her, He had sent me to comfort her in her suffering, and He had sent me to be Christ's love to her. She had prayed and I was God's answer, I would be God's miracle in her life.

And then the even bigger truth washed over me. I could see that all across the world people were crying out in desperation to God for help, for comfort; widows, orphans, the sick, the disabled, the poor and the exploited. These millions of prayers were being lifted up to God, and we, each of us who claim to be His followers, were to be His answer. We were the ones who would bring the "good news" of Christ to the poor, the sick, and the downtrodden. God had not turned His back on the poor in their suffering. God had sent us. This was the good news of the gospel—good news indeed for the poor.

I will return to my comfortable home in a few days. I'll tuck my children into their comfortable beds and read them a story. The familiar routines of my life will resume again. But tonight, Octaviana is still on that mountain in her run-down adobe house. She will sleep on the hard floor with her three children coughing and shivering through the night— hungry and afraid, and she will pray again to her God.

I promised her that I would not forget her. I promised her that I would help. I promised her that I would be the answer to her prayers. May God help me to keep those promises.

POSTSCRIPT

After my visit, World Vision did come alongside Octaviana and her children, bringing clean water and latrines to her and her community, helping her with food and nutrition through improved gardening, and training her in basic health and sanitation. Not all stories have happy endings. Several years after my visit, it was discovered that Octaviana had advanced breast cancer. Virginia, one of World Vision's caregivers, walked with her through her illness, taking her to the health center in Quiquijana and then to the main hospital in Cuzco, looking for a relief treatment, since she was in a great deal of pain. World Vision made arrangements for a surgery that allowed her to live for another year. Meanwhile, Virginia visited her constantly and made contact with the local church for additional spiritual support. When Octaviana died, World Vision paid for all of her funeral expenses. After her death, Virginia looked for a safe place for her three children.

In addition to the children I wrote of in my field notes, Octaviana also had older children, who had grown up and left the community. Her oldest son, Florencio, who had a family of his own, agreed to take in the three young children. World Vision then committed to help Florencio support his expanded family. He came to participate in World Vision agriculture and livestock programs. He was given guinea pigs for breeding—a food source in Peru—and also received technical assistance to run his farm plot and raise his animals. World Vision also provided medicines and extra food for the family for the first few years, and the children received school supplies for the duration. Today, Justo and Francisco still live with Florencio in his community.

Octaviana, a courageous woman whom I met only briefly, enriched my life and taught me much about faith, perseverance, and prayer. She had no title, rank, or formal education, and she lived thousands of miles from me both geographically and culturally. But she blessed me deeply through the few hours we spent together. Jesus said that when we feed the hungry, visit the sick, and clothe the naked, we are doing the same for Him. The day I met Octaviana, I saw Jesus in her eyes. I'm certain I did.

PART 4

A HOLE IN THE CHURCH

We've drifted away from being fishers of men to being keepers of the aquarium.

—PAUL HARVEY

Baseball is like church. Many attend, few understand.

—LEO DUROCHER

CHAPTER FIFTEEN

A TALE OF TWO CHURCHES

I am far from the people who have money.
The rich man closes his door in my face.

—FOUA, A WOMAN FROM EGYPT[1]

If a man shuts his ears to the cry of the poor, he too
will cry out and not be answered.

—PROVERBS 21:13

Where was the Church of Jesus Christ? That was the question I cried out that first day in Rakai, Uganda, after seeing the suffering of orphans living in child-headed households. That question has troubled me ever since. Where, indeed, *was* the Church? If the world as I have described it truly is wracked with poverty, injustice, and suffering, and God has clearly called us to embrace the whole gospel—characterized by love for our fellow man, a commitment to justice, and a proclamation of the good news of His salvation to all people—then we must next look at His Church and ask whether it is being faithful in its responsibility to bring the whole gospel to the whole world. This section of the book will look both at the big-*C* Church, meaning all, regardless of denomination, who claim to follow Jesus Christ, and also little-*c* churches—the local congregations in which we come together for worship, fellowship, and service.

Let me say something at the outset. Some of the things I am going to say in this section are very critical of the Church universal and also some of our individual churches. They were hard to write and may be even harder to read. I love the Church and truly believe that it is at the center of God's plan for the world. I also believe that our pastors have the most challenging jobs imaginable. They must be teachers, preachers, counselors, administrators, leaders, peacemakers, and visionaries, not to mention husbands, wives, fathers, and mothers. Their commitment to us is 24/7 as they try to respond to the overwhelming demands of needy congregations. My intent is not to heap even more on their crowded plates but rather to replace some of what is already heaped there with more nutritious fare. Remember, too, that the faithfulness and effectiveness of any individual church is not carried by its pastors alone but by all who are part of it. My words in this section are directed more to those of us who sit in the pews—not our leaders. If *we* fail to give, serve, pray, and sacrifice, we cannot expect our pastors to compensate for our own lack of commitment.

As a nation of Christians, we are blessed. Never has there been a nation with more educational opportunities, financial resources, technological tools, Bible study materials, training seminars, or Christian books and music. We have been given much, and much is now expected. My goal is to set a high bar of expectation not just for our pastors but for all of us who have been so blessed by the Lord.

When I am critical of some of the shortcomings of our churches, many of you will be tempted to say, "Wait! This is not true of *my* church," and you will be correct. I know of many congregations that are doing incredibly inspiring work in our world and making great sacrifices to do so. To all of them I humbly say, "Well done." I shudder to think what would happen to our country and to the world if the staggering sum total of all of the good deeds of the body of Christ were suddenly removed. But the Church in America must confront the uncomfortable challenge of being endowed with an abundance of blessings in an extremely poor world. We cannot be satisfied with glasses half full. Rather, we must strive to fill our "glasses" until they overflow, bringing blessings to our communities, our nation, and the world. It is with this spirit that I now write.

I want to begin by describing for you two different *imaginary churches* as they might exist in our world today. One might feel very familiar to you, while the other will probably not. When I'm done, you may have a sense of what God sees when He looks at His churches, rich and poor.

Our first church is a suburban congregation in middle America.

THE CHURCH OF GOD'S BLESSINGS

The Church of God's Blessings, as its name suggests, has been blessed by God, growing in just ten years from a small group of founding members to some three thousand strong, after breaking off from a larger church over a doctrinal dispute. Today, after much hard work, they have a beautiful new facility with a sanctuary that holds fifteen hundred and a resource center that houses the burgeoning Sunday school classes, youth programs, church library, and administrative offices. Their pastoral staff has grown to twelve and includes pastors for music and worship, high school, junior high, children's ministries, small groups, missions, men's and women's ministries, and administration. The music program boasts both a worship leader and a choir director, not to mention a marvelous pipe organ and a sound system that was the crowning achievement of the recent building campaign.

This is a church that has impacted the community as well. Located in a prosperous area, it has drawn hundreds of professionals from law, medicine, and many of the booming corporations in the area. Quite a few CEOs and entrepreneurs populate the Sunday services, and the church has also drawn effectively from the students and professors at the university. The annual Christmas pageant has been one of the key outreach events for the church, as each year hundreds of nonbelievers hear the gospel through festive music and drama.

As churches go, this one has been blessed financially. While there is the usual struggle each year to hit the budget, the year-end appeals always seem to pull the iron out of the fire. The various ministries within the church have grown quickly in order to keep up with the diverse needs of the growing congregation. The list of offerings in the church bulletin is impressive: Bible studies; apologetics courses; premarital seminars; divorce recovery sessions; aerobics classes; and support groups for substance abuse, depression, cancer patients and their families, parents of teenagers, and women who have had abortions. There are also group activities for seniors, singles, single parents, college students, young professionals, and young parents.

One of the highlights of the year is a missions focus week during which progress reports are given from the field. The fellowship hall is turned into an international theme park for the children, where foods from different cultures can be sampled and craft projects from around the world are displayed. The church supports twenty missionaries, and more than 5 percent of the church budget is devoted to missions.

On this particular Sunday, the parking lot begins to fill for the first of three morning worship services. Music style has been a divisive issue at the church, ultimately resulting in three different formats offered each week. The first service features traditional hymns and organ music; the second is contemporary; while the third is a blend of both. The choir this morning is impressive as its sixty voices are raised in praise to God.

The Scripture reading this day is from the gospel of Luke:

> And he told them this parable: "The ground of a certain rich man produced a good crop. He thought to himself, 'What shall I do? I have no place to store my crops.' Then he said, 'This is what I'll do. I will tear down my barns and build bigger ones, and there I will store all my grain and my goods.' And I'll say to myself, 'You have plenty of good things laid up for many years. Take life easy; eat, drink and be merry.' But God said to him, 'You fool! This very night your life will be demanded from you. Then who will get what you have prepared for yourself?' This is how it will be with anyone who stores up things for himself but is not rich toward God." (12:16–21)

The pastor preaches a sermon entitled "Investing in God's Kingdom," mindful of the shortfall in the annual operating budget and careful to end on a positive note. (When he gets too "preachy," especially about money, he hears about it after the service.) The offering is then taken, and the parking lot begins to empty to make room for the eleven o'clock crowd.

THE CHURCH OF THE SUFFERING SERVANT

Our second church is located in Africa. The Church of the Suffering Servant is a small congregation of fifty that meets under a large shade tree because they have no building. Its members live a simple life of subsistence as they work the land to provide the food they need to survive. There is great joy in their worship as these people cry out to the Lord and feel His comfort in the midst of their need. They rely on God for every mouthful of food they eat, for every child who is born to them, and for the rain that waters their crops. There is pain in this church, born of illness and hardship; they are well acquainted with grief. They have endured two decades of civil war in their country due to political instability. Every family has suffered some loss at the hands of the armed rebels who have ravaged the land in wave after wave. Men have been killed, houses burned, women raped, children kidnapped, and land and possessions stolen. Food is scarce, and the children often go to bed hungry. Clean water is not available, and the two-hour treks to the waterhole may quench the thirst, but they also sow the seeds of disease. The many sicknesses bring terror, because there is no doctor to visit when things become grim. It is not unusual for children to die from simple diarrhea (many before their fifth birthday) or for mothers to die in childbirth—and there is growing death from AIDS. It has left so many children orphaned.

A school is available, but few can attend, because the children are needed to fetch water, work the fields, and tend the livestock. Money is in short supply; most live on barely a dollar a day, so even the basic necessities are out of reach, like medicines, clothing, and supplemental food. No new farming tools, fertilizers, or better seeds are available, and there is no vehicle with which the community can transport its heavy crops to the market twenty miles away. Only what can be carried can be taken.

But it is Sunday, and this small community comes together to worship and to celebrate the gospel. Such good news, such amazing news—that God loves them and has actually sent His Son to die for their sins, save them in their brokenness, and grant them eternal life with Him!

Today they read from Isaiah 61:

> The Spirit of the Sovereign Lord is on me,
>> because the Lord has anointed me
>> to preach good news to the poor.
>> He has sent me to bind up the brokenhearted,
>> to proclaim freedom for the captives
>> and release from darkness for the prisoners,
> to proclaim the year of the Lord's favor
>> and the day of vengeance of our God,

> to comfort all who mourn,
> and provide for those who grieve in Zion—
> > to bestow on them a crown of beauty
> > instead of ashes,
> > the oil of gladness
> > instead of mourning,
> > and a garment of praise
> > instead of a spirit of despair. (vv. 1–3)

The little congregation breaks into spontaneous and jubilant singing and praise as they contemplate these promises of God. So much comfort, so much love. The pastor cries out in prayer, "Lord, give us the strength to endure. Hear us in our suffering. Deliver us from our circumstances. Help us, Lord; please help us in our need." He then preaches a sermon of hope and reminds his congregation that they must face hardships *together*, loving one another as brothers and sisters in Christ. The service ends, but the singing continues as families disperse and walk together back to their homes. Even on Sunday, there is work to be done.

These two different churches with circumstances poles apart are reasonably accurate portrayals of typical churches in different parts of the world. Neither church is even aware of the other. But what if we could connect them for just a few minutes on a Sunday morning? I'd like you to use your imagination again for a moment. Imagine that you are the pastor of that African church and that through an amazing set of circumstances, you are actually transported to America on a Sunday morning to visit the Church of God's Blessings.

Imagine how awestruck you would be as you entered the parking lot to see all of the shiny cars and this great church building with thousands of God's people streaming in. You have never dreamed of such prosperity— never imagined a church so grand. Your heart leaps at the notion that you have discovered a group of fellow believers that may be able to help your poor congregation in the midst of their suffering.

As you sit in your pew, you are overwhelmed by the music and the chorus of voices that fill the great hall. Brilliant stained-glass windows surround you, and colorful banners hang from the ceiling. The great choir

Karen Homer/World Vision

"I wasn't supposed to be there ..." Rich's encounter with Richard Sseremba and his brothers in Rakai, Uganda (pictured here at their mother's gravesite), awakened him to the plight of children living alone after losing their parents to AIDS (*see page 7*).

Photos courtesy of Richard Stearns

Above: Reneé and Rich around
the time they met at Cornell.
Center: The young Parker
Brothers executive celebrated
the 50th anniversary of the
Monopoly™ board game in style.
Left: Rich left his position as
CEO of Lenox in 1998 to join
World Vision.

Top: Reneé has accompanied Rich on many international trips, including India, where Reneé visited with Chitra, 10, a girl with a brighter future because of her sponsor's support. Above: *"The day I met Octaviana, I saw Jesus in her eyes,"* Rich recalls of the woman he and Reneé met in the Peruvian Andes (*see page 165*).

Top: In Zambia, Rich met Maggie, 7, orphaned by AIDS and living in deep poverty with her great-grandmother, Finedia. Left: Four years later, Maggie attended private school, and she and Finedia lived in a new house World Vision built (*see page 152, 298*).

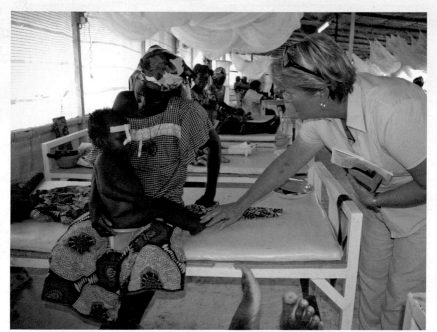

Kari Costanza/World Vision

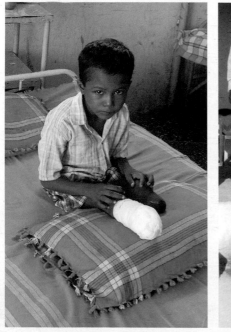

Top: Reneé encountered the effects of severe hunger in a *Médecins Sans Frontières* unit in Niger. Above, left: Rich made a personal commitment to help Vikas Prajapati, 6, after he lost his legs in an earthquake in Gujarat, India. Above, right: This photo of Vikas standing on his prosthetic legs hangs in Rich's office (*see page 111*).

Pastors embracing the "whole" gospel: facing page—Pastor Rath Ourng in Cambodia (*see page 70*); top—Pastor John Thomas of Fish Hoek Baptist Church in South Africa, with Pumla, a member of his AIDS ministry team (*see page 99*); above—struggling and sacrificial church leaders in rural Malawi walked barefoot for miles to see Rich (*see page 188*); right—Morgan Chilulu, who pastors the world's smallest "megachurch" in Zambia, told Rich, "A church that lives within its four walls is no church at all" (*see page 180*).

People who inspired Rich: top left—Hoops of Hope founder Austin Gutwein (*see page 265*); top right—clean-water provider Leon McLaughlin (*see page 267*); above—former President Jimmy Carter during Habitat for Humanity's 1999 Jimmy Carter Work Project in the Philippines (*see page 98*).

Others who inspired Rich: top—Rodrick Ngoma, a Zambian entrepreneur who started 13 businesses (*see page 128*); above—Lida Sargsyan, who runs an apparel business in Armenia thanks to small loans through World Vision's separate microloan institution (*see page 154*).

In Northern Uganda, Rich and Reneé saw evidence of the gospel's light piercing the darkness of brutal conflict. Top: Rich greeted Michael and Joseph, two youths who had been forced combatants in the Lord's Resistance Army, as they arrived at World Vision's Children of War center in Gulu. Center: The center helped rehabilitate young men and women haunted by atrocities they were forced to commit. Bottom: Michael and Joseph listened to Rich preach on the parable of the prodigal son (*see page 61*).

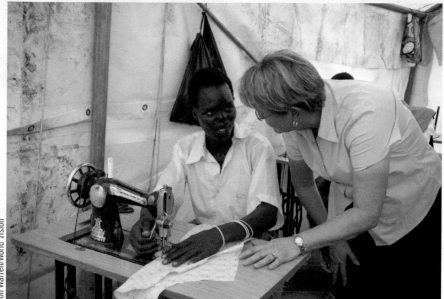

Jon Warren/World Vision

Margaret Alerotek/World Vision

Top: Reneé met Margaret Achiro, who was starting over and learning to sew after being horribly disfigured and left for dead by LRA rebels. Above: Margaret forgave the former rebel who maimed her (*see page 159*).

Top: In Kpalang village, Ghana, this was the only water source for 600 people.
Above: This picturesque scene from Kpalang captures the time-consuming labor of women trying to keep their children alive. Facing page: In nearby Gbum Gbum, Rich and Steve Hilton, head of the Conrad N. Hilton Foundation, saw the impact of clean water—school attendance had leapt from 40 students to 400 (*see page 138*).

Developing-world travel has become a Stearns family affair. Facing page: Rich and Reneé brought Peter and Grace to India (*see page 145*). Top: Andy and his wife, Kirsten, sponsored another child, Chaltu, in Ethiopia. Center: Sarah and Reneé sampled home cooking in Malawi. Right: Hannah cuddled babies in Uganda.

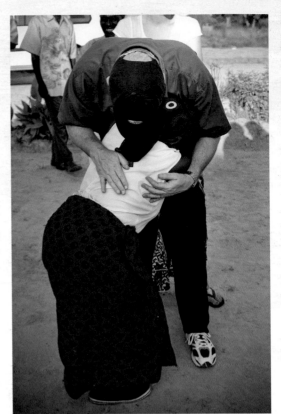

Zambian grandmother Mary Bwalya thanked Rich (top) for sponsoring her orphaned grandsons Jackson and Morgan (below), expressing her belief that God had replaced the parents the boys had lost to AIDS (*see page 270*).

sings, and you feel as if you have gone to heaven. Then the pastor stands and preaches familiar words from the same Scriptures you teach each Sunday in your village. Seated there, you begin to pray—prayers of hope as you ponder how you will say to these brothers and sisters what is on your heart. You will tell them of the children's suffering, the dirty water, the failed crops, and the lack of food. You'll tell them about the sorrow of the widows and the orphans struggling to cope with the ravages of the devastating AIDS epidemic. You'll share how you have prayed so fervently for deliverance and help, crying out to God for a miracle, and now it is here. *They* are your miracle. You have been brought to the place where your story can finally be heard, and help will surely be found.

After the last song, you arise and walk to the front of the sanctuary, carefully ordering in your mind what you will say. You move to the podium, but just as you begin to speak, the people begin to leave. Something is wrong. "Please wait! Listen!" But they are *not* listening. They don't even seem to hear you. It's as if you are invisible to them. Your pleas become more and more urgent as you now follow them out the door to the parking lot, begging them to stop, hoping that even one of them might turn around. But one at a time, they get into their cars and drive away, until you are left alone, your eyes full of tears. Why wouldn't they listen? Why couldn't they see you? *Lord, why didn't You open their eyes and ears to hear and see?*

Can you see the problem? The American church in my little parable was not a "bad" church; it was just oblivious to the suffering of the little church in Africa. It wasn't that they wouldn't help the African congregation; they were just so preoccupied with their own programs and people that they failed to see the bigger picture: the reality of the church across the world. There are some 340,000 individual congregations in the United States, which together possess unprecedented resources and capabilities. There are also hundreds of thousands of poor churches in the developing world, whose members struggle with daily survival. I try to imagine how this looks to God as He sees all of His churches—the wealthy and the needy—and wonders why the churches He has blessed have not reached out to their poor, burdened brothers and sisters.

Let's look again at 2 Corinthians, where this very issue was addressed in the first century. Paul challenged the church in Corinth to give to relieve the suffering of the churches in Jerusalem who were living in extreme poverty. The Macedonian churches, also poor, had taken up a generous collection to assist them; now Paul wanted the Corinthian church to follow their example. Here is how Paul described the Macedonians' sacrificial giving: "Out of the most severe trial, their overflowing joy and their extreme poverty welled up in rich generosity. For I testify that they gave as much as they were able, and even beyond their ability. Entirely on their own, they urgently pleaded with us for the privilege of sharing in this service to the saints" (8:1–4). Though under trial and in "extreme poverty" themselves, they had nonetheless responded to help their brothers and sisters in Jerusalem. The Corinthian church, though, had failed to complete their offering to help, and Paul was urging them to rise to the occasion. "I am not commanding you, but I want to test the sincerity of your love by comparing it with the earnestness of others. For you know the grace of our Lord Jesus Christ, that though he was rich, yet for your sakes he became poor, so that you through his poverty might become rich" (vv. 8–9). Paul framed this as a test of their faith and the genuineness of their love. Then he went on to say, "Our desire is not that others might be relieved while you are hard pressed, but that there might be equality. At the present time your plenty will supply what they need, so that in turn their plenty will supply what you need. Then there will be equality, as it is written: 'He who gathered much did not have too much, and he who gathered little did not have too little'" (vv. 13–15). *That there might be equality.* Notice that the notion of equality comes up twice in this passage. This must be an important concept to God.

So we in the twenty-first century must ask why we have not done more to come to the aid of Christians (and those of other faiths) found in "extreme poverty" in our own time. One reason is surely lack of awareness. For most of my life, I gave little thought to the circumstances of Christians in faraway countries—mostly out of ignorance about their plight. But I think the other reason is self-absorption. We are so preoccupied with our own lives and the daily issues in our own churches that we overlook the challenges faced by churches in other lands. Our sin is not one of *commission* but rather of *omission*. Sins of omission are sometimes the most difficult ones to address. To do so requires intentional and relentless self-examination, a commitment to serve those in greatest need, and a keen awareness of the broader world in which God has placed us. Only then can we become consistent and effective in using our considerable resources for the benefit of the church worldwide.

THE CHURCH IS THE HOPE OF THE WORLD

The Lord says: "These people come near to me with their mouth and honor me with their lips, but their hearts are far from me. Their worship of me is made up only of rules taught by men." —Isaiah 29:13

It's important to understand why churches are so strategically important to carrying out the mission that Jesus described in Luke 4, of bringing the good news of the kingdom of God to the whole world. As individuals, we all have an important role to play in demonstrating the gospel through our lives. We can pray, give, volunteer, and become effective personal ambassadors for the gospel. However, our greatest power to change the world is released when we come together in collective action to organize and focus the resources of the whole body of Christ. A church of one thousand members can have a much more powerful impact by harnessing the power of the whole than its individual members can have acting alone. God established the institution of the Church as a key strategy for building His kingdom and for leading the social revolution required by the gospel—"on earth as it is in heaven" (Matt. 6:10). Said another way, without the collective and organizing power of churches, the ability of Christians to impact the world is greatly compromised.

Bill Hybels, pastor of Willow Creek Church in Illinois, has said, "The local church is the hope of the world, and its future rests primarily in the hands of its leaders." He's right. If Church leaders do not have an outward vision to become salt and light in our world, to promote social and spiritual transformation, pursue justice, and proclaim the whole gospel, then the Church will fail to realize its potential as an agent of change. It will become inwardly focused on meeting the needs of its members, to the exclusion of its nonmembers. It will be a spiritual cocoon, where Christians can retreat from a hostile world, rather than a "transformation station" whose primary objective is to change the world. We need only to read our church bulletin to see where our priorities have been placed. How many of the announcements involve programs that focus more on meeting our needs than the needs of those outside the church? I've been in churches whose bulletins read like the table of contents for *Psychology Today*, listing programs and support groups for depression, anxiety, divorce recovery, bipolar disorder, sexual dysfunction, eating disorders, and dieting, not to mention aerobics, Pilates, cooking classes, and Tae Kwon Do. It's not that churches shouldn't minister to their own members, but there should be a balance between internal and external ministry. As I'll show you in a later chapter, the way our churches spend their budgets provides a pretty sobering glimpse into this matter of balance. When our churches become spiritual spas in which we retreat from the world, our salt loses its saltiness, and we are no longer able to impact the culture.

> When our churches become spiritual spas in which we retreat from the world, our salt loses its saltiness, and we are no longer able to impact the culture.

Morgan Chilulu, an African pastor of a small and humble church in the midst of the AIDS pandemic, once told me, "A church that lives within its four walls is no church at all."

That says it all.

CHAPTER SIXTEEN

THE GREAT OMISSION

The world can no longer be left to mere diplomats, politicians
and business leaders. They have done the best they could, no doubt.
But this is an age for spiritual heroes—a time for men and
women to be heroic in their faith and in spiritual character
and power. The greatest danger to the Christian church today
is that of pitching its message too low.

—DALLAS WILLARD, *THE SPIRIT OF THE DISCIPLINES*

A number of years ago, long before I came to World Vision, my wife chaired our church's annual missions conference. The purpose of the conference was to raise both awareness and money to support our annual foreign missions budget. Many congregations have a similar "missions week," and in our church it was a pretty big deal. The kids' program used astounding creativity to help young children learn about different cultures and the importance of global missions. Great speakers told us firsthand about what was happening in different parts of the globe and how the programs we supported were changing lives.

As with most such conferences, we had a fund-raising goal to support the work. As I recall, for our church it was about seven hundred thousand dollars that year—a very substantial commitment. The conference concluded with an appeal for pledges, and all of the pledge cards were collected at the end of the week.

The following Sunday I expected an announcement from the pulpit regarding how much we had raised in light of our goal—but it never came.

Reneé and I wondered how the congregation had done, so I called one of the pastors that week to find out. "Oh," he said, "we raised pledges of about six hundred thousand dollars, so we are one hundred thousand short of our goal." When I asked what he was planning to do to make up the shortfall, he said, "Well, we're just going to cut back on our programs. What choice do we have?"

"Cut back?" I said. "Why don't we go back to the congregation and tell them we need more money to do the work the Lord has given our church to do?"

The young man then explained that the senior pastor felt that it wouldn't go over very well if he asked for more money. This really bothered me, so I asked him if I, as a layperson, could address the congregation at the three services the next Sunday to make an appeal to give more.

"You would be willing to do that?" he asked, somewhat skeptically.

"Absolutely," I said. "If God has given us this work to do, then we need to rise to the challenge and do it."

And so, the next Sunday, there I was, making my pitch. "Friends," I said, "two weeks ago we concluded our annual missions conference. As you know, we were seeking to raise seven hundred thousand dollars to do the work God has given our church to do. Unfortunately, when all of the pledges were counted up, we fell short by a little more than a hundred thousand. So this morning we've got a little family business to take care of. I'm going to ask all of you to help us reach our goal by making another pledge. Right now I'd like to ask you to just find a piece of paper somewhere in your pew. Tear a page out of your hymnal if you need to—just kidding!

"Now, the first people I want to address are those who haven't made any pledge at all. You need to make one right now. I don't care if it's just for one dollar, but everyone needs to participate in supporting the Lord's work at a level they can afford. Write down your name and address and the amount of your pledge, and throw it in the offering plate.

"Now, for those of you who already made a pledge, you need to make another one. That's right, another pledge. I am going to bet that all of us this year will spend money on something less important than this. We'll buy a new piece of furniture, maybe a new car, we'll go out to movies and restaurants, and we'll take family vacations. So I'm guessing we have the money to support this; we've just decided to spend it on something else. You heard all week about the needs and the effective programs we support around the world. So let's step up and get it done."

I could tell that this straight talk had freaked people out a bit. They had never heard anything quite like this from the pulpit. Nonetheless, I heard a rustling of papers, and people seemed to be responding to my request. I thanked them, prayed, and sat down.

After the first service, I saw one of the pastors and asked what he thought. He said that the senior pastor was irritated that I had gone over my time by two minutes, and that he didn't appreciate the comment about tearing a page out of the hymnal. A bit discouraged by this chastisement, I did the other two services in less time and then went home.

A couple of days later I still hadn't heard from the church on how it had all come out, so I called again to ask. I was told that a little over one hundred thousand dollars in additional pledges had come in. It had worked, people had responded, and we achieved our goal. But even though this had taken us over the top, I still had the distinct impression that I was viewed as a nuisance. The senior pastor hadn't wanted to rock the boat. Ours was a good church, a faithful church in so many ways, but a church whose leaders, both pastoral and lay, had perhaps lost the sense of urgency for God's kingdom advancing across our world. "Missions" had become just one more program, not a nonnegotiable commitment. This has always been a problem with God's people; we tend to drift away from God's bold vision, replacing it with a safer, tamer vision of our own.

But in Isaiah 1, we can see exactly what God thinks when His people have lost their zeal for serving Him. While written to the people of Judah, these scathing words can easily be applied to the twenty-first-century Church:

> Listen to my Message,
>> you Sodom-schooled leaders.
> Receive God's revelation,
>> you Gomorrah-schooled people.
> "Why this frenzy of sacrifices?"
>> God's asking.
> "Don't you think I've had my fill of burnt sacrifices,

rams and plump grain-fed calves?
Don't you think I've had my fill
   of blood from bulls, lambs, and goats?
When you come before me,
   whoever gave you the idea of acting like this,
running here and there, doing this and that—
   all this sheer commotion in the place provided for worship?
Quit your worship charades.
   I can't stand your trivial religious games:
monthly conferences, weekly Sabbaths, special meetings—
   meetings, meetings, meetings—I can't stand one more!
Meetings for this, meetings for that. I hate them!
   You've worn me out!
I'm sick of your religion, religion, religion,
   while you go right on sinning.
When you put on your next prayer-performance,
   I'll be looking the other way.
No matter how long or loud or often you pray,
   I'll not be listening.
And do you know why? Because you've been tearing
   people to pieces, and your hands are bloody.
Go home and wash up.
   Clean up your act.
Sweep your lives clean of your evildoings
   so I don't have to look at them any longer.
Say no to wrong.
   Learn to do good.
Work for justice.
   Help the down-and-out.
Stand up for the homeless.
   Go to bat for the defenseless. (vv. 10–17 MSG)

Do you hear what God is saying in these blistering verses? He is sick
of churches and people who just "go through the motions." And He is
weary of seeing a shiny veneer of faith but no depth of commitment. That

is the *hole in our gospel*, and until we fill it, ours is an empty religion, one that God despises. Notice that in this passage, He is so angry that He says He won't even listen to our prayers or pay attention to our worship rituals. "But doesn't God *want* us to worship Him?" you might be asking. "Didn't He *command* us to pray?" Yes, of course, but one of the highest and best ways of expressing our love for God is by demonstrating His love tangibly to those around us. We achieve this by showing compassion to the most vulnerable of God's children and fighting for justice.

A few years ago World Vision did a survey of pastors, in which we asked them to rate the things they considered real priorities for their churches. Based on a list of items that we provided, these ministers were to tell us which ones they thought took precedence over the others. In the highest-priority category, 79 percent listed worship; 57 percent, evangelism; 55 percent, children's ministry; and 47 percent, discipleship programs. Just 18 percent said that "helping poor and disadvantaged people overseas" was of "highest priority."[1] Startling when you consider the words of the apostle James: "Religion that God our Father accepts as pure and faultless is this: to look after orphans and widows in their distress and to keep oneself from being polluted by the world" (James 1:27). *The Message* puts it this way: "Anyone who sets himself up as 'religious' by talking a good game is self-deceived. This kind of religion is hot air and only hot air. Real religion, the kind that passes muster before God the Father, is this: Reach out to the homeless and loveless in their plight, and guard against corruption from the godless world" (vv. 26–27).

God wants to see the authenticity of our faith put into action, not the emptiness of a faith without deeds. But if we look at the things that God condemns when He looks at the behavior of His followers, once again it seems that sins of *omission* grieve Him even more than sins of *commission*, yet it is these on which we tend to be fixated. Sins of commission occur when we do something to violate God's commands. These include murder, violence, theft, adultery, profanity, gossip, sexual promiscuity, exploiting the poor, among others. Most Christians and churches speak to these sins quite directly. In fact, our zeal to condemn these sins of commission often causes Christians to be perceived as judgmental and intolerant, always defined by what we are against rather than what we're for. But notice that

God seems to get angrier about those things that He has commanded us but we have failed to do. Again, the book of James says it bluntly: "Anyone, then, who knows the good he ought to do and doesn't do it, sins" (4:17).

What was Isaiah's antidote for this kind of shallow, going-through-the-motions worship of God? Again, the very same elements I have described as being parts of the whole gospel:

> Work for justice.
> > Help the down-and-out.
> > Stand up for the homeless.
> > Go to bat for the defenseless. (Isa. 1:16–17 MSG)

> Is not this the kind of fasting I have chosen:
> > to loose the chains of injustice
> > and untie the cords of the yoke,
> > to set the oppressed free
> > and break every yoke?
> Is it not to share your food with the hungry
> > and to provide the poor wanderer with shelter—
> > when you see the naked, to clothe him,
> > and not to turn away from your own flesh and blood? (58:6–7)

These are the *do's* rather than the *don'ts* of our faith, and they are the very things that make Christ attractive to the world. In fact, the two greatest commandments of our faith—to love God and love our neighbors as ourselves—are also the do's, not the don'ts. When we *do* the gospel—the *whole* gospel—the world takes notice and likes what it sees. That's why Mother Teresa, Billy Graham, Bishop Desmond Tutu, and Pope John Paul II have been such winsome and beloved figures.

THE BEGGARS AT OUR GATE

One of the most provocative parables in Scripture is the story of the beggar Lazarus and a rich man. It begins like this: "There was a rich man who was dressed in purple and fine linen and lived in luxury every day. At his gate was laid a beggar named Lazarus, covered with sores and longing to eat what fell from the rich man's table. Even the dogs came and licked his sores" (Luke 16:19–21).

The picture painted here is graphic and compelling. The rich man lives in indulgence, yet right outside his gate is poor Lazarus, plastered with unsightly, oozing abscesses, and hungering for even crumbs of food. We can be sure that the rich man was well aware of Lazarus; he knew him by name and probably walked by him each day as he came and went from his opulent home. It is interesting that we are told that "at his gate was laid a beggar named Lazarus," perhaps suggesting that God placed him there intentionally to see how the rich man would respond.

We know the eternal fates of both men: "When the beggar died . . . the angels carried him to Abraham's side. The rich man also died and was buried. In hell, where he was in torment, he looked up and saw Abraham far away, with Lazarus by his side" (vv. 22–23). Lazarus found comfort; the rich man went to hell.

Do you see what's important about this? The rich man did not abuse Lazarus, didn't beat him or mistreat him; he simply ignored him, passing by him, day after day, with indifference. His sin was not one of commission but of omission.

> If we in the Church are *truly* dedicated to the Great Commission, then we will first have to do something about the "Great Omission." We will never effectively demonstrate Christ's love to the world, if we cannot first demonstrate it to the Church—the *whole* Church, and that includes those struggling just to survive.

He knew, as the apostle James wrote, the "good" he ought to have done, but he failed to do it (James 4:17). The plain conclusion is that the rich man went to hell because of his appalling apathy and failure to act in the face of the gross disparity between his wealth and Lazarus's poverty. He was aware of the beggar's plight, had the power to relieve his suffering—and yet chose to do nothing. I see in this parable a great metaphor for the Church of Jesus Christ in the third millennium. Has God not laid a beggar at our gate as well? Outside of our comfortable homes and great church buildings lie the poorest of the poor in our world, suffering, hungry, and sick, longing for just a few crumbs from our "rich man's" table. And like the rich man, we cannot say that we do not know about the suffering poor; we cannot claim that we don't have the means to help. We, too, will one day stand before God and give an accounting.

Thinking back to my "Tale of Two Churches," can you see now that the same contrast between Lazarus and the rich man is evident between our rich churches and those of the poor? Can you also see that God has provided enough resources for all of His churches to thrive? It's just that they are not distributed evenly—that's our task.

The little church I described earlier, the Church of the Suffering Servant, was fictional, but it was not far from the truth. A few years ago I traveled to Malawi in southern Africa and had a chance to meet with a group of rural African pastors who were struggling to survive the AIDS pandemic. These twenty or so pastors had walked from their villages to meet me. It broke my heart to see that some of them had come miles—in bare feet! They didn't even own a pair of shoes.

World Vision Malawi staff had helped organize these clergymen into a group, to better address the many challenges that AIDS had been presenting them. (Some of these pastors were performing three to five funerals a week, sometimes two or three in a day.) After all of the introductions, their leader stood up and unfolded a carefully handwritten summary of the activities and needs of their group. This is what he read to me that day:

Our committee is formed of twenty-six pastors with the following aims:
- To preach the gospel of our Lord Jesus Christ
- To strengthen the unity between all churches
- To organize interdenominational prayers
- To work together in fighting HIV/AIDS

The role we play is as follows:
- We visit and pray for those who are affected
- We visit and pray for the orphans
- Building houses and toilets for the aged
- Providing orphans with clothing and maize flour

- Teaching Christians how HIV can be prevented
- We have youth clubs in our churches

He then listed the challenges they are facing:

- Lack of funds for supporting orphans
- Lack of drugs for orphans
- Lack of food for the orphans
- Lack of transport for visiting the orphans and the aged [I had been told that because the community did not own a vehicle, children sometimes had to carry their parents' dead bodies as much as a mile to be buried.]

This paints a pretty vivid picture of the real contrast between our churches and theirs. Over *there* is the church of Jesus Christ in Malawi, facing the greatest challenge of their generation. But they lack the critical things they need to prevail. And *here* is the church in America, brimming over with the very skills, influence, and resources so desperately needed. If we in the Church are *truly* dedicated to the Great Commission, then we will first have to do something about the "Great Omission." We will never effectively demonstrate Christ's love to the world, if we cannot first demonstrate it to the Church—the *whole* Church, and that includes those struggling just to survive.

CHAPTER SEVENTEEN

AWOL for the Greatest Humanitarian Crisis of All Time

We will have to repent in this generation not merely for the vitriolic words and actions of the bad people, but for the appalling silence of the good people.

—MARTIN LUTHER KING JR., "LETTER FROM BIRMINGHAM JAIL"

But then my cynicism got another helping hand—a tiny virus called AIDS. And the religious community, in large part, missed it. The ones who didn't miss it could see it only as a divine retribution for bad behavior. Even on children.

—BONO, *ON THE MOVE*

One of the disturbing things about Church history is the Church's appalling track record of being on the wrong side of the great social issues of the day. If the Church is indeed a revolutionary kind of institution, called to foment a social revolution by promoting justice, lifting up the sanctity of human life, fighting for the underdog, and challenging the prevailing value systems in our world, then it seems we should be out in front on social justice issues rather than bringing up the rear. But what we see when we look historically at the Church is a kind of pronounced "culture blindness," an inability to see the dominant culture through God's eyes.

When I was growing up, TV shows and movies were dominated by "cowboys and Indians." It was just accepted that the cowboys were the good guys and the Indians the bad guys, perpetuating a demeaning racial stereotype. Then, when I was in college, I read Dee Alexander Brown's book *Bury My Heart at Wounded Knee*, which told a more accurate story.[1] In this account, Native Americans had been flourishing for centuries— until the arrival of European colonists, who helped themselves to the land, with little or no regard for the rights of the people already living there. Many tribes sought peaceful coexistence with the settlers, but the treaties they signed were broken as new demands for land and expansion arose. And while certain tribes indeed committed violent acts, these were often provoked by the colonists' actions. We all know that this story ultimately ended in the decimation of Native Americans as they were killed, forced onto reservations, robbed of their lands, and forced to watch as their homes and herds were destroyed. Today we would call it genocide.

So what does this have to do with the Church? Virtually all of the settlers in colonial America had come here for religious freedom; they were Christians. Yet for the most part, Christian settlers and churches either participated in the marginalization of Native Americans or, at the very least, turned a blind eye toward the atrocities committed by their neighbors and our own government.

Slavery, of course, is another dark blot on the reputation of the Church, another example of culture blindness. The slave trade and the inhumane treatment of slaves flourished for hundreds of years, not just in sight of the Church, but within the Church itself. Southern plantation owners would ride off to church in their surreys, while their slaves were picking cotton to line their masters' wallets. Never mind the beatings, lynchings, and rapes that were regularly visited upon the slaves. There were, in fact, many Southern ministers who campaigned strongly against the abolitionist movement. One such person was Rev. James H. Thornwell, who wrote in an 1850 editorial in the *New York Herald* that those who supported the abolition of slavery (and women's suffrage) were "atheists, socialists, communists and red republicans." He denounced putting "all races, sexes and colors upon a footing of equality" as actions that would cause the devil and his angels to be "jubilant."[2]

Perhaps those dark periods happened too long ago to convict you of the sins of the Church, so let's fast-forward and look at civil rights in the 1950s and '60s. This was another sad chapter for American Christians.

The segregated society of those years was very much created and sustained by and with the complicity of Christians and churches in both the North and the South. African-Americans were forced to sit at different lunch counters, drink from different fountains, ride in the backs of buses, and attend different schools. Meanwhile, Martin Luther King Jr. was vilified as an extremist and enemy of decent, God-fearing people because he dared to challenge the social injustice of his day. Like Paul, Dr. King penned some amazingly prophetic words on scraps of paper from a jail cell. In his "Letter from Birmingham Jail," he addressed this label of "extremist":

> But . . . as I continued to think about the matter I gradually gained a measure of satisfaction from the label. Was not Jesus an extremist for love: "Love your enemies, bless them that curse you, do good to them that hate you, and pray for them that despitefully use you, and persecute you." Was not Amos an extremist for justice: "Let justice roll down like waters and righteousness like an ever-flowing stream." Was not Paul an extremist for the Christian gospel: "I bear in my body the marks of the Lord Jesus." Was not Martin Luther an extremist: "Here I stand; I cannot do otherwise, so help me God." And John Bunyan: "I will stay in jail to the end of my days before I make a butchery of my conscience." And Abraham Lincoln: "This nation cannot survive half slave and half free." And Thomas Jefferson: "We hold these truths to be self-evident, that all men are created equal . . ." So the question is not whether we will be extremists, but what kind of extremists will we be. Will we be extremists for hate or for love? Will we be extremist for the preservation of injustice or for the extension of justice? In that dramatic scene on Calvary's hill three men were crucified. We must never forget that all three were crucified for the same crime—the crime of extremism. Two were extremists for immorality, and thus fell below their environment. The other, Jesus Christ, was an extremist for love, truth and goodness, and thereby rose above his environment. Perhaps the South, the nation and the world are in dire need of creative extremists.[3]

Here again, the Church was found guilty, some members of sins of commission, and others of sins of omission. Later in his letter King spoke directly to the Church's failure in this time of need. These are visionary words that should cause us even today to pause and examine our consciences.

> Let me take note of my other major disappointment. I have been so greatly disappointed with the white church and its leadership . . . I do not say this as one of those negative critics who can always find something wrong with the church. I say this as a minister of the gospel, who loves the church; who was nurtured in its bosom; who has been sustained by its spiritual blessings and who will remain true to it as long as the cord of life shall lengthen.
>
> When I was suddenly catapulted into the leadership of the bus protest in Montgomery, Alabama, a few years ago, I felt we would be supported by the white church, felt that the white ministers, priests and rabbis of the South would be among our strongest allies. Instead, some have been outright opponents, refusing to understand the freedom movement and misrepresenting its leader; all too many others have been more cautious than courageous and have remained silent behind the anesthetizing security of stained-glass windows.[4]

"More cautious than courageous." "Silent behind the anesthetizing security of stained-glass windows." Are these things still true of us today? King then went on to conclude that a Church that has lost its voice for justice is a Church that has lost its relevance in the world.

> The contemporary church is a weak, ineffectual voice with an uncertain sound. So often it is an archdefender of the status quo. Far from being disturbed by the presence of the church, the power structure of the average community is consoled by the church's silent and often even vocal sanction of things as they are.
>
> But the judgment of God is upon the church as never before. If today's church does not recapture the sacrificial spirit of the early church, it will lose its authenticity, forfeit the loyalty of millions, and be dismissed as an irrelevant social club with no meaning for the twentieth century. Every day I meet young people whose disappointment with the church has turned into outright disgust.[5]

Perhaps you're like me, wondering how my parents and grandparents sat by and tolerated the hateful discrimination against African-Americans in their generation. How had they missed something that in hindsight seems so clear? Were they just "frogs in the kettle" of a culture that had gotten comfortable in the waters of racism and segregation? Is it really their fault that they didn't challenge the prevailing values? Listen to what Jesus said in Mark 7, as He challenged the Pharisees, another set of people who clearly "missed it": "Isaiah was right when he prophesied about you hypocrites; as it is written: 'These people honor me with their lips, but their hearts are far from me. They worship me in vain; their teachings are but rules taught by men.' You have let go of the commands of God and are holding on to the traditions of men" (vv. 6–8).

"Holding on to the traditions of men" is exactly the problem we struggle with when we are called to challenge our culture instead of being absorbed by it. If nothing else, these lessons from history should cause us to ask where our justice "blind spots" are today. What will our grandchildren ask us when they look back twenty-five or fifty years from now and wonder how we could have just sat by and watched when justice was demanded?

A G-RATED MINISTRY IN AN R-RATED WORLD

For we are taking pains to do what is right, not only in the eyes of the
Lord but also in the eyes of men. —2 Corinthians 8:21

As the brand-new president of World Vision U.S., when I returned from Rakai, Uganda, after that first encounter with the AIDS pandemic, I was both heartbroken and angry that the world was not doing enough to help. I began to ask questions all around World Vision about what we were doing to care for the orphans and widows and how we planned to battle this terrible disease. Even World Vision, which had been eyewitness to the impact of AIDS in community development work throughout Africa, had to be shaken awake before fully realizing the extent of what they were facing. We were responding to the fallout from AIDS, but we didn't yet have a coherent plan to either address the disease's impact on the poor or to raise the financial support we would need to expand our response. I can remember distinctly the discomfort in the room as I brought together some of our marketing people and tried to marshal cooperation to raise both awareness and money in our donor community. There were awkward glances as I asked how we might take this issue out to our support base. Finally someone spoke up and said, "We're a G-rated ministry focused on children and families. AIDS is an R-rated issue. I don't think our donors are going to be willing to give for this, and if we push too hard, it could hurt our reputation."

There. It was on the table. My staff knew that the evangelical community and the broader population had been more than apathetic about the issue of AIDS; they had been downright hostile toward it. AIDS was perceived as a gay disease contracted through a homosexual and promiscuous lifestyle. During most of the 1980s, it had been a key battleground in the "culture wars" that had dominated the dialogue between the evangelical Christian community and secular society. It was not one of our proudest moments. Most Americans didn't even realize that, globally, AIDS was a primarily heterosexually transmitted disease. (I even had a well-educated friend ask me, when he heard how AIDS had affected African countries, if everyone in Africa was gay!) The prevailing view was that if you had AIDS, you deserved it.

"But," I reasoned, "much of the impact of AIDS is actually on women who become infected by their husbands, and children who end up orphaned through no fault of their own. Surely people understand that. I refuse to believe that Christians will not feel compassion for children who have become orphans because of AIDS. And didn't Jesus tell us to love people unconditionally? Even if someone contracted the disease because of extramarital sex or homosexual behavior, are we to judgmentally withhold our compassion?" I was getting angry again.

We decided that before launching any national program to raise support for our AIDS ministry, we should first conduct a research study to ask real people to tell us how they actually felt about this issue. We needed to know what we were up against, so we contacted the Barna Group and fielded a survey on the willingness of Christians to help people affected by AIDS. The results?

When evangelical Christians were asked whether they would be willing to donate money to help *children* orphaned by AIDS, assuming they were asked by a reputable Christian organization that was doing this work . . .

- only 3 percent answered that they definitely would help;
- 52 percent said that they probably or definitely would *not* help![6]

These were evangelical Christians! Sadly, virtually every other demographic group we surveyed, including non-Christians, showed a greater willingness to help.

"Houston, we've got a problem!"

When it came to rising above the prevailing culture, seeing the plight of AIDS orphans and widows as an issue of justice, and reaching out of their comfort zone to help, the Christian community was failing. When it came to showing compassion to AIDS victims, culture blindness obscured our sins of apathy and judgment, just as it blinded Christians in previous generations to slavery and racism. We see this same exact pattern in God's people in the Old Testament, condemned by Isaiah and other prophets, and again in the hypocrisy of the Pharisees, which Jesus denounced in the strongest of terms. The message should be plain for us to see—history demonstrates that the institutional Church often fails to rise above and challenge the popular culture and values.

However, it is also true that there are always faithful "extremist" voices within the Church. Some Christians opposed the exploitation and genocide of Native Americans. Slavery was ultimately ended by committed abolitionists standing on *scriptural* truth. William Wilberforce and the Clapham sect in England were determined to challenge the injustice of slavery based on their passionate Christian values. Abraham Lincoln challenged slavery in the United States out of his own deeply held Christian convictions that it was morally wrong in the sight of God. Bishop Desmond Tutu, who fought to topple apartheid in South Africa, did so as a Christian fighting for justice. Martin Luther King Jr. was a Christian minister, and many of those who marched with him, white and black, did so out of their own commitment to biblical justice. On each of these historic social justice issues, there were voices in the churches speaking up for truth and righteousness, but they were often drowned out by the majority, who had become comfortable with, or profited from, the status quo.

Our track record here should be sobering. What are the injustices in our world right now that we cannot see? Where have we been co-opted by our prevailing culture? What are the implications of this for pastors and church leaders? How can we avoid the same mistakes that we see so clearly in hindsight in our predecessors?

Every speaker at an Alcoholics Anonymous meeting begins by saying, "My name is _____, and I am an alcoholic." Doing this forces the person to acknowledge his failure with humility and prevents him from playing any denial games that could trick him into believing he doesn't really have a problem. May I suggest that we take this same approach with respect to our culture blindness? We should neither be surprised at our own blindness nor be judgmental of our leaders for theirs. All of us are susceptible to the strong pull of our prevailing culture. And so, we, like the alcoholic, must approach our society's blindness with humility, acknowledging first the "plank" in our *own* eye, *then* pointing out the "speck" in the eye of our culture (see Matthew 7:3–5 and Luke 6:41–42). The fact of the matter is, *we are all blind*, and our only solution is to pray that God will *show* us our blindness.

Speaking of the blindness of the religious leaders of His day, Jesus quoted the prophet Isaiah:

Though seeing, they do not see;
    though hearing, they do not hear or understand.
In them is fulfilled the prophecy of Isaiah:
    "You will be ever hearing but never understanding;
        you will be ever seeing but never perceiving.
For this people's heart has become calloused;
    they hardly hear with their ears,
    and they have closed their eyes.
Otherwise they might see with their eyes,
    hear with their ears,
    understand with their hearts
    and turn, and I would heal them." (Matt. 13:13–15)

These were leaders who didn't have a clue. They needed God to open their eyes. The apostle Paul, writing to the Ephesians, also recognized the need to be enlightened by God. He prayed that God would open the eyes of those he loved, so they would see and understand: "I keep asking that the God of our Lord Jesus Christ, the glorious Father, may give you the

Spirit of wisdom and revelation . . . I pray also that the eyes of your heart may be enlightened" (Eph. 1:17–18).

Perhaps every pastor, church leader, and parachurch ministry leader should begin their daily devotions with something similar to the Alcoholics Anonymous recitation as they pray that God would open their eyes to their own blind spots so they can lead their congregations through the strong currents of our secular culture. *My name is _____, and I am blind to the injustices and sins of omission committed by my own church. Open the eyes of my heart, Lord, to see the world as You see it. Let my heart be broken by the things that break Your heart. Give me the ability to see through our culture and to lead my people with Your vision, instead of the world's.*

We must also listen to the prophetic voices both within and outside of our churches. Bono, Tutu, King, Mother Teresa, and many, many others have all spoken prophetically to the Church. We need to pay heed.

HOW FAITH KILLED WORKS

> *But someone will say, "You have faith; I have deeds." Show me your faith without deeds, and I will show you my faith by what I do.*
> —James 2:18

One of the things drummed into my head as a young Christian was the doctrine that we are saved by faith alone and not by works. Understanding and applying this simple truth has been at the root of fierce and contentious debates throughout the long history of the Christian faith. Indeed, the notion that one could be saved by doing enough good works—and could even purchase one's justification through the buying of "indulgences"— was ultimately the root cause of Martin Luther's rebellion against the Roman Catholic system in the sixteenth century, leading to the Protestant Reformation. This same basic debate has seesawed back and forth within the Church ever since, with the pendulum swinging more toward *faith* in some groups and, in certain times, more toward *works* in others. But faith and works were never meant to be in dichotomy. We need only to look at the primary proof text for salvation by faith alone to see the unity of faith and works intended in Scripture: "For it is by grace you have been saved, through faith—and this not from yourselves, it is the gift of God—not by works, so that no one can boast" (Eph. 2:8–9).

For the "faith-only" crowd, this one verse seems to win the argument—but if we look at the very next verse, we will understand the harmony between faith and works: "For we are God's workmanship, created in Christ Jesus to do *good works*, which God prepared in advance for us to do" (v. 10; emphasis added). Taken together, this powerful passage tells us that we are indeed saved through faith alone, the amazing gift of a loving God, but that we are saved for a *purpose*: to do the good works God actually prepared beforehand for us to carry out. Simply put, we are:

- saved *by* faith
- saved *for* works

> Our Christian habit is to bewail the world's deteriorating standards with an air of rather self-righteous dismay. We criticize its violence, dishonesty, immorality, disregard for human life, and materialistic greed. "The world is going down the drain," we say with a shrug. But whose fault is it? Who is to blame? Let me put it like this. If the house is dark when nightfall comes, there is no sense in blaming the house; that is what happens when the sun goes down. The question to ask is "Where is the light?" Similarly, if the meat goes bad and becomes inedible, there is no sense in blaming the meat; that is what happens when bacteria are left alone to breed. The question to ask is "Where is the salt?" Just so, if society deteriorates and its standards decline until it becomes like a dark night or a stinking fish, there is no sense in blaming society; that is what happens when fallen men and women are left to themselves, and human selfishness is unchecked. The question to ask is "Where is the Church? Why are the salt and light of Jesus Christ not permeating and changing our society?" It is sheer hypocrisy on our part to raise our eyebrows, shrug our shoulders, or wring our hands. The Lord Jesus told us to be the world's salt and light. If therefore darkness and rottenness abound, it is largely our fault and we must accept the blame. —John Stott[7]

As we saw in Matthew 7, Christ's true disciple, like the good tree, will bear good fruit: "By their fruit you will recognize them" (v. 16). It also follows that he who does not bear good fruit is not a true disciple. This, again, is not an argument that salvation comes through works, but rather an assertion that one who has committed his life to Jesus will bear good fruit as evidence of the lordship of Christ in his life. "No good tree bears bad fruit, nor does a bad tree bear good fruit. Each tree is recognized by its own fruit" (Luke 6:43–44). Therefore, faith and works should be seen not as two opposing ideas but as two manifestations of the same idea. A tree and its fruit are not different ideas in conflict with each other; rather, one is the natural product of the other. The tree is recognized by its fruit, and the fruit is produced inevitably by the tree.

But this ongoing argument about the nature of salvation has regrettably caused different groups of Christians to take sides in a conflict that should never have occurred. Prior to the twentieth century, the integration of faith and works as essential ingredients to Christian character and mission was largely understood. The great revivals in England and America were characterized by tremendous social reforms in both nations. In England, John Wesley's followers not only played a major role in the abolition of the slave trade but also had an effect on prison reform, labor laws and factory working conditions, and the availability of education for the poor. Further, they challenged Britain's colonial domination of India, and they were central to the fight against gambling, drunkenness, and other social vices.

J. Wesley Bready, in his book *England: Before and After Wesley*, said that the evangelical revival sparked by Wesley "did more to transfigure the moral character of the general populace, than any other movement British history can record."[8] In America, evangelist Charles G. Finney, historically associated with the great revival of 1830, was also passionate for social reform. He and his followers were instrumental in the abolition of slavery in America, and they fought passionately for women's rights, temperance, and education reform. As you can see, the notion of the integration of faith and works, or faith and social reform, was readily apparent in these eighteenth- and nineteenth-century movements in Britain and America.

But in the early part of the twentieth century, a split in Christian theology resulted in a deep divide over the respective roles of faith and works. Liberals within the Church, as well as the wider society, began to attack historic, biblical Christianity. This liberal faction no longer saw the Church's mission as "saving souls" but rather, transforming society through humanitarianism—in other words, a "social gospel" based on *works*.

On the other side were those who staunchly defended a salvation by faith alone, offered only because of the *grace of God*, which they strongly emphasized. And because of a rise in premillennial eschatology, Christians in this group reasoned that since Jesus was coming back (and would cure all evil Himself during His millennial reign), why bother trying to fix the world now? It was beyond redemption, riddled with evil, so the focus *ought* to be on saving souls for the *next* life. (Besides, in the aftermath of World War I, much of the world was pessimistic regarding social reform anyway. They believed any such efforts were impotent in the face of the type of human evil they had seen during the war.) As a result, these "conservatives" reacted vehemently against the theological "liberals" and the social gospel they espoused.

And so began a kind of war between faith and works. It continues to be played out today. The "works" proponents downplayed the importance of soul-winning and instead emphasized the works of caring for the poor and fighting injustice wherever it is found. The "faith-only" proponents, on the other hand, considered this view worldly. They focused *solely* on efforts to get the world to accept God's redeeming grace—a salvation by faith alone.

It's easy to see how this dividing of the gospel left both sides with only half a gospel, that is, a gospel with a hole in it, as each became satisfied with their particular piece. But this diminution of the whole gospel left both camps with just a shadow of the tremendous power of the good news proclaimed by Jesus. His gospel encompassed not only the forgiveness of sins and the saving of our souls but also the fullness of the coming kingdom of God through a society transformed by His followers. This "holey" gospel, on the other hand, reduced the full gospel of Christ to a series of transactions that, for one side, involved the mechanics of soul winning and, for the other, would reform the world through social and legislative changes.

Thankfully, the second half of the twentieth century saw a remarriage of the concepts of faith and works. Several key events—including the Wheaton Declaration of 1966; the Lausanne Covenant of 1974; and Salt and Light, a gathering of church leaders in Britain in 1988—caused the Church to begin to reunite evangelism and social action as indivisible parts of the whole gospel. *An Evangelical Call to Civic Responsibility*, a wonderful document produced by the National Association of Evangelicals in 2004, reemphasized the responsibility of Christians to fight for the poor, for justice, for human rights, for the environment, and for the sanctity of life, through both personal and collective civic *action*.

Nevertheless, there lingers in some conservative American churches a suspicion that social action and reform are somehow part of a liberal theology that substitutes good works for evangelism. Working to reclaim and reform our world today is of little import, they say, because we'll all soon be "beaming up" to heaven. Further, the notion persists that committing one's life to Christ begins and ends by reciting a brief prayer that activates one's "fire insurance." The parts about helping the poor, working for justice, and being salt and light to redeem a rebellious planet are seen as optional.

But that's not what Jesus taught. "You are the salt of the earth," He said, "but if the salt loses its saltiness . . . [it] is no longer good for anything" (Matt. 5:13). In the next verse He added, "You are the light of the world" (v. 14). If the Christian community is truly to be salt and light in a dark world, we will only succeed by embracing the whole gospel. Faith and works must be put back together again. We must move beyond an anemic view of our faith as something only personal and private, with no public dimension, and instead see it as the source of power that can change the world. Faith is the fuel that powers the light that shines in darkness. We must not keep that light under a basket. We must instead put it "on a lampstand, so it gives light to all" (v. 15 NKJV). "Let your light so shine before men," Jesus said, "that they may see your good works and glorify your Father in heaven" (v. 16 NKJV).

CHAPTER EIGHTEEN

PUTTING THE AMERICAN DREAM TO DEATH

Mankind wants glory. We want health. We want wealth.
We want happiness. We want all our felt needs met, all our little
human itches scratched. We want a painless life. We want the
crown without the cross. We want the gain without the pain.
We want the words of Christ's salvation to be easy.

—JOHN MACARTHUR

But seek first his kingdom and his righteousness, and all
these things will be given to you as well.

—MATTHEW 6:33

Perhaps the dominant cultural paradigm in our time and culture is the "American Dream." Here are two definitions I found online:

> The U.S. ideal according to which equality of opportunity permits any American to aspire to high attainment and material success.[1]

> A life of personal happiness and material comfort as traditionally sought by individuals in the U.S.[2]

This cultural aspiration is so ingrained in our thinking that most of us embrace it without thinking twice about whether it is consistent with our faith values or whether it might be harmful in any way. But if we scrutinize the values inherent in it, we should begin to feel somewhat uncomfortable with their implications. Certainly there is nothing wrong with the idea of equal opportunity, allowing any person to pursue his or her dreams without being limited by race, economic class, gender, or religion. Compared to so many nations in our world, that promise has held out hope to generations of American immigrants. But not all parts of the American Dream are consistent with Christian values. Aspiring to material comfort and success are not necessarily core Christian values. A person who dreams of becoming wealthy so she can indulge her every selfish fantasy is not in alignment with God's ideals. Neither the person who wants to become famous nor the one who steps on other people to get ahead is walking in Jesus' footsteps. And can we rightfully delight in our own personal happiness and material comfort when we know that they are out of reach for billions of people in our world?

And what about money? The American Dream often promotes this view of it: *I worked hard, I earned it, and it's mine to do with as I please.* This suggests that we are "entitled" to any income that comes to us because we worked for it. But that's not what the Bible tells us about our money and possessions. In fact, the biblical view of our resources is just the opposite. It teaches that all we have or receive comes from God; He has simply *entrusted* it to us. There's a big difference between *entitled* and *entrusted.*

Listen to what Moses told the nation of Israel just before they entered the promised land. Note especially God's view of the source of prosperity.

> When you have eaten and are satisfied, praise the LORD your God for the good land he has given you. Be careful that you do not forget the LORD your God . . . Otherwise, when you eat and are satisfied, when you build fine houses and settle down, and when your herds and flocks grow large and your silver and gold increase and all you have is multiplied, then your heart will become proud and you will forget the LORD your God, who brought you out of Egypt, out of the land of slavery. He led you through the vast and dreadful desert, that thirsty and waterless land, with its venomous snakes and scorpions. He brought you water out of hard rock. He gave you manna to eat in the desert, something your fathers had never known . . . You may say to yourself, "My power and the strength of my hands have produced this wealth for me." But remember the LORD

your God, for it is he who gives you the ability to produce wealth. (Deut. 8:10–18)

God wanted Israel to understand that any prosperity they enjoyed came from His hand, not their own. He also addressed the arrogance of those who take credit for their prosperity, believing that their own hard work and talent produced it. Are you gifted, attractive, eloquent, brilliant, creative, or clever? Are your opportunities in life favorable because you were born in the right family or the right country? If you have any of these traits or good circumstances, you have only God to thank for them. Even your hard work can be traced to the personality He gave you and perhaps the upbringing He arranged for you. Indeed, the very notion that we are entitled to anything that comes from God's hand is wrong.

My own "American Dream" came true as I overcame a challenging childhood and went on to get an education and climb to the top of the corporate ladder. At times I acted as though I deserved all the credit, but God showed me otherwise—sometimes the hard way as I got fired from jobs, went through periods of unemployment, and suffered financial setbacks. As my own understanding grew, I realized that I was to be a steward of those things God had given me—my education, my CEO position, and the financial resources I had acquired. They were not mine to do with as I pleased.

King David, with a title even higher than CEO, understood this when he thanked God for the money and talents that God's people generously and freely offered to build the temple:

> Yours, O LORD, is the greatness and the power
>> and the glory and the majesty and the splendor,
>> for everything in heaven and earth is yours.
>> Yours, O LORD, is the kingdom;
>> you are exalted as head over all.
> Wealth and honor come from you;
>> you are the ruler of all things.
>> In your hands are strength and power
>> to exalt and give strength to all.
> Now, our God, we give you thanks,
>> and praise your glorious name.

But who am I, and who are my people, that we should be able to give as generously as this? Everything comes from you, and we have given you only what comes from your hand. We are aliens and strangers in your sight, as were all our forefathers. Our days on earth are like a shadow, without hope. O LORD our God, as for all this abundance that we have provided for building you a temple for your Holy Name, it comes from your hand, and all of it belongs to you. (1 Chron. 29:11–16)

According to God's Word, it is He who owns "the cattle on a thousand hills" (Ps. 50:10). He just *entrusts* us with resources and giftedness, as we might entrust our money to a stockbroker. This is a pretty radical idea, because it means that we do not rightfully *own* our capital—it is God's. Therefore, we are not free to use it as we please. God, the rightful owner, expects us to use it for His purposes. If you were to put twenty-five thousand dollars in the hands of a stockbroker, how would you feel if you later went to withdraw the money only to find that your broker had used it to buy himself a new car? You would understandably explain to your broker that he had no right to spend your money as he saw fit. As a steward of your money, he should obviously receive a reasonable *commission*, which he could spend on his needs, but you would have expected him to invest your money on *your* behalf.

That's exactly what God expects of us. He wants us to invest His money on His behalf by undertaking His kingdom work. This is precisely the view Jesus presented in the parable of the talents: "[The kingdom of heaven] will be like a man going on a journey, who called his servants and entrusted his property to them. To one he gave five talents of money, to another two talents, and to another one talent, each according to his ability" (Matt. 25:14–15). Jesus was telling us that it is God—compared to a traveler in this parable—who distributed the money to three different men, "each according to his ability" (abilities also given to them by God). He *entrusted* them with the various sums while he was away. When he returned, he came back with expectations. In other words, the master wanted a return on his investment. He therefore asked each man what he had done with the money entrusted to him. The two who had invested wisely and gotten a return for the master were praised and rewarded:

The man who had received the five talents brought the other five. "Master," he said, "you entrusted me with five talents. See, I have gained five more."

His master replied, "Well done, good and faithful servant! You have been faithful with a few things; I will put you in charge of many things. Come and share your master's happiness!"

The man with the two talents also came. "Master," he said, "you entrusted me with two talents; see, I have gained two more."

His master replied, "Well done, good and faithful servant! You have been faithful with a few things; I will put you in charge of many things. Come and share your master's happiness!" (vv. 20–23)

But the one who had gotten no return, who had done nothing for his master with the entrusted sum, was chastised. "You wicked, lazy servant!" he was told (v. 26). Then his angry master said, "Take the talent from him and give it to the one who has the ten talents . . . And throw that worthless servant outside, into the darkness" (vv. 28, 30).

It is important to note here that God is a generous giver. He does not begrudge us the things He gives us. In fact, He is pleased when we enjoy them. The point is that He wants us to embrace a kingdom view of our money, possessions, and abilities, recognizing that all we have comes from Him. He wants us to hold them lightly and be willing to use them on His behalf.

Three clear principles, then, differentiate the scriptural view of our money from the "American Dream" view:

1. It's not our money—it all comes from God.
2. We are not *entitled to* it but *entrusted with* it.
3. God expects us to use it in the interest of His kingdom.

How about you? How do you look at your assets (car, bank accounts, home)? What about your giftings? Are you *entitled* to them to do with as you please, or were they *entrusted* to you for a purpose—God's purpose? If we see them as God sees them, we must think differently about how we use them: *Should I buy this new car? take this vacation? add this new insurance policy? increase my savings account? Maybe, but not until I prayerfully consider what God would have me do with His money.* It's not easy being a steward.

In Acts 2 we read about the early church's view of possessions, a standpoint that not only challenged the culture of the day but actually began to change it: "All the believers were together and had everything in common. Selling their possessions and goods, they gave to anyone as he had need" (vv. 44–45). Here we see a community of believers who held things loosely, making whatever they had available for the greater good of the community of believers. This view of money and community was so radical that the prevailing culture sat up and took notice. The early church enjoyed "the favor of all the people," and not only that, but "the Lord added to their number daily those who were being saved" (v. 47). These folks were transforming the culture, not letting the culture transform them. Can you imagine the impact on our own culture if American Christians began using their riches as if they belonged to God and were intended primarily to further God's kingdom? I'm pretty certain the world would take notice.

> Can you imagine the impact on our own culture if American Christians began using their riches as if they belonged to God?

GETTING IN THE GAME

Several months after I came to World Vision and moved my family to Seattle, my son Andy and I were running some errands around town. All of this had been a pretty major family and lifestyle adjustment, and even the kids were hurting, as they struggled to fit in and make new friends. That day Andy and I were sitting at a traffic light in our six-year-old minivan, not a cool vehicle by any standard for a seventeen-year-old boy. Just then a shiny new Jaguar XK-8 pulled up next to us, one just like the company car that had been mine a few months earlier. Andy looked at it wistfully and sighed.

"Dad, I guess those days are gone," he said.

"Yeah, Andy, I think they are," I answered.

"But, Dad," Andy went on, "do you think you'll ever get back in the game, for one last kill?"

I had to laugh at his choice of words. He was asking whether I thought that someday I would leave World Vision and become a corporate CEO again, with all of the associated perks. "Andy," I said, "for the first time in my life, I feel like I'm in the real game; I'm in *God's* game."

That's the bottom line for all of us—whose "game" are we in? Our own? Or God's? We don't have to be in full-time ministry to be in God's game, but we do have to serve God full-time—as stewards of all that He has given us. If we're in God's game, we need to put the American Dream to death, because God's game is a different game altogether.

TWO PERCENT OF TWO PERCENT

How different our standard is from Christ's. We ask how much a man gives. He asks how much he keeps.

—ANDREW MURRAY

If charity cost nothing, the world would be full of philanthropists.

—JEWISH PROVERB

Now we have to talk money. Yes, I know that money is not the most popular topic in the church, but that's exactly *why* we have to discuss it. Jesus did not hesitate to discuss money. It was, in fact, one of His most common themes. The Bible devotes twice as many verses to money as it does to faith and prayer combined, and fully 15 percent of Jesus' recorded words dealt with money, more than He said about heaven and hell combined.[1] Jesus understood that our relationship to our money and possessions is an indicator of our spiritual condition: "For where your treasure is," He said, "there your heart will be also" (Luke 12:34). And it's true. If you look at the "power lines" that flow through our society and our world, money is the current that flows through them. So, to better understand the spiritual priorities of our churches—and ourselves—we have to do what any detective would do: "follow the money."

One of the great principles in Scripture, intended to govern our relationship to our material goods, is the tithe. According to the book of

Leviticus, the first 10 percent of our income is to be offered to God: "A tithe of everything from the land, whether grain from the soil or fruit from the trees, belongs to the LORD; it is holy to the LORD" (27:30). The tithe was not considered a gift to God—it *belonged* to God. There were other provisions that spoke to freewill giving, but any such offerings were to be over and above the 10 percent required for the tithe. That first 10 percent was seen as a bare minimum one would set aside for the Lord.

But why did God require it? It is critical to understand that God did not command His people to give the tithe because *He* needed the money. No, instead it served two main purposes. First, it provided for the work of God's kingdom by supporting the levitical temple worship system. The money was managed by the Levites (priests), and part of it was meant to take care of the needs of not only the temple (items pertaining to sacrifices and worship) but the priests as well. But a portion of the tithe was also intended to care for "the aliens, the fatherless and the widows" (Deut. 14:29), which, along with the year of Jubilee, was a critical part of God's system of economic justice. In New Testament terms, the tithe is the fuel that runs the work of the church around the world. It funds the operation of our churches and programs, pays the salaries of the ministers and staff, supports local and global missions, and provides for the poor and the vulnerable. The tithe is a way of redistributing the wealth of a community to ensure that important spiritual and social priorities are not overlooked or left to chance.

> To better understand the spiritual priorities of our churches—and ourselves—we have to do what any detective would do: "follow the money."

The second reason for the tithe was that it helped God's people understand their utter dependence on Him. Can you imagine living several thousand years ago in a completely subsistence-based economy, wherein you lived or died based on whether your fields produced enough crops and your animals survived? Think of the faith it would require to give the first fruits of your produce to God instead of the "last fruits." This was almost a reckless way of saying, "We trust You and are totally dependent on You, God, and if we starve, we starve." God had reinforced His desire for their complete dependence during the forty years Israel had wandered in the desert. Each morning God had miraculously provided manna, the bread from heaven, for them to eat, and they were not allowed to store up more than they needed for that day. God wanted them to depend only on Him. When they did try to hoard the manna, it rotted and became riddled with maggots. This forty-year-long lesson from God was to teach them to rely on Him only—even when they reached the land flowing with milk and honey. So important was this symbol of dependence on God that a jar of manna became one of the three things contained in the sacred ark of the covenant.

In Leviticus, the tithe was instituted to again underscore our total dependence on God. God recognized that the chief competitor to our dependence on Him is our money. When we have enough cash, food, and possessions, we can become *self*-reliant. Therefore, money is not seen by God as a benign and neutral thing. Money is power, and power competes with God for supremacy in our lives. Jesus recognized this very thing in the Sermon on the Mount. "No one can serve two masters," He said. "Either he will hate the one and love the other, or he will be devoted to the one and despise the other. You cannot serve both God and money" (Matt. 6:24).

Note that both God and money are portrayed in a master-slave relationship to the person. Jesus recognized that we will be a slave to one or the other but not to both. In fact, Jesus often talked about money as if it were battery acid—something to handle with extreme caution!

R. Scott Rodin, in his book *Stewards in the Kingdom,* has vividly described the relationship of money to our faith:

> We must never for a single moment lose sight of the stark realization that whenever we deal with money, we are dealing with dynamite. What is one day that which we control, the next day becomes the controller. Such dynamite must be defused, and the greatest defuser that we as Christians have at our disposal is the opportunity to take that which seeks to dominate us and simply give it away. Think about it. There is no greater expression of money's total lack of dominance over us or of its low priority in our lives than when we can with joy and peace, give it away for the Lord's work. You cannot worship the God of mammon and be a free and cheerful giver. Likewise, you cannot serve the living God and be a hoarder of his resources. Giving, both how we give and how much we

give, is the clearest outward expression of who our God really is. Our check stubs speak more honestly of our priorities than our church memberships.[2]

I have often thought of the tithe in a different way, as a kind of "inoculation" against the power that money can sometimes hold over us. When we are vaccinated against a deadly virus, our bodies are injected with a small amount of that virus, weakened so that it won't hurt us. By putting this small amount into our systems, we develop an immunity to the virus, and it can no longer harm us. Metaphorically speaking, paying a tithe on our income has the same effect. By cheerfully giving away a small portion of our money, we become immune to the corrupting power it can have in our lives. When we tithe, not out of obligation, but out of love and obedience for God, we are making the bold statement that money has no power over us. Even when we give it away freely, we know that we can depend on God to replenish it and sustain us.

In 1987, the largest single-day stock market crash since 1929 took place. In one day, Reneé and I lost more than one-third of our life's savings and the money we had put aside for our kids' college education. I was horrified and became like a man obsessed, each night working past midnight, analyzing on spreadsheets all that we had lost, and the next day calling in orders to sell our remaining stocks and mutual funds to prevent further losses. (Of course that turned out to be the absolute worst thing I could have done.) I was consumed with anguish over our lost money—and it showed.

One night, when I was burning the midnight oil, Reneé came and sat beside me. "Honey," she said, "this thing is consuming you in an unhealthy way. It's only money. We have our marriage, our health, our friends, our children, and a good income—so much to be thankful for. You need to let go of this and trust God."

Don't you hate it when someone crashes your pity party? I didn't *want* to let go of it. I told her that I felt responsible for our family and that she didn't understand. It was my job to worry about things like this. She suggested we stop and pray about it—something that hadn't occurred to me—so we did.

At the end of the prayer, to my bewilderment, Reneé said, "Now I think we need to get out the checkbook and write some big checks to our church and the ministries we support. We need to show God that we know this is His money and not ours." I was flabbergasted at the audacity of this suggestion, but in my heart I knew she was right. So that night we wrote some sizeable checks, put them in envelopes addressed to various ministries, and sealed them. And that's when I felt the wave of relief. We had broken the spell that money had cast over me. It freed me from the worries that had consumed me. I actually felt reckless and giddy—"God, please catch us, because we just took a *crazy* leap of faith."

And He did.

I love the recklessness of faith. First you leap, and then you grow wings.
—William Sloane Coffin

Of course, we are also told in Scripture that when we are faithful with our money, God will indeed bless us. This is another of the great paradoxes of our faith: that when we give our money to God, His blessings come back to us—not always in the form of money, but in so many other ways. The book of Malachi bears this out. But the same book warns that to *fail* to pay our tithes is nothing less than *robbing God*. Listen to God's own words:

> "Will a man rob God? Yet you rob me. But you ask, 'How do we rob you?' In tithes and offerings. You are under a curse—the whole nation of you—because you are robbing me. Bring the whole tithe into the storehouse, that there may be food in my house. Test me in this," says the LORD Almighty, "and see if I will not throw open the floodgates of heaven and pour out so much blessing that you will not have room enough for it. I will prevent pests from devouring your crops, and the vines in your fields will not cast their fruit," says the LORD Almighty. "Then all the nations will call you blessed, for yours will be a delightful land," says the LORD Almighty. (3:8–12)

The consequence of financial unfaithfulness is severe: God's people are "under a curse." That means that not only are God's ministries starved for resources, but the nation as a whole is denied God's blessings and protection.

Now contrast these stiff penalties to the rewards of generous and faithful stewardship:

- God opens the "floodgates of heaven" and pours out blessings.
- God will protect our "harvests."
- *All* the nations will call us blessed.

To summarize, when we do as we are told with regard to the tithe, God will reward us richly. But when we fail to give that portion back to God, not only do we compromise God's blessings within our own community, but we also miss the opportunity to show His blessings to the watching world.

The Wealthiest Church in History

Obedience to the Great Commission has more consistently been poisoned by affluence than by anything else. —Ralph Winter

Command those who are rich in this present world not to be arrogant nor to put their hope in wealth, which is so uncertain, but to put their hope in God, who richly provides us with everything for our enjoyment. Command them to do good, to be rich in good deeds, and to be generous and willing to share. In this way they will lay up treasure for themselves as a firm foundation for the coming age, so that they may take hold of the life that is truly life. —1 Timothy 6:17–19

Let me start with the good news. You're rich, we're rich, and the Church in America is rich. And now I am sure you are thinking that I am wrong, that you're not rich, and neither is your church. But bear with me, because wealth is always measured in relative terms. Brace yourselves for this good news! If your income is $25,000 per year, you are wealthier than approximately 90 percent of the world's population! If you make $50,000 per year, you are wealthier than 99 percent of the world![3] Does this shock you? Remember, of the 6.7 billion people on earth, almost half of them live on less than two dollars a day. If you don't feel rich, it's because you are comparing yourself to people who have more than you do—those living above even the 99th percentile of global wealth. It's also because we tend to gauge whether or not we are wealthy based on the things we *don't* have. If we think we need a bigger house or apartment, a nicer car, more clothes, or the ability to go out for dinner more often, we don't feel "rich." Again, it's all relative to our expectations. When you realize that 93 percent of the world's people don't own a car,[4] your old clunker starts to look pretty good. Our difficulty is that we see our American lifestyles as normative, when in fact they are grossly distorted compared to the rest of the world. We don't *believe* we are wealthy, so we don't see it as our responsibility to help the poor. We are deceived.

It is important to put the American Church in perspective. Simply stated, it is the wealthiest community of Christians in the history of Christendom. How wealthy? The total income of American churchgoers is $5.2 trillion.[5] (That's more than five thousand billion dollars.) It would take just a little over 1 percent of the income of American Christians to lift the poorest one billion people in the world out of extreme poverty.[6] Said another way, American Christians, who make up about 5 percent of the Church worldwide, control about half of global Christian wealth;[7] a lack of money is not our problem.

So as the wealthiest nation of Christians in the world, how do we do on tithing our income? Here is the bad news. If we define tithing as giving 10 percent or more of our pretax income to the church or to nonprofit ministries, *only about 5 percent of American households tithe.*[8] If we look at "born again" Christians in America (those who claim to have made a personal commitment to Christ), the number of tithers improves to 9 percent.[9] For "evangelical Christians," those who claim their faith has the greatest influence on their life and conduct, still only 24 percent tithe.[10] Given our relative wealth, might the remaining 76 percent not be "robbing God" as defined—and condemned—in the book of Malachi? Listen to the words James used to address wealthy first-century Christians who hoarded their money to spend on themselves:

> Listen, you rich people, weep and wail because of the misery that is
> coming upon you. Your wealth has rotted, and moths have eaten your
> clothes. Your gold and silver are corroded. Their corrosion will testify

against you and eat your flesh like fire. You have hoarded wealth in the last days . . . You have lived on earth in luxury and self-indulgence. You have fattened yourselves in the day of slaughter. (James 5:1–5)

So if we are not tithing, how much are we giving? The average giving of American church members in 2005 was just 2.58 percent of their income, about 75 percent less than the biblical standard of 10 percent. Sadly, as our incomes have increased, our giving has significantly declined. In 1933, at the height of the Great Depression, giving averaged 3.3 percent, 27 percent more than we gave in 2005.[11] But this is just the first part of the equation. If we then look at where the money goes after it is received by the churches, we find that just about 2 percent of it goes to overseas missions of any kind, whether evangelistic or to assist the poor.[12] The other 98 percent stays right here, within our churches and communities. The bottom line is that the commitment that American Christians, the wealthiest Christians in all history, are making to the world is just about 2 percent of 2 percent—actually *about five ten-thousandths of our income*. In simpler terms, that amounts to about six pennies per person per day that we give through our churches to the rest of the world—*six cents!*[13]

The point of all of these numbers is to pose the question, what if? What if American Christians did "bring the whole tithe into the storehouse"? How might the manifestation of the kingdom of God on earth be different? Earlier I told the story about me standing before my congregation and telling them that God had given us work to do but that we had not given enough money to do it. I appealed to them to make an additional pledge to completely fund our church's missions program. What if we applied that same logic to all of our churches and Christians?[14] Here is what would happen if we all paid our tithe—that is,

> The bottom line is that the commitment that American Christians, the wealthiest Christians in all history, are making to the world is just about 2 percent of 2 percent—actually *about five ten-thousandths of our income*.

10 percent of our incomes instead of the 2.5 percent we actually give: *we would have an extra $168 billion to spend in funding the work of the Church worldwide!*

Now I realize that big numbers are hard to put into perspective, so let me help.

$168 billion	the extra money available if all American churchgoers tithed
$705 billion	amount Americans spend on entertainment and recreation[15]
$179 billion	amount spent by teenagers ages 12–17 (2006)[16]
$65 billion	amount we spend on jewelry (2008)[17]
$58 billion	amount spent on state lottery tickets (2007)[18]
$39.5 billion	total U.S.-government foreign assistance budget for the world[19]
$31 billion	amount spent on pets (2003)[20]
$13 billion	amount spent by Americans on cosmetic surgery (2007)[21]
$5 billion	total Overseas ministries income to 700 Protestant mission agencies, including denominational, interdenominational, and independent agencies (2005)[22]

If every American churchgoer tithed, we could literally change the world. In fact, as I mentioned in chapter 13, $65 billion—less than 40 percent of the extra $168 billion—could eliminate the most extreme poverty on the planet for more than a billion people.[23] Universal primary education for children would cost just $6 billion; the cost to bring clean water to most of the world's poor, an estimated $9 billion; and basic health and nutrition for everyone in the world, $13 billion.[24]

Can you begin to catch a vision of not only what this would mean to the world's poor but what it would do for the image of the world's

Christians? Imagine how stunning it would be to the watching world for American Christians to give so generously that it:

- brought an end to world hunger;
- solved the clean water crisis;
- provided universal access to drugs and medical care for the millions suffering from AIDS, malaria, and tuberculosis;
- virtually eliminated the more than twenty-six thousand daily child deaths;[25]
- guaranteed education for all the world's children;
- provided a safety net for the world's tens of millions of orphans.

Think about the statement it would make if American Christian citizens stepped up and gave more than all of the governments of the world combined because they took Jesus seriously when He said to love our neighbors as ourselves. Terrorists might have a harder time recruiting young men to attack a nation so compassionate. Other wealthy nations might be shamed—or inspired to follow our example. Adherents of other religions would surely wonder what motivates the Christians to be so loving and generous. The global social revolution brought forth by the body of Christ would be on the lips of every citizen in the world and in the pages of every newspaper—in a good way. The world would see the whole gospel— the good news of the kingdom of God—not just spoken but *demonstrated*, by people whose faith is not devoid of deeds but defined by love and backed up with *action*. His kingdom come, His will be done, on earth, as it is in heaven. This was the whole gospel that Jesus proclaimed in Luke 4, and if we would embrace it, it would literally change everything.

> The Spirit of the Lord is on me,
>> because he has anointed me
>> to preach good news to the poor.
> He has sent me to proclaim freedom for the prisoners
>> and recovery of sight for the blind,
> to release the oppressed,
>> to proclaim the year of the Lord's favor. (Luke 4:18–19)

This is the vision that should capture the imagination of every follower of Christ and every church. And this is the vision that can cause us to rise above what Isaiah 1 calls our "worship charades" and "trivial religious games" (v. 13 MSG)—and truly be salt and light to the world.

> *Let your light shine before men, that they may see your good deeds and praise your Father in heaven.* —Matthew 5:16

CHAPTER TWENTY

A LETTER TO THE CHURCH IN AMERICA

*Action springs not from thought, but from
a readiness for responsibility.*

—DIETRICH BONHOEFFER

Several years ago, while I was reading the book of Revelation, I was struck by the vividness of the letters to the seven churches in Asia. The one that grabbed me the most was the last of the seven, the one to the church at Laodicea, because much like many churches in America, the Laodicean church was wealthy.

Laodicea was an important center of trade and communication, strategically located on a main Roman road stretching from Ephesus, on the coast, inland to Asia. This city was famous for both its banking industry and a great school of medicine. In fact, the Laodiceans produced a well-known ointment for the eyes. They also boasted a one-of-a-kind, glossy black wool for weaving, which created great wealth for their city. They were even rich enough to refuse help from Rome when their city suffered a major earthquake in AD 60. And because they had achieved prosperity by themselves, Laodicea had a reputation for self-sufficiency and pride.

But as far as God was concerned, they had nothing to be proud of. "I know your works, that you are neither cold nor hot," He told them. "I . . . wish you were cold or hot [but] because you are lukewarm . . . I will vomit you out of My mouth" (Rev. 3:15–16 NKJV).

In contrast to its glowing attributes, Laodicea was also known for its poor water. On the other hand, nearby Hierapolis was famous for its hot springs, which boasted medicinal properties. People traveled there daily for a dip in the healing waters. Colossae, also a neighbor, was known as well for its cold, pure waters. A drink from the springs of Colossae was refreshing to many a traveler in the heat of the day. But Laodicea's waters were brought in by aqueduct and were neither hot nor cold—but lukewarm. Interestingly, as Christ looked at His church there, He was essentially saying that their works—like their waters—were so tepid that they were good for neither spiritual healing nor spiritual refreshment. The result? "You make me want to vomit" (v. 16 MSG). The Lord found them thoroughly disgusting.

WRETCHED, PITIFUL, POOR, BLIND, AND NAKED

If ever there were five adjectives that we should not want to see in a sentence describing our churches today, it is these. Yet these five words are the exact ones chosen by the Lord to describe the church at Laodicea: "You say, 'I am rich; I have acquired wealth and do not need a thing,'" He mocked. "But you do not realize that you are wretched, pitiful, poor, blind and naked" (v. 17). Isn't it ironic that the "wealthy" Laodicea, in spite of their delusional claim of self-sufficiency, was actually dirt-poor? Despite their fine black wool, they were naked. And regardless of their famed eye ointment, they were blind. They had deluded themselves into thinking God was pleased with them and that their prosperity was a sure sign of His favor.

The Lord told them that they desperately needed clothes and the kind of eye salve that only He could give, and He would provide them—*if they would repent.* God made the offer—then He stood at their door and knocked, waiting for them to let Him in: "I counsel you to buy from Me gold refined in the fire, that you may be rich; and white garments, that you may be clothed, that the shame of your nakedness may not be revealed; and anoint your eyes with eye salve, that you may see. As many as I love, I rebuke and chasten. Therefore be zealous and repent. Behold, I stand at the door and knock. If anyone hears My voice and opens the door, I will come in to him and dine with him, and he with Me" (vv. 18–20 NKJV).

As I studied these verses, I could not help but make application to the modern Church. We, too, are comfortable, wealthy, and self-sufficient. We, too, blindly believe that we are prosperous because we are God's "favorites." And our deeds are every bit as "lukewarm" as those of the Laodicean assembly. So what, I wondered, would Christ say if He were to write a letter to the Church in America?

I pondered this for some weeks as I was preparing a talk for a large World Vision conference of our donors and supporting pastors. I had decided that my topic would be "A Letter to the Church in America." I actually wanted to write such a letter, the kind I imagined Christ might write to us. But I struggled again and again to do it, without success. (It's not easy to speak with God's voice.)

And then it dawned on me. He has *already* written that letter to us. It is contained in the Bible; we just have to read it and apply it. So I spent several days pulling verses together and compiling them in the style of a letter. I realize this violated every rule of sound biblical exegesis, but I think you'll agree that it works—it speaks to us with truth and with bluntness. Here is that letter.

A LETTER TO THE CHURCH IN AMERICA

He who has an ear to hear, let him hear what the Spirit says to the churches. —Revelation 2:7 NKJV

To the angel of the Church in America write:

These are the words of the One who holds the seven stars and walks among the golden lampstands. I know your deeds. You live in luxury and self-indulgence, and you have forsaken your first love. I hold this against you. Woe to those of you who add house to house and join field to field till no space is left. Surely the great houses will become desolate, the fine mansions left without occupants.

Give careful thought to your ways. You have planted much, but have harvested little. You eat, but never have enough. You drink, but never have your fill. You put on clothes, but are not warm. You earn wages, only to put them in a purse with holes in it. Your wealth has rotted, and moths have eaten your clothes.

Your gold and silver are corroded. Their corrosion will testify against you and eat your flesh like fire. You have hoarded your wealth in the last days. You say, "I am rich; I have acquired wealth and do not need a thing." Yet it is those who are poor in the eyes of the world that are rich in faith. I have chosen them to inherit the kingdom I have promised to those who love Me. Therefore, do not store up for yourselves treasures on earth, where moth and rust destroy, and where thieves break in and steal. But store up for yourselves treasure in heaven, where moth and rust do not destroy, and thieves do not break in and steal. For where your treasure is, there your heart will be also. Seek first My kingdom and My righteousness, and all these other things will be given to you as well. Remember, even I, the Lord Jesus Christ, though I was rich, for your sakes became poor, so that you, through My poverty, might become rich.

Why do you call Me, "Lord, Lord," but do not do what I say? Do not merely listen to the Word, and so deceive yourselves. Do what it says, for whoever obeys My commands—that is the one who loves Me.

What does the Lord require of you, you ask? To act justly, love mercy, and walk humbly with your God. In fact, the entire law is summed up in a single command: "Love your neighbor as yourself."

There will always be poor people in the land. I command you to be openhanded toward your brothers and toward the poor and needy in the land. Defend the cause of the weak and the fatherless; maintain the rights of the poor and the oppressed.

Now let's talk about fasting. You cannot fast as you do today and expect your voice to be heard on high. Is this the kind of fast I have chosen, only a day for a man to humble himself? Is it only for bowing one's head like a reed and for lying on sackcloth and ashes? Is that what you call a fast, a day acceptable to the Lord? No, this is the fast that I have chosen: to loose the chains of injustice and untie the cords of the yoke, to set the oppressed free and break every yoke. It is to share your food with the hungry and to provide the poor wanderer with shelter—when you see the naked, to clothe him, and not to turn away from your own flesh and blood. If anyone has material possessions and sees his brother in need but has no pity on him, how can the love of God be in him?

Even now, return to Me with all your heart, with fasting and weeping and mourning. Rend your heart and not your garments. Return to the Lord your God, for He is gracious and compassionate, slow to anger and abounding in love, and He relents from sending calamity.

I urge you to live a life worthy of the calling you have received. Be completely humble and gentle; be patient, bearing with one another in love. Do not be conformed to the pattern of this world, but be transformed by the renewing of your mind. Why spend money on what is not bread and labor on what does not satisfy? Listen, listen to Me, and eat what is good, and your soul will delight in the richest of fare. Then you will call, and I will answer; you will cry for help, and I will say, "Here am I." If you do away with the yoke of oppression, with the pointing finger and the malicious talk, and if you spend yourselves in behalf of the hungry and satisfy the needs of the oppressed, then your light will rise in the darkness, and your night will become as the noonday. I will guide you always; I will satisfy your needs in a sun-scorched land and will strengthen your frame. You will be like a well-watered garden, like a spring whose waters never fail.

Therefore, My dear brothers and sisters, stand firm. Let nothing move you. Always give yourselves fully to the work of the Lord, because you know that your labor in the Lord is not in vain.

—Jesus

P.S. I am coming soon! My reward is with Me, and I will give to everyone according to what he has done.[1]

CHAPTER TWENTY-ONE

WHY WE'RE NOT SO POPULAR ANYMORE

The Jubilee movement wasn't a bless-me club; it wasn't a holy huddle. These religious guys were willing to get on the streets, get their boots dirty, wave the placards and follow their convictions with actions. Making it really hard for people like me to keep their distance. It was amazing. I almost started to like these church people.

—BONO, *ON THE MOVE*

Endeavor to live so that when you die, even the undertaker will be sorry.

—ANONYMOUS

I like your Christ, I do not like your Christians. Your Christians are so unlike your Christ.

—MOHANDAS GANDHI

For most of my life, being a "Christian" has been perceived as a good thing in our culture. I don't remember many negative connotations associated with the word. For years, in fact, it was kind of assumed that most people in America *were* Christians. I can still remember, shortly after making my own commitment to follow Christ at age twenty-three, eagerly speaking to my mother about my newfound Christian faith and asking whether she, too, considered herself a Christian. "Doesn't everybody?" she asked.[1] In her view, of course everyone was a Christian; America was

Christian. *Christian*, after all, was a synonym for "good people," and Americans are good people. Everyone wanted to be a "Christian" in bygone days.

But it feels as though that has changed. In the last thirty or so years, the word *Christian*, and even more so the word *evangelical*, has become associated with an ideological battle raging in our country, sometimes called the "culture war." Galvanized by *Roe v. Wade*'s legalization of abortion, and with growing concern over the consequences of the sexual revolution, the prevalence of divorce, and the rise of the homosexual political agenda, conservative Christians have "gone to war" with the popular culture, becoming increasingly involved in politics and trying to grab a share of the media spotlight. This thirty-year battle and the vitriolic debate it has produced have taken a toll on the formerly positive image of Christians and especially evangelicals in our society.

Much has been written about this, and I will not attempt to rehash all of it here. However, I will say that the Christian "brand," as perceived by those on the outside who don't consider themselves to be Christians, has taken a beating. According to Barna researchers, as recently as 1996, 85 percent of "outsiders"—individuals who had no strong religious convictions themselves—still felt favorably toward Christianity's role in society. But just about ten years later, only 16 percent of them had a good impression of Christianity. Worse, only 3 percent have a favorable impression of "evangelicals," with 49 percent saying they have a bad impression![2] One interviewee put it this way: "Most people I meet assume that Christian means very conservative, entrenched in their thinking, antigay, antichoice, angry, violent, illogical, empire builders; they want to convert everyone, and they generally cannot live peacefully with anyone who doesn't believe what they believe."[3]

Ouch! This is serious business. If we are trying to reach out with the positive message of the gospel—the *good* news—to those who have not accepted the Christian faith, then we either have a major problem with our message or with our methodology—or both! To help you better understand how the Christian faith is perceived by the outsiders (and the "insiders" as well), I have reproduced one of the key tables from the Barna research on which a recent book, titled *UnChristian*, is based.

THE STRUGGLE OF YOUNG CHURCHGOERS[4]

Question: Here are some words or phrases that people could use to describe religious faith. Please indicate if you think each of these phrases describes present-day Christianity.

Among Americans 16–29	Outsiders	Churchgoers
Antihomosexual	91%	80%
Judgmental	87	52
Hypocritical	85	47
Old-fashioned	78	36
Too involved in politics	75	50
Out of touch with reality	72	32
Insensitive to others	70	29
Boring	68	27
Not accepting other faiths	64	39
Confusing	61	44

Those of you reading this may be inclined to say that this is not true, Christians are not like this, and these outsiders have it all wrong. That's not unusual. Over my years as a manager doing performance reviews, I learned that my staff often disagreed with my assessments of their behavior and accomplishments. Some would even deny that my various assertions were accurate, and we would end up wasting a lot of time debating over whether or not my opinions and those of their coworkers were correct. Now I explain to them a simple but compelling truth: *perception is reality*. In other words, you may not *think* you are this way or that way, but if that is how you are perceived by others, then you have to change either the reality or the perception, or both. If you look at the list of characteristics attributed to Christians by outsiders, they paint a very unflattering picture and suggest that whatever we have been doing, right or wrong, justified or not, we have been perceived badly. If we are to represent the attractiveness of Christ and His gospel, we need to change that perception.

The data also suggests that we have become defined by those things we are *against* rather than those we are *for*. We're seen to be *against* homosexuality and gay marriage, *against* pornography and sexual promiscuity, *against* alcohol and drug use, abortion, divorce, Islam, evolution . . . *even* against those who believe that global warming is a threat. Can you see why people get the feeling that we are judging them and looking down on them with a sense of moral superiority?

Perhaps the only thing worse than coming across as judgmental is doing so hypocritically. It is one thing to judge when you can actually demonstrate moral superiority, but entirely another when you are guilty of the very same things you condemn in others. Everyone hates a hypocrite, and we have been hypocrites.

Based on a study released in 2007, we found that most of the lifestyle activities of born-again Christians were statistically equivalent to those of non-born-agains . . . Born-again believers were just as likely to bet or gamble, to visit a pornographic website, to take something that did not belong to them, to consult a medium or psychic, to physically fight or abuse someone, to have consumed enough alcohol to be considered legally drunk, to have used an illegal, non-prescription drug, to have said something to someone that was not true, to have gotten back at someone for something he or she did, and to have said mean things behind another person's back. No difference.

One study we conducted examined Americans' engagement in some type of sexually inappropriate behavior, including looking at on-line pornography, viewing sexually explicit magazines or movies, or having an intimate sexual encounter outside of marriage. In all, we found that 30 percent of born-again Christians admitted to at least one of these activities in the past thirty days, compared with 35 percent of other Americans. In statistical and practical terms, this means the two groups are essentially no different from each other.[5]

Might this be why Jesus told us to not judge others? "Do not judge," He preached, "and you will not be judged. Do not condemn, and you will not be condemned. Forgive, and you will be forgiven" (Luke 6:37). But as I read through the list of perceptions that people have of Christians, I can't

help but observe how opposite these attributes are from what Jesus taught—
not to mention those we see in His own life! Let's compare . . .

Perceptions of Christians	Attributes of Christ
Antihomosexual	Loving to all
Judgmental	Forgiving
Hypocritical	Genuine
Old-fashioned	Revolutionary
Too involved with politics	Involved with people
Out of touch with reality	Truthful and aware
Insensitive to others	Loving
Boring	Radical
Not accepting of other faiths	Inviting to members of all faiths
Confusing	Simple in presenting truth

Jesus showed us another way. *Don't* hate the sinner, but *do* show him
love. *Don't* be judgmental, but *do* offer forgiveness. In a phrase, the "do's"
of our faith are so much more powerful than the "don'ts." If we are to
truly let our lights shine before the world, it must be through those do's
that the world finds so attractive. The first-century world was amazed by
Christ because of what He *did*: Jesus healed the sick, loved the poor,
touched the leper, stood up for the down-and-out, forgave the sinner,
condemned the religious hypocrites, dined with prostitutes and corrupt
tax collectors, challenged the wealthy and powerful, fought for justice for
the oppressed, defied His culture, renounced materialism, demonstrated
that greatness is found in serving—and then died that others might live.
These actions—performed by one man—changed the world.

These same actions, when carried out by His followers, still change the
world today.

Be ye doers of the word, and not hearers only, deceiving your own
selves. —James 1:22 KJV

CHAPTER TWENTY-TWO

A TALE OF TWO REAL CHURCHES

Going to church doesn't make you a Christian any more than standing in a garage makes you a car.

—BILLY SUNDAY

To the angel of the church in Thyatira write:
These are the words of the Son of God, whose eyes are like blazing fire and whose feet are like burnished bronze. I know your deeds, your love and faith, your service and perseverance, and that you are now doing more than you did at first.

—REVELATION 2:18–19

THE MOST SOUTHERN BAPTIST CHURCH IN THE WORLD

This was not something we chose. It is something God put in our path. Wherever He leads, we will follow. —John Thomas, pastor, Fish Hoek Baptist Church

In 1999, Pastor John Thomas heard a shocking statistic at a local minister's meeting. Forty-four percent[1] of the population of Masiphumelele, a shanty-town slum community of black migrants, embedded near the tiny seaside town of Fish Hoek, South Africa, were HIV-positive. This high percentage stunned Pastor Thomas, whose predominantly white church of about

315 members had little awareness of the impact of AIDS in their own backyard. Just five years after the end of apartheid, relations between black and white were still strained in South Africa, a country that now had more HIV infections than any nation in the world. Thomas was provoked. *How can I face God on judgment day*, he thought, *realizing I've done nothing about the greatest problem that lies on our doorstep?*

The troubled pastor decided to share his heart with his church—and nothing has been the same since. Fish Hoek Baptist Church is now known around town as "the church that cares." Today, almost ten years later, the AIDS ministry of Fish Hoek Baptist Church, known as Living Hope, has a budget of $1.2 million a year and a full-time staff of 147. By comparison, the church's annual budget is just $300,000 with a staff of 10. The AIDS ministry now dwarfs the church in size and scope.

I met Pastor Thomas in 2007 at the Willow Creek Leadership Summit near Chicago, where Fish Hoek Baptist had been selected as the first winner of the Courageous Leadership Award, an honor presented by Willow Creek and World Vision to the church whose AIDS ministry most embodies excellence, compassion, creativity, and the love of Christ. The award is intended not only to recognize congregations who are doing amazing work in AIDS prevention and care, but also to inspire other churches to do the same. Pastor Thomas invited me to visit Living Hope to see for myself the effect his AIDS ministry is having on his society.

In February 2008, I took him up on his invitation and found that what was perhaps most striking was the sheer breadth of their vision. Living Hope encompasses virtually every dimension of the impact of AIDS in the lives of the poor. A sister church has been established in the heart of Masiphumelele to provide a permanent and accessible spiritual presence for the community. A twenty-bed clinic, Living Hope Health Care Centre, for treating the gravest cases of AIDS has been built and staffed with a full complement of health care workers and counselors. Alongside the center is the Living Way ministry, where HIV support groups can meet and men and women can receive training in job skills so they can support themselves economically after leaving the clinic. Because the patients are receiving antiretroviral drug therapy, most of them recover and reenter their communities. ("Charity has its place," said one of the staff, "but it's not sustainable.")

Across the street is a retail store that sells some of the crafts and jewelry made by the women from Living Hope.

Down the road and in the middle of the poorest part of Masiphumelele, we visited a community health clinic staffed by many Living Hope volunteers and lay counselors.

These personnel meet with community members who are about to be tested for HIV, as well as those who are receiving their test results. The clinic's counselors are literally Christ's hands and feet to individuals who are hearing for the first time that they are HIV-positive. After the terrifying news is given to patients, the clinic's staff counsel and pray with them, connect them with available treatments, and help them begin living positively with the disease. There's even a prenatal clinic that assists HIV-positive women through their pregnancies, ensuring that their babies are born HIV-free. Pumla, one of the lay counselors, told me, "Living Hope showed me, if you are Christian, you have to practice what you preach. The Word of God has changed my life." (Pumla became a Christian through this same ministry.) Another staff member, Bongani, came to Pumla last year, pregnant and HIV-positive. She was very ill and was cared for during the pregnancy by home-based caregivers, also sent by Living Hope. Pumla counseled her through the pregnancy, and her baby was born healthy. Today, Bongani is a support-group facilitator who counsels other women who are in the same situation she had faced.

AIDS is best fought by *prevention*, so Living Hope has trained an army of life skills educators who go into the community to work, especially with young people. This is a community rife with drug use, gangs, prostitution, rape, and alcoholism. Speaking about the plight of young people in these slums, Pastor Thomas says, "There are no dreams. It's the poverty of the mind." Hence, life skills education starts in kindergarten and helps kids make wise choices.

Living Hope initially started their counseling in high school but quickly realized that they had to start far earlier. In the darkness of poverty, children as young as six or seven may have drug and alcohol issues. Seventy percent of the sixth and seventh graders are sexually active. Pastor Thomas tells the story of one fourteen-year-old girl who told him why she had become sexually active so young. With nothing to look forward to, no future job or opportunity, her friends told her that sex was good, and sex was fun. She, like them, saw a future with no job, no education, and no hope. "I decided to have as much sex as I can. Hopefully I'll have AIDS by the time I am fifteen and be dead by the time I am twenty," she told him. "And, Pastor, I'm right on track."

While in Fish Hoek, we were also able to visit Fish Hoek Baptist's homeless ministry and the relief effort they were undertaking in an area destroyed weeks earlier by a fire. The fingerprints of this church were evident everywhere we turned. They were literally transforming their culture, reaching across racial and economic barriers, and bringing hope to some of the darkest places I have ever seen. Pastor Thomas was honest about the struggles they have faced. Some in the church were not as enthusiastic about his vision, and there were divisions, often leading him to wonder whether he would be able to keep his job. There was also what he called "AIDS fatigue"; it isn't easy to face the bleakness of AIDS and poverty every single day. This weary pastor acknowledges that this is a constant struggle and that it has been difficult to get other churches involved. Why? "This is not the prosperity gospel," he says.

Thankfully, Living Hope has seven volunteer missionaries from the United States and Canada, and about eight U.S. churches partner with them consistently, sending additional volunteers. Brentwood Baptist Church in Tennessee has been a particularly significant partner for them.

Meanwhile, Fish Hoek Baptist, this one small church near the bottom of the globe, has garnered the attention of the world. John Thomas has been invited to the White House to be commended for their work by President Bush himself. USAID has granted his ministry its financial support, and the local state government has even asked them—a Christian church—to consider taking over the running of parts of the government health infrastructure! Why? Because this single congregation chose to not walk by "the beggar laid at their gate" but stopped, instead, to minister Christ's love to him. There is no hole in their gospel; they are transforming their community, changing lives, showing people the love of Christ, and bringing the good news to the poor. Theirs is the *whole* gospel, and it has great power. Their audacious vision provokes the imagination of what could be if even one-tenth of our churches gave themselves away to the world, as they have.

A MEGACHURCH—WITH 120 MEMBERS

A church that lives within its four walls is no church at all. —Pastor Morgan Chilulu

In case you think that only wealthy churches can be salt and light to the world, and only large churches can really make a difference, let me help you: *that is simply not true.* As Americans, we tend to be impressed with bigness. God is not. I've always liked the saying "It's not the size of the dog in the fight that matters; it's the size of the fight in the dog." Christian Family Church is a small dog *full* of fight.

This church of about 120 members sits on a busy road in Kamfinsa, Zambia, in southern Africa. The congregation meets in a modest building of scrap lumber, cement, and corrugated tin. Twenty wooden pews and a simple pine cross, all hand-hewn by a young orphan named Milton, who grew up in the church, define the spare sanctuary. A lone lightbulb hangs from a wire above.

Christian Family Church, started in the 1970s, found itself besieged by the growing AIDS pandemic in the 1980s and '90s. With shame in his voice, Pastor Morgan Chilulu told me, "We looked at being HIV-positive as negative. We related HIV to sin. We would say people were not living right with God. Our church pushed people away." But in 2003, World Vision invited Chilulu and thirty other pastors to a workshop to help African churches cope with the impact of AIDS on their communities. "It had a very big impact," he said. "The Bible says, 'Do not judge.' We were driving people away from God. Now we are winning people back." The workshop was a wake-up call to Pastor Chilulu, and it transformed his vision for Christian Family Church. "Now our vision is to empower believers. This church has 120 members, but we are a megachurch," he told me.

How did he transform his biased congregation? First, he had to deal with the stigma that surrounded HIV and AIDS. He challenged his flock to see people through God's eyes. The church began to organize six-member "Hope Teams" to serve people affected by AIDS. One of the Hope Team members said, "Before when I saw people who were infected, I thought, *Just let them be like that.* Now I know that we are just the same. Even if I am not infected, I am affected. I have compassion for them now.

I am a different person." And the church is now a different church. Hope Teams go out into the community to visit and care for widows and orphans. The weekly rounds are organized such that no one is left out. The church prepares meals for the sick and the orphans and offers counseling as well. Team members also clean houses and care for children, and those who are trained in basic medicine offer home-based care to the sick, equipped with Caregiver Kits supplied by U.S. churches. The church also connects AIDS patients to antiretroviral drugs available through the government. If patients are too sick to travel, the Hope Teams bring the drugs to them. People who were dying are getting well now. Mothers are staying alive to raise their children. And hope is being restored.

But now that so many people are regaining their strength, they need a livelihood, so the church has branched out to equip them in their poverty-ridden community. Milton, the young man who furnished the church, now teaches carpentry to others, and their wares are sold to passersby on the highway. An orphan himself, Milton understands hopelessness. But now, filled with enthusiasm for his work, he said, "We want to leave a legacy. When we die, we hope what we did is remembered."

The church has also begun a welding business, both to train young men in the trade and to raise money to support the other ministries of the church. To buy the materials they needed, the congregation conducted a capital fund-raising campaign. Sacrificially, this modest church raised one million *kwacha*, about three hundred dollars, to get the welding business started. Next they started raising chickens, something the widows and children could get involved with. A nursery school, buzzing with the voices of children, sits just in front of the church, educating many of the local orphans and giving some of the community's mothers a needed break from their child-rearing responsibilities. Pastor Chilulu's next dream is for a farm that will supply adequate food for the whole community.

Pastor Chilulu brimmed with excitement as he talked about his vision for his church. But he was also excited about the other churches in his community that had now come together. He showed me a sophisticated thirty-five-page, five-year strategy that had been put together by thirty churches in the region to address the impact of AIDS. "All the churches have become one," he said. "There is no Pentecostal; there is no Evangelical; there is no Seventh-day Adventist. Thirty churches have come together.

Now thirty churches are speaking the same language. We work together without any quarrel." Here is the body of Christ in a very poor corner of the world, embracing the whole gospel—taking their stand against the AIDS pandemic and reaching out to the hurting and lost in their own community. The Church in Zambia is moving outside of its four walls to be the hands and feet of Christ to the needy in their midst. They are truly lighting a candle in the darkness.

Christian Family Church itself is at a disadvantage. Most of its 120 members are transients, people passing through, looking for work. They come, and then a few months later they are gone. But instead of seeing this as a negative, Pastor Chilulu has a larger perspective. "It's good that people come and go," he said. "Those that pass through this church are never the same. Maybe they will take our ideas and teach others. What they learn here, they take to other churches. You never know what seeds you might be planting. They could be blossoming everywhere."

Indeed they could.

Our Defining Moment

We are therefore Christ's ambassadors, as though God were making his appeal through us. —2 Corinthians 5:20

There are some 340,000 Christian churches in the United States and about 155 million regular churchgoers.[2] Let those numbers sink in for just a minute. Think of the possibilities. Think of the resources. Ponder the potential to change the world if all of these churchgoers "activated" and ramped up their commitment to love their neighbors to a new, even higher level. I said at the beginning of this section that so many of our churches are already doing amazing things right here in our own country and around the world. Many Christians are already volunteering their time, giving their money, and using their talents to serve God and their neighbors. My contention is not that

> The question is not, as the saying goes, the size of the dog in the fight. Clearly, the American Church is a very large "dog."

we're doing nothing, only that we could do so much more. With regard to American Christians, the question is not, as the saying goes, the size of the dog in the fight. Clearly, the American Church is a very large "dog." But what size is the *fight* in our dog? Are we fighting the good fight to be faithful stewards of the abundance entrusted to us by God, or does He expect *more* fight out of us? Are we fighting hard on behalf of the poor; that is, are we giving it all we've got? These are the questions we must each ask, not only of our churches, but of ourselves individually. And they are not easy to answer.

There is much at stake. The world we live in is under siege—three billion are desperately poor, one billion hungry, millions are trafficked in human slavery, ten million children die needlessly each year, wars and conflicts are wreaking havoc, pandemic diseases are spreading, ethnic hatred is flaming, and terrorism is growing. Most of our brothers and sisters in Christ in the developing world live in grinding poverty. And in the midst of this stands the Church of Jesus Christ in America, with resources, knowledge, and tools unequaled in the history of Christendom. I believe that we stand on the brink of a defining moment. We have a choice to make.

When historians look back in one hundred years, what will they write about this nation of 340,000 churches? What will they say of the Church's response to the great challenges of our time—AIDS, poverty, hunger, terrorism, war? Will they say that these authentic Christians rose up courageously and responded to the tide of human suffering, that they rushed to the front lines to comfort the afflicted and to douse the flames of hatred? Will they write of an unprecedented outpouring of generosity to meet the urgent needs of the world's poor? Will they speak of the moral leadership and compelling vision of our leaders? Will they write that this, the beginning of the twenty-first century, was the Church's finest hour?

Or will they look back and see a Church too comfortable, insulated from the pain of the rest of the world, empty of compassion, and devoid of deeds? Will they write about a people who stood by and watched while a hundred million died of AIDS and fifty million children were orphaned, of Christians who lived in luxury and self-indulgence while millions died for lack of food and water? Will schoolchildren read in disgust about a Church that had the wealth to build great sanctuaries but lacked the will to build schools, hospitals, and clinics? In short, will we be remembered as the Church with a gaping hole in its gospel?

I believe that much more is at stake than global economics or world missions. More is at risk even than the lives of the poor and the orphaned. The heart and soul of the Church of Jesus Christ, the very integrity of our faith and our relevance in the world, hang in the balance.

The gospel of Mark tells of a remarkable encounter between Jesus and a leper. In this brief story we get a glimpse of how God would have us approach the sick, the broken, and the downtrodden in our world. We see the "good news" made manifest.

The leper was sick, and he was poor. He lived his life isolated from those who were whole. This man was marginalized, ostracized, devalued. Healthy people believed that those with leprosy were sinners, and their afflictions were a judgment from God. That this man would even dare to approach Jesus was scandalous. Lepers were "unclean" and untouchable. But his suffering and desperate need compelled him. He came to Jesus "and begged him on his knees, 'If you are willing, you can make me clean'" (1:40).

Begged him on his knees. Can you feel the anguish in this man's soul as he cries out for help? The disciples were undoubtedly horrified as this unclean man approached their master. Any other rabbi would have been unwilling to become ceremonially defiled by any contact with a leper. But Jesus did the *unthinkable* to the *untouchable*: "Filled with compassion, Jesus reached out his hand and touched the man" (v. 41).

Did you catch that? Jesus' heart was not filled with disgust,
> with fear,
>> with hatred,
>>> with judgment,
>>>> with indifference,
>>>>> with anger, or
>>>>>> with condescension.

Jesus was filled with *compassion*. "I am willing," He answered the man. "Be clean!" (v. 41). And the Bible tells us that the once-leprous man was instantly cured.

If you are willing . . . This same petition hangs before every follower of Christ today.

Are we willing?

How will the Church of Jesus Christ respond to the "lepers" in our midst—the poor, the sick, and the oppressed, in our country and in our world? Are we, like Christ, *willing* to respond with compassion and urgency to those who suffer? *Are we willing?* Do we have the kind of faith, the moral courage, the depth of love, and the strength of will to rise up off of our padded pews to demonstrate the good news to the world?

One way or the other, this will be our defining moment.

PART 5

REPAIRING THE HOLE

Never doubt that a small group of thoughtful, committed citizens can change the world; indeed, it's the only thing that ever has.

—MARGARET MEAD

The creation waits in eager expectation for the sons of God to be revealed.

—ROMANS 8:19

CHAPTER TWENTY-THREE

WHAT ARE YOU GOING TO DO ABOUT IT?

Vision without action is merely a dream. Action without vision just passes the time. Vision with action can change the world.

—JOEL BARKER

The probability that we may fail in the struggle ought not to deter us from the support of a cause we believe to be just.

—ABRAHAM LINCOLN

So far I have spent twenty-two chapters arguing the case that there is a hole in our gospel and that, as a result, we have embraced a view of our faith that is far too tame. We have, in fact, reduced the gospel to a mere transaction involving the right beliefs rather than seeing in it the power to change the world. I have painted a picture of a world aflame with violence, poverty, injustice, disease, corruption, and human suffering—a world in need of revolution. But I have also attempted to make clear from Scripture that the whole gospel—the very social revolution Jesus intended as His kingdom unfolded "in earth as it is in heaven"—has been entrusted to *us*, those who claim to follow Christ. Jesus seeks a new world order in which this whole gospel, hallmarked by compassion, justice, and proclamation of the good news, becomes a reality, first in our hearts and minds, and then in the wider world through our influence. This is not to be a far-off and distant kingdom to be experienced only in the afterlife. Christ's vision was of a redeemed world order populated by redeemed people—*now*. To accomplish this, we are to be salt and light in a dark and fallen world, the "yeast" that leavens the whole loaf of bread (the whole of society). We are the ones God has called to be His Church. It's up to us. *We* are to be the change.

But a changed world requires *change agents*, and change agents are people who have first been changed themselves.

SLEEPING IN GETHSEMANE

It is hard to believe that just eleven of Jesus' disciples—and particularly those men—actually changed the world. Do you remember them the night before His crucifixion? Jesus had taken them to the Garden of Gethsemane. He'd asked them to keep watch while He prayed. We are told that as Jesus called on God, He was "deeply distressed and troubled" and that His soul was "overwhelmed with sorrow" (Mark 14:33–34). If ever He needed His friends, it was this night. But when Jesus returned to check on the disciples, He found them sleeping, not once, but twice! And worse, after His arrest "everyone deserted him and fled" (v. 50)—the disciples scattered in fear! Peter denied Christ three times that night, and the others were found three days later behind locked doors, for fear of what might happen to them.

These were the same unlikely men who would later give their lives for Christ and change the world.

What possibly could have happened to transform them from cowardly to courageous? Something spectacular: they encountered the resurrected Christ in bodily form! After the Resurrection, we read that Jesus' disciples became such incredible agents of change that they literally altered the course of history. The communities they started and the values they practiced were so striking to the world around them that they ignited a social revolution that drew thousands and ultimately billions to faith in Christ. The difference between the pre- and postresurrection disciples was astonishing.

Fear became courage;
     timidity became boldness;
          uncertainty became confidence
as their lives were given over to the revolution that the gospel—the good

news—envisioned. Everything changed because *they* had been changed, and they had been changed because Christ had risen.

He is risen indeed.

You and I are not meant to act like preresurrection disciples, racked with fear, doubt, and timidity. We are *postresurrection* disciples, and if we are to live like postresurrection disciples, everything in our lives must change. The question for us is whether we are willing to make that commitment— to live and act differently, and to repair the hole in our own gospel. If we are, then God will use us as parts of His amazing plan to change our world. But becoming this kind of disciple, one who is determined to *be* the gospel to the world around him, involves an intentional decision. It doesn't just happen. Any of us who have ever been on a diet or embarked on an exercise regimen know that fitness and weight loss don't just happen. They require us to make a choice and then change our behaviors in deliberate ways—it cannot be "business as usual." And it's not easy. The same is true of discipleship. We won't really become change agents for Christ just by going to church every Sunday. We will have to make some "on purpose" life choices and then change our priorities and behavior. Only then can God transform us and use us to change the world.

RADIOACTIVE CHRISTIANS AND SLEEPER CELLS

Therefore, if anyone is in Christ, he is a new creation; the old has gone, the new has come! —2 Corinthians 5:17

People who work around radioactive materials are required to wear radiation badges, called *dosimeters*, that change color as soon as they have been exposed to a dangerous level of radiation. The exposure is cumulative, so the badges are designed to measure the workers' cumulative exposure.

Reneé and I have attended wonderful churches throughout all the years of our marriage. We've gone faithfully every Sunday, with our children in tow. We have gone to Sunday school classes each week, met in small-group Bible studies during the week, and listened to approximately twelve hundred sermons from the pulpit. We have had daily times of Scripture study and have prayed for God's guidance in our lives. We've just kept absorbing more and more biblical knowledge and values—more "radiation." If we had been wearing dosimeters, they would have been turning a brighter and brighter shade of red.

I can still remember when our good friends Bob and Pam Snyder went on a short-term missions trip to Latvia, not too long after the dissolution of the Soviet Union. When they returned, they spoke to our Sunday school class about their experiences and about the great needs they had seen. Bob was a physician and had a particular concern for the crumbling health care system and the Christian medical personnel in these former Soviet republics. One Sunday they came to class and announced that they were moving— lock, stock, and barrel—to Hungary, kids and all. They planned to start a nonprofit organization to build up and minister to health professionals, helping them to integrate their faith into their work.[1] Just like that they were leaving everything behind: their home, their friends and family, Bob's medical practice, and their financial security. Reneé and I were stunned. "I don't think I could do that—leave everything, just like that," I said to Reneé. The Snyders seemed just like us. What had happened?

Bob and Pam had absorbed a lot of "radiation" too. They, too, had listened to hundreds of sermons, participated in Bible studies, gone to Sunday school classes, studied their Bibles daily, and prayed. And finally, when all of this cumulative exposure reached a critical level, they went "radioactive." Their faith had encountered a human need through an opportunity provided by God—and they had responded. This gospel we embrace and this Jesus we follow are dangerous—and they can change us.

Bob, Pam, and their three daughters left a few weeks later to begin their new life in Budapest. Their willingness to follow God, *no matter what*, challenged many of their friends. I know it challenged us.

It was about two or three years later that my own moment of decision came, through that phone call from World Vision. We now faced the same kind of choice Bob and Pam had faced. In the end, Reneé and I went radioactive too. We, too, came to Sunday school one day to announce that we were leaving. Our friends were stunned as well. Some of my professional colleagues and our neighbors were particularly perplexed, wondering why we were making such a radical decision.

A few years later, after 9/11, a terrorist sleeper cell in the United States was uncovered and the terror suspects arrested. Sleeper cells are small groups of extremists living undercover and waiting to be "activated" to carry out the purpose for which they have been prepared. I remember watching the news as these terrorists' neighbors were being interviewed by the news media. "They seemed so normal," one neighbor would say. "They were nice young men, who never bothered anyone," said others. Imagine their shock when they learned that these neighbors, who had lived among them, had been planning a terrorist attack all along.

I'm pretty sure some of our friends and neighbors may have also experienced shock concerning us when we made the radical decision to move across the country. "The Stearnses seemed so normal—nice people, really. How strange for them to pack up and leave like that. Maybe they were part of some cult . . ." You see, we had been a "sleeper cell" for Jesus, and we had finally been activated. We were confronted with a choice, which required us to reorder our priorities and our lives to become completely available to God, without conditions. We had become *radio-active, postresurrection* Christians. We had joined the social revolution envisioned by Jesus for His coming kingdom in a deeper way than ever before.

More than sixty years ago World Vision's founder, Bob Pierce, had been confronted with his own life-changing choice. His story, and the question he answered, stand as a challenge to each of us.

CHINA, 1948

> *Why do you call me, "Lord, Lord," and do not do what I say? I will show you what he is like who comes to me and hears my words and puts them into practice. He is like a man building a house, who dug down deep and laid the foundation on rock. When a flood came, the torrent struck that house but could not shake it, because it was well built.*
> —Luke 6:46–48

In 1948, Bob Pierce was finishing up a long tour in Asia, where he had been preaching at large evangelistic meetings representing Youth for Christ. Just a couple of days before he was scheduled to return to the States, he preached a message to some children at a missionary school in China, on Amoy Island, just off the coast. As was his practice, he exhorted them to give their lives to Christ. One little girl, named White Jade, went home that night and told her parents that she had become a Christian, not understanding that her parents' reaction would be severe. They were angry, and she was beaten by her father, disowned, and cast out of her home.

The next morning Tena Hoelkeboer, the missionary director of the school, found White Jade crying and huddled at the front gate. She took her in, comforted her, and listened to her story. When Bob arrived at the school that day, he saw Tena approaching him with a bloodied and crying little girl in her arms. He asked what had happened. "This little girl did what you told her to do, and now she has lost everything!" Tena declared angrily, thrusting the child into his arms.

Shocked and dismayed, Bob stammered, "How will she live? Will you take her in and feed her and care for her?"

The feisty school director answered, "I am already sharing my rice bowl with six other children who have no homes, and I cannot take in even one more. The question isn't what *I* am going to do. The question is, what are *you* going to do? You created this problem, Mr. Pierce. Now, *what are you going to do about it?*"

At that moment, Bob Pierce was confronted with the dilemma of his life. He was leaving for home the next day. What could he possibly do to help? And yet he had to do something. Flustered, he reached into his pocket, pulled out all he had—about five dollars—and gave it to the woman. "Here," he said. "I'm terribly sorry. Please accept this for now; it's all I have. I promise you that I will send more soon as I get back home." He and Tena then discussed what would be required to ensure that White Jade would be properly cared for, and Pierce left for the States.

What are you going to do about it? That was the question that confronted Bob Pierce that day in 1948, when he was met head-on with the desperate plight of one child. And in one moment he learned something groundbreaking about the gospel that he so freely preached: the *whole* gospel involves more than preaching; it also means caring about the *whole person* and finding ways to meet that individual's needs. When we look around our world and see children beaten and crying, huddling in their broken-down houses, aren't we confronted with the very same question that challenged Bob Pierce? For him, it was life changing. He wasn't a wealthy man; he was just a poor evangelist who had barely raised enough money to go to Asia in the first place. The fact that he had only five dollars in his pocket at the end tells you how little he had. But Pierce had had an encounter with God, and nothing for him was ever the same again.

He returned to the United States and raised more money to help White Jade. He also began telling stories of the great needs of other children in Asia to friends and churches. Then, at the outset of the Korean War, he returned to Asia and saw the appalling condition of thousands of war widows and orphans. So, again, he came back to the States, this time with 16-millimeter films to better show the pressing needs he had encountered. Then . . . *he* started asking people what they were going to do about it.

On an ordinary day in China, six decades ago, World Vision was born in the heart of an ordinary man. He had gone *radioactive*. Today World Vision operates in one hundred countries with more than thirty thousand full-time staff. And the lives of hundreds of millions of men, women, and children have been changed—because one man decided to *do something about it.*

> *Then the King will say, "I'm telling the solemn truth: Whenever you did one of these things to someone overlooked or ignored, that was me—you did it to me."* —Matthew 25:40 MSG

CHAPTER TWENTY-FOUR

How Many Loaves Do You Have?

If you think you are too small to make a difference,
try spending the night in a closed room with a mosquito.

—AFRICAN SAYING

There are no ordinary people. You have
never talked to a mere mortal.

—C. S. LEWIS

Bob Pierce's story is proof of the amazing truth that God does indeed use ordinary people to accomplish extraordinary things. David, a mere boy, killed a giant and became king of Israel. Mary, a teenage girl, gave birth to the Messiah. Peter, a fisherman, established the early church and changed the world. It is no different today. If the gospel is to be proclaimed, poverty defeated, racism overcome, the tide of AIDS turned back, or injustice challenged, it will be done by such people—ordinary people like you and me.

We might imagine that God's vision for our world is like a great jigsaw puzzle. You and I are the pieces in His hand, and He places them in just the spots where our particular shapes, sizes, and patterns best fit with the other pieces. The full picture only takes shape as all of the pieces come together in their proper places. In this view, no single piece is insignificant. Have you ever completed a puzzle only to find that one or two pieces were missing? I have, and the missing pieces compelled me to pull the cushions out of the couch, lift the tables and chairs, and scour the room to find them. Those mislaid pieces made a huge difference to the outcome. They were obviously not insignificant.

God has created each of us with a unique contribution to make to our world and our times. No other person has our same abilities, motivations, network of friends and relationships, perspectives, ideas, or experiences. When we, like misplaced puzzle pieces, fail to show up, the overall picture is diminished.

One of the most common mistakes we can make is to believe that we have nothing of significance to offer—that we're not rich enough, smart enough, skilled enough, or spiritual enough to make much difference at all, especially in the face of huge global problems. Remember the words of Moses, when God asked him to go to Pharaoh and lead His people out of Egypt? "O Lord, please send *someone else* to do it." He had his excuse too: he wasn't eloquent enough. And we're just like him. Deluded, we sit on the bench, watching the game from a distance, content to let others play. But the very good news for those of us who want to follow Christ and be part of God's plan for our world is that He uses what we have to offer, no matter how unimportant we think it might be.

In the New Testament, the story of the feeding of the five thousand is found in all four Gospels. Jesus used it to change the way we think about *underwhelming* resources in the face of *overwhelming* challenges. We are told that as Jesus and the disciples attempted to retreat to a quiet place to rest, a large crowd of people, eager to hear Jesus' teaching and to be healed, followed them.

The first thing we notice is how differently Jesus and His disciples viewed the situation. The disciples saw only a large *problem*: "This is a remote place," they said, "and it's already very late. Send the people away so they can go to the surrounding countryside and villages and buy themselves something to eat" (Mark 6:35–36). But Jesus looked at the exact same situation and saw an *opportunity*: "When Jesus . . . saw the large crowd, he had compassion on them, because they were like sheep without a shepherd. So he began teaching them many things" (v. 34). And according to the gospel of Luke, "He welcomed them and spoke to them about the kingdom of God, and healed those who needed healing" (9:11).

When we see poverty and sickness, hunger and famine, cruelty and abuse, do we see them as problems, or do we, like Jesus, filled with compassion, see their human faces and immediately begin to respond—as a shepherd to his vulnerable sheep? The disciples told Jesus that *He* needed to do something: He should send the crowd away, so they could buy food. In other words, "Jesus, You need to deal with this problem!"

Of course, Jesus did not tell them what they wanted to hear. Instead, He calmly put it right back on them. "They do not need to go away. *You* give them something to eat" (Matt. 14:16; emphasis added).

Now, this was an overwhelming predicament, from the disciples' point of view. There were five thousand men present, "besides women and children" (v. 21). Theoretically, then, there may have been as many as ten or even twenty thousand people present. At this point the disciples were getting a bit exasperated, and they panicked; Jesus *couldn't* expect them to do the impossible, could He? They even did some calculations to demonstrate to Jesus the absurdity of His response. "That would take eight months of a man's wages!" they told Him. "Are we to go and spend that much on bread and give it to them to eat?" (Mark 6:37).

There. Surely Jesus gets it now, they thought. *There is no earthly way all these people can be fed. There are too many; it would be too costly; it's not possible.* But Jesus persisted.

"How many loaves do you have?" He asked. "Go and see" (v. 38). Notice that Jesus did not fall into the same trap His disciples had, by being overwhelmed by the size of the problem. He didn't ask about magnitude or strategy or feasibility. He asked not how much it would take to solve the problem, but only how much *they* had to offer. The disciples told Him that one boy had five loaves and two fishes that he was willing to give. "Bring them here to me," He said (Matt. 14:18).

The disciples had found just one boy who was willing to give what he had. Presumably there were others, too, that had some food. Thousands, even. They could have offered it, but instead they kept it to themselves, perhaps rationalizing that "someone else" would respond. And one did— just one. So Jesus received this generous but meager offering and showed the disciples what God can do with even the smallest gift offered in faith. "Taking the five loaves and the two fish and looking up to heaven, he gave thanks and broke the loaves. Then he gave them to the disciples, and the disciples gave them to the people. They all ate and were satisfied, and the disciples picked up twelve basketfuls of broken pieces that were left over" (vv. 19–20).

Can you see the real miracle at work here? Confronted with an overwhelming problem, Jesus did not ask the disciples to do the impossible; He asked only for them to bring to Him what they had. He then multiplied the small offering and used it to do the impossible. The principle here is so very important for those of us who are overwhelmed with the immensity of human suffering and need in our world: God never asks us to give what we do not have . . . But he cannot use what we will not give.

I used to wonder why we are told so specifically at the end of this story that there were twelve basketfuls of leftovers collected. Why twelve? Might it be because there were twelve disciples who needed a tangible reminder of their lack of faith? Each one now had his own basketful of God's surplus. And as the little boy who had given his lunch looked on, can you imagine the joy *he* must have felt, seeing his gift multiplied by God to feed thousands of hungry people, many of whom he probably knew? It was his lone "puzzle piece" that completed this miracle of God. When we, as Christians, are willing to lay our pieces down on the table, we, too, can take part in God's "multiplication." But if we are *un*willing, we will assuredly miss out on every opportunity to be used by God in a powerful and amazing way.

The Power of the Possible

Be the change that you want to see in the world. —Mohandas Gandhi

If we turn to Scripture once again, we will find another compelling example of the power of ordinary people who are willing to be pieces in God's puzzle. It comes from the book of Nehemiah.

Here is the scenario: Jerusalem, the holy city of God, lay in ruins. It had been sacked by the Babylonians in 586 BC. The temple had been destroyed; the great wall around the city, toppled; and the people of God, slaughtered, with a remnant carried off to Babylon as slaves. Think for a moment about the gravity of this situation. The people God had set aside as His chosen ones; the magnificent temple built by Solomon to glorify and worship God; and the great city of Jerusalem, with its imposing walls, had been destroyed and pillaged by a heathen army. The very image and presence of God in the world had been smashed and defaced. Why? Because for generation after generation the kings of Judah and the Jewish people had sinned, disobeying God's laws, worshiping other gods, and conforming to the pagan cultures surrounding them. Finally, God's anger could be held back no more.

But now forty-seven years had passed, and the Babylonians were themselves conquered by the Persian king Cyrus, who then opened the way for Jews to return to Jerusalem. Under this new, Persian occupation, it would actually be possible for the city and its temple to be rebuilt, thereby restoring the physical manifestation of God's presence among His people. Over the next decades many Jews returned to Jerusalem. Led by Ezra and exhorted by the prophets Haggai and Zechariah, they also succeeded in rebuilding the temple, seventy years after it had been destroyed. The effort was plagued by political opposition, as well as by the continued sin and apathy of God's people; but in the end, the Jews met with some success.

But the job was only partially completed—the great walls needed to protect the city still lay in ruins nearly a century and a half after they were destroyed.

Years passed, but then one day a man named Nehemiah, one of the Jews in exile in the city of Susa, eagerly questioned some men who had just come back from Jerusalem. He wanted to know if the Jews who had returned to Jerusalem were thriving and if the city itself had been rebuilt. The news was not good.

"Those who survived the exile and are back in the province are in great trouble and disgrace," Nehemiah was told. "The wall of Jerusalem is broken down, and its gates have been burned with fire" (Neh. 1:3).

Nehemiah's reaction to this news tells us a great deal about his heart: "When I heard these things, I sat down and wept. For some days I mourned and fasted and prayed before the God of heaven" (v. 4). Nehemiah was devastated by the report of his countrymen, but why? Why would he weep just because some *walls* had not been rebuilt?

Because Nehemiah saw Jerusalem through God's eyes. He understood that it was the city of God's chosen people, *covenant* people. Within its walls was the temple of the one God and the holy of holies, the very place where God forgave man's sin. The wall around Jerusalem was the structure that set God's people apart from the polytheistic cultures that surrounded them. The holy city, its place of worship, and the walls that encircled them represented *God's very presence and identity in the world*. This is why Nehemiah wept, mourned, and fasted. In his eyes the ruins of Jerusalem were an affront to God; they also epitomized the slander of God's image in the pagan world.

Let me now draw a symbolic comparison. In our world today, God's image and identity are still defaced. They are slandered by poverty, by injustice, by corruption, by disease, and by human exploitation and suffering. And God's name is defiled when His people willingly and apathetically accept the status quo, lacking the vision to lift up God's holiness, goodness, and justice in a crumbling world. God's heart was broken over the condition of Jerusalem in Nehemiah's time, and His heart is broken today by the condition of our world and our failure to challenge it.

> God's image and identity are still defaced. They are slandered by poverty, by injustice, by corruption, by disease, and by human exploitation and suffering.

Nehemiah was not willing to accept the status quo. He had a different vision. After weeping and fasting, Nehemiah prayed, first asking forgiveness for himself and the apathy and sin of God's people. Then he challenged the Jews of Jerusalem to act: "You see the trouble we are in: Jerusalem lies in ruins, and its gates have been burned with fire. Come, let us rebuild the wall of Jerusalem, and we will no longer be in disgrace" (2:17).

Nehemiah's approach was simple and inspiring. He was first a man of prayer. We see him praying at all times through the story, understanding that success would depend on God and not himself. He was also a man of vision. And above all, Nehemiah was a man of action—he was a doer. He was never overwhelmed by the enormity of the task; instead he was focused on using what he had to accomplish the goal. He divided the bigger goal into smaller pieces. He then developed detailed plans, raised money, and organized people to complete the task. Despite opposition and discouragement, he encouraged and inspired each person to do only what that individual could do—*his own* part. And he reminded people of the great truths in Scripture. In fact, Nehemiah had the Book of the Law read aloud to the people *from daybreak till noon*, and we are told that they wept as they listened, repenting of their sins.

The result was amazing. The great wall that had lain in ruin for more than 150 years was rebuilt in fifty-two days! But how? One stone at a time. In Nehemiah 3 alone, we read of more than forty different people and groups who each rebuilt the section of the wall that was nearest to them. Each person did the doable, the part that *he* could accomplish, that which was within *his own* reach. Then their collective power, when it was harnessed and channeled in alignment with God's will—changed everything. *Together,* they did the impossible—in less than two months.

Our world, like Nehemiah's, also lies in ruins, and we, too, need a fresh vision. Nehemiah's vision was to rebuild the broken places and to lift up God's righteousness to a scoffing world. Our vision should be the same. If we can capture that vision, then we, too, can accomplish the impossible— one stone at a time—everybody doing something. If each child of God does his or her *doable* part, then collectively we *can* set aright a topsy-turvy world. "And we will no longer be in disgrace." But we must *each* give what we have to the cause of Christ, who beckons to each of His followers . . .

How many loaves do you have? Bring them here to Me.

CHAPTER TWENTY-FIVE

TIME, TALENT, AND TREASURE

*Use what talents you possess: the woods would be very silent if no
birds sang there except those that sang best.*

—HENRY VAN DYKE

*But we have this treasure in jars of clay to show that this
all-surpassing power is from God and not from us.*

—2 CORINTHIANS 4:7

It's time to commit. What are you going to do about it? In the end God
works in our world one person at a time. The hungry are fed, the thirsty
are refreshed, the naked are clothed, the sick are treated, the illiterate are
educated, and the grieving are comforted, just *one person at a time.* You
have the opportunity to be that one person to someone who needs what you
have to offer. And what you have to offer is never small and insignificant.
Again, the great picture of what God is doing in our world is incomplete
without your unique puzzle piece—the one that only *you* possess. But you
must choose to place your piece in the puzzle.

My hope is that you have already made that choice—that you've
decided to bring your "loaves" and offer them to the Lord. But in my experience, most people don't really have a good sense of what it is they have
to offer. They are willing to sign up and *show* up but are confused about
just what they might possess that could be of value to God's kingdom. One
of the traditional ways to think about this involves looking at our three

t's—*time*, *talent*, and *treasure*. Each of us has resources in all three of these categories, and we often have far more to offer than we think.

When I was just twenty-six and two years out of business school, Reneé and I went to our church's weeklong missions conference every night. One evening we hosted one of the missionary speakers, a man named Andy, in our home for dinner. Andy worked for World Relief, an organization that specializes in working with churches to help the poor around the world. After dinner the three of us sat talking for quite some time.

Sensing that I had a real interest in missions, Andy asked me if I had ever considered serving full-time in missions work. He said that World Relief might be able to use someone like me. Somewhat awkwardly I explained that I really hadn't and that my business degree didn't seem to be a very good background for missions. Over the next days, though, I felt convicted about our conversation. *Maybe*, I thought, *I should pursue something full-time where my faith and my career could come together.* So I made an appointment to discuss this with my pastor, Dr. Paul Toms. I remember explaining my dilemma—that I really liked my job in the marketing department of Parker Brothers Games but that I felt guilty that I wasn't making myself available to God in full-time service. Dr. Toms listened carefully, asked me a few questions, and then told me what he thought.

"Rich," he began, "we are all in full-time Christian service. It's just that some of us serve the Lord in secular jobs, and others in ministry jobs. But either way, we should be using our gifts to represent Christ in the best possible way. You seem to really love your business job, and it seems like God has given you a knack for it. I think you should stay where you are." Then he laughed and added, "Who knows? Maybe you'll make a lot of money someday that can be used for the kingdom. And if God really wants you to move into full-time service down the road, He'll let you know." (Boy, did that turn out to be a prophetic word!)

In the twenty years that followed, I climbed the corporate ladder and deepened my business and management skills. I tried to be an ambassador for Christ in the workplace as best I could, and as our income grew, we were able to support more and more ministries financially. But Reneé and I would still sometimes talk of retiring early and going to the mission field. I used to laugh because I felt I would be the absolute worst missionary in the world. As I saw it, I had no useful skills at all. Didn't missionaries have to speak multiple languages, know how to improve crop yields, perform surgeries with a machete, and be able to build irrigation systems out of bamboo with that same machete? I was so klutzy that when asked to even hang a picture, I was tempted to make a call from the Yellow Pages. I really had a passion for missions and for helping the poor, but I just didn't think I had anything to offer besides a monthly check. I completely failed to see the "loaves and fishes" that God had given me, even though they were right under my own nose:

- a zeal for missions
- a deep concern for the poor
- senior executive leadership experience
- a career in connecting people with products through marketing
- a knack for writing and public speaking
- a heart for giving financially to support ministry
- a wife who also wanted to serve the poor

Those were the things that World Vision saw when they were looking for a new leader in 1998, even though I couldn't see them at the time. That was where my pieces of the puzzle fit perfectly. I just had to discover what God had uniquely given me and be willing to offer them in His service.

What has God given you? Moses had a stick (remember chapter 7?). David had a slingshot, and Paul had a pen. Mother Teresa possessed a love for the poor; Billy Graham, a gift for preaching; and Joni Eareckson Tada, a disability. What did they have in common? A willingness to let God use whatever they had, even when it didn't seem very useful. If you will assess what *you* have to offer in terms of your time, your treasure, and your talents, you will have a better understanding of how you might uniquely serve.

TIME

Of the three categories of assets we have to offer, the one we often consider least is time. Whether we are generous or stingy, most of us are much more careful and deliberate about what we do with our treasure than with our time. The same is true of our talents. If you are a gifted teacher, a brilliant scientist, or a superb organizer, you may not have a full understanding of how you can best use your talent in serving God, but you probably think and pray more about that than you do about how you use your time. Even though time is a finite resource, most of us waste a lot of it. How many hours do we spend watching TV, strolling through the mall, or sitting in traffic, which could be better spent in building God's kingdom?

Time has value—many of us are paid by the hour or the week because our employers understand the value of our time. If you doubt the value of time as a kingdom resource, consider this. Let's say that each of us on average has about two hours each day that might be available for service if we so chose. Over the course of the year, if we valued our time at just $10 an hour, that would be the equivalent of more than $7,000 that each of us could make available for ministry. The total asset value for 120 million American Christians would be more than $800 billion! Even if we all just volunteered one hour a week to serve a charitable cause, it would be worth $62 billion each year. That's what it would cost if our churches and nonprofit organizations had to pay for that time. As the saying goes, "Time is money." But giving our time to kingdom causes has an even more important dimension because of the eternal impact it can have. God can multiply the impact of the time, treasure, and talents that we make available to Him.

Last year I met a Korean man who lives and works in New York. He knew I was the president of World Vision, and he told me how important the work of organizations like ours had been to him when he was a child right after the Korean War. He and his family, he said, desperate and dislocated by the war, had been helped enormously by the shipments of clothing, food, and even school supplies that they received—lovingly donated, sorted, and organized by people of goodwill in America and perhaps other countries. These donors had given of their time, treasure, and talents to help the people suffering in a foreign nation. And the young Korean boy benefited immeasurably from their kindness; he was able to finish school. He was so grateful for the generosity he and his family had experienced.

Today, that "boy" is the secretary general of the United Nations—his name is Ban Ki-moon. I wonder if the people who donated their time, treasure, and talent back in the early 1950s had any idea of the impact they would have.

We never know how God might use our efforts, no matter how insignificant they may seem to us, to influence important issues and needs in our world. Listen to this story of a senior citizen who made a difference.

When Bread for the World member Connie Wick of Indianapolis, Indiana, wrote a letter to her senator supporting the Millennium Challenge Account (MCA)[1] and HIV/AIDS funding, she didn't know it would be mentioned at the White House. But that's what happened on July 13, 2004. Bread for the World President David Beckmann[2] was attending a White House signing ceremony when he had the opportunity to talk with President Bush about the importance of full funding for the MCA. Mr. Bush called over two key senators, Majority Leader Sen. Bill Frist (R-TN) and Sen. Richard Lugar (R-IN), and asked them to help secure the MCA funding that he had requested.

Just after this conversation, Sen. Lugar said to Beckmann, "You know, I am just now responding to a letter from a constituent, Connie Wick. She is saying just what you are saying, that we should fully fund the MCA, the AIDS initiative, and not cut funding for ongoing programs of assistance to poor people."

Connie Wick, the longtime leader of a Bread for the World group at the Robin Run Retirement Community in Indianapolis, said reports of the conversation with the President were "heart-stopping." She has worked on behalf of hungry and poor people most of her life. "Robin Run has a lot of committed activists," said regional organizer Mariah Priggen. "But Connie is really the one who gets everyone and everything organized. It's been her passion and vision that anchors the group and keeps it moving."

"I was again impressed by the power of Bread for the World members," said Beckmann afterward. "The Chair of the Senate Foreign Relations Committee had just been asked by the President of the United States to help get full funding for the MCA. What immediately came to the senator's mind was a recent letter from an active constituent—Connie Wick at the Robin Run Retirement Community in Indianapolis."

Wick's experience offers encouragement to all who have wondered whether their letter writing on hunger and poverty issues really makes a difference.[3]

One of the most remarkable insights I have ever had regarding how God uses our seemingly insignificant puzzle pieces to accomplish significant things is the story of a young man from Boston, named Edward

Kimball. Edward taught Sunday school at his church because he felt called to invest himself in the lives of young boys and men. To get to know his students better, he would often visit them during the week where they lived or worked.

One Sunday a challenging teenager showed up in his class. The boy was seventeen, a bit rough hewn, poorly educated, and prone to outbursts of anger and profanity. Edward thought about how he might reach this boy and one day decided to visit him at the shoe store where he worked for his uncle. Kimball passed by the store once, trying to get up the courage to speak to the boy. What would he say, he wondered, and how would he be received?

Finally, he entered and found the boy in the back, wrapping shoes and putting them on the shelves. Edward went to him, simply put his hand on the young man's shoulder, and mumbled some words about Christ's love for him. And apparently his timing was just right, because right there in the shoe store, the boy was moved to commit his life to Christ.[4] His name was Dwight L. Moody, and he became the most successful evangelist of the nineteenth century, preaching to an estimated one hundred million people during his lifetime and traveling perhaps a million miles—before the time of radio, television, automobiles, and air travel!

But the story gets better. Moody himself, in 1879, was instrumental in the conversion of another young man, F. B. Meyer, who also grew up to become a minister. Meyer subsequently mentored J. W. Chapman and led him to Christ. Chapman also became a pastor and evangelist and started an outreach ministry to professional baseball players. One of the players he met, Billy Sunday, became Chapman's assistant and advance man for many of his evangelistic meetings.

In time, Sunday, having learned the art of preaching from Chapman, started to hold his own evangelistic meetings. He went on to become the greatest evangelist of the first two decades of the twentieth century in America. One of his revivals, in Charlotte, North Carolina, in the 1920s, was so successful that an associate of his named Mordecai Ham, who years earlier had given his life to Christ at one of his crusades, was asked to come back to Charlotte a few years later to hold a second series of evangelistic meetings. On one of the final nights, when Ham was preaching, a gangly teenager came forward and responded to his call to "give your life to Christ." His name was Billy Graham.

Do you sometimes feel that you have nothing worthwhile to offer—that you are a nobody when it comes to doing great things for God? I wonder if Edward Kimball felt the same way. He never did anything spectacular or particularly newsworthy. He just showed up out of faithfulness to God, an hour or two each week, to teach the boys in his class. And yet Edward Kimball's dedication to teaching Sunday school faithfully and caring about those boys changed the world.

TALENT

My faith demands—this is not optional—my faith demands that I do whatever I can, wherever I am, whenever I can, for as long as I can with whatever I have to try to make a difference. —Jimmy Carter

Unfortunately the word *talent* is often misunderstood. We automatically think of special abilities, such as playing the bassoon, singing opera, writing poetry, dancing ballet, or perhaps athletic abilities in soccer or tennis. But in the context of evaluating those things we possess that may be useful in service, the word *talent* has a much wider meaning. Yes, it does include those artistic and athletic abilities we usually think of, but it also encompasses much more. Let me try to expand the way you look at the talents God has given to you. Let's start with your unique personality and character traits. Are you outgoing, contemplative, determined, stubborn, visionary, thoughtful, funny? All of those parts of you describe how God uniquely made you.

They are also characteristics that God intends to use in your service to Him. Your *talents* also include your life experiences. Each of us has a unique life history, made up of our family background, education, professional and work history, experiences and the wisdom gained from them, relationships, and connections. No one has ever lived the same life as you, and that is one of the things that makes your "puzzle piece" extraordinary. We also have interests and passions that God has placed in our hearts. Bono has a passion for Africa; William Wilberforce, a burning desire to end slavery; and Connie Wick, an interest in lobbying on behalf of the poor. You may love animals or care deeply about the environment. You may be fascinated by politics or passionate about running marathons. But whatever your objects of deepest interest, they may provide clues to your particular way of serving.

Thus, when considering our talents, we need to consider all of the above—our abilities, personalities, passions, pursuits, knowledge, experiences, and relationships and networks. These things are all resources we possess that can be used in one way or another.

Finally, the Bible tells us that each of us has been given "spiritual gifts" that we are to use in building up the Church, the body of Christ. (These gifts are listed in Romans 12:6–10; 1 Corinthians 12:1–12, 28; and Ephesians 4:11.) These include such gifts as spiritual discernment, giving, leadership, mercy, administration, teaching, evangelism, wisdom, and exhortation. We are told that God has distributed these gifts throughout the Church to equip His people to do kingdom work. For a follower of Christ, discerning one's spiritual gifts is an important part of understanding just how and where he or she can best serve in furthering the work of the Church. To help, various organizations have made a number of assessment tools available on the Internet.[5] I challenge you to check them out.

When you think about what talents *you* have to offer, think in these broader terms, not just in terms of a specific ability you might have. Most of us have a lot more to offer than we give ourselves credit for. The apostle Peter was an impulsive and passionate person—a fisherman by trade. God used his passion and impulsiveness to make him a "fisher of men." Peter became the entrepreneur God used to launch the first-century church. Paul, a man who persecuted the Church in the same century, was a zealot with a brilliant mind, a deep knowledge of Jewish theology, and a gift for scholarship and writing. He was also a Roman citizen, something that played heavily in his various arrests and imprisonments, leading him ultimately to Rome for his trial. God used every dimension of Paul's abilities and circumstances after his conversion on the Damascus Road. Even his imprisonment turned out to be a "talent" used by God, as Paul wrote most of his letters from his prison cells.

Sometimes just the position we occupy—not even our abilities or personalities—can be used by God. In the book of Esther, we see the amazing story of how God used a queen to save the entire Jewish race.

Yes, you can definitely impact the world if you are royalty . . .

But you can have just as much impact if you're a nine-year-old boy.

HOOPS OF HOPE

Austin Gutwein was just nine when he learned about children in Africa who had become orphaned because of AIDS. Most adults would laugh at the idea of a nine-year-old tackling the global AIDS pandemic, but Austin believed he could do something—that he had a "talent" that God could use. Austin described his journey in this letter, found on the Hoops of Hope Web site:

> In the spring of 2004, I watched a video that showed children who had lost their parents to a disease called AIDS. After watching the video, I realized these kids weren't any different from me except they were suffering. I felt God calling me to do something to help them. I decided to shoot free throws and on World AIDS Day, 2004, I shot 2,057 free throws to represent the 2,057 kids who would be orphaned during my day at school. People sponsored me and we were able to raise almost $3,000. That year, the money was used by World Vision to provide hope to 8 orphan children.
>
> From that year forward, thousands of people have joined me in a basketball shoot-a-thon called Hoops of Hope. By doing something as simple as shooting free throws, Hoops of Hope participants have raised over $500,000. The children left behind by AIDS now have access to food, clothing, shelter, a new school and finally, a medical testing facility.
>
> Last year, our goal was to raise $150,000 to build a medical testing lab in Sinazongwe, Zambia. This lab will enable medical staff to test parents for HIV/AIDS prior to administering medication for the disease. The medication will allow parents suffering from HIV/AIDS to prolong their life and keep their children from becoming among the 15 million children already orphaned by this disease.
>
> Not only did Hoops of Hope participants raise enough money to fund the building of the lab, they also supplied the lab with 1,000 medical Caregiver Kits. This will allow those caring for HIV/AIDS infected moms and dads to have the basic supplies they need. We also were able to furnish the 2006 Johnathan Sim[6] Legacy School.
>
> In 2008, we would like to build a second medical lab in Twatchiyanda,

Zambia (also the site of the 2006 Johnathan Sim Legacy School), provide Caregiver Kits and provide bicycles for caregivers to ride. The lab combined with Caregiver Kits and bicycles will help to keep parents healthier and alive longer so they can provide for their children.

I hope you'll join us by participating or sponsoring a participant. It's an awesome event that will leave an impact not only on the lives of the kids we're helping, but on yours as well.

In Him,
Austin[7]

Today, Austin has thousands of kids in two hundred different locations doing "Hoops of Hope" in most of the fifty states and in other countries around the world. His cumulative fund-raising is approaching one million dollars. Think of it: a million bucks—for *shooting hoops!* Talk about using your talents to change the world!

TREASURE

That bread which you keep belongs to the hungry; that coat which you preserve in your wardrobe, to the naked; those shoes which are rotting in your possession, to the shoeless; that gold which you have hidden in the ground, to the needy. Wherefore, as often as you are able to help others, and refuse, so often did you do them wrong. —Augustine

Earlier in the book I stated that anyone earning fifty thousand a year has an income higher than 99 percent of the people in the world. Simply stated, by comparison the average American is, well, wealthy. The question is, what does God expect us to do with our wealth? In assessing our time, treasure, and talents, we must give adequate consideration to the financial resources God has entrusted to us. Too often we cop out of this responsibility by saying something like, "I volunteer my *time* to help those in need," or "I use my *talents* to raise funds for philanthropic causes . . . so I don't really have to give my *money*. People wealthier than me can do that." But following Christ is not an either-or proposition. We need to be stewards of our time, our treasure, and our talent—all three.

Imagine for a moment that Bill Gates was trying to discern how he could best make the world a better place. How would you react if he concluded that, instead of investing a single dollar, he would spend one week each year in Mexico, shovel in hand, digging latrines for people who have no toilets? One of the wealthiest men in the world, with a net worth greater than $50 billion, phenomenal business skills, and matchless influence, deciding that the *best* way he can help is by shoveling dirt for seven days a year! I think we would all say, "Give me a break!" Thankfully, that's not what Bill Gates did. He looked at the highest and best use of all of his assets—time, talent, *and* treasure—and created an innovative foundation endowed with billions of his own dollars to tackle some of the world's biggest challenges: global health, education, and development issues.

> It doesn't take billions of dollars to make a difference.

But it doesn't take billions of dollars to make a difference.

The lack of clean water causes millions of needless child deaths each year. Yet the cost to bring clean water to one person costs only *one dollar per year*![8] When you realize that a gift as small as a dollar can save a life, it is hard to argue that you're not wealthy enough to make a difference. We might instead want to ask just how many lives our own wealth would enable us to save. In truth, the cost to feed the hungry, to educate children, to make microloans to poor farmers, to inoculate children, and even to provide needed surgeries to the poorest of the poor is extremely affordable and within the reach of most of us.

Now, you're probably thinking, *Sure, Bill Gates has time, treasure (lots of it), and the talent (lots of that too) to make a difference, but I'm not Bill Gates.* Well, Leon McLaughlin isn't Bill Gates either—and his talent was shining shoes! But he believed that he could make a difference.[9]

Leon works at a shoe shine stand in a large office building in Seattle. Several years ago, while traveling in Mexico, Leon met a woman who told him a story that changed his life. The woman had hosted an American tourist in her home. The tourist, when using her bathroom, noticed that the bathtub was filled with water, so he pulled out the plug to drain it, thinking he was doing the woman a favor. When he told the woman what he had done, she began to cry. *He had just drained the only clean water she would have for a month.*

Leon returned to Seattle, determined to learn as much as he could about the crisis caused by a lack of clean water in the developing world. He took his interest further by taking online classes in the repair and maintenance of water distribution systems and becoming an agent for First Water, a Georgia-based manufacturer of a filtration machine that can produce 740 gallons of clean water per hour.

Following a spate of flooding in Bolivia, Leon approached World Vision to see if the organization could use one of his machines to assist the thousands displaced by floodwaters there. World Vision said it could, but they would need Leon to donate the machine and pay for its transportation and ongoing technical support and maintenance. Leon was not put off. He remembered that he was shining the shoes of some of the top lawyers, business executives, and bankers in the city. So he taped pictures of the flooded Bolivian community on the walls of his shoe shine stand to stimulate conversation, and he then began to talk to his clients about his dream to help bring clean water to communities that didn't have it.

It worked. Through his shoe shine contacts, Leon was able to fund his first machine for Bolivia. World Vision Bolivia staff were so impressed with it that they soon ordered five more. An additional ten machines have since been ordered to supply schools and hospitals in Bolivia, and Leon is now setting his sights on other countries that struggle for lack of water.

Leon works three different jobs to support his "habit" of helping others. Dean Salisbury, World Vision's director of supply-chain management, told me that other corporations had been approached to donate filtration systems like this, but Leon was the only one who agreed to do it and to provide the additional money for transportation, technical training, and maintenance. "His goal in life," said Salisbury, "is not to make money, but to help people. It's very refreshing in the corporate world."

Indeed it is. Leon did not allow himself to be overwhelmed by the magnitude of a problem. Instead, he brought the "loaves" he had and offered them to help others.

A SHARP ELBOW IN MY CONSCIENCE

I seem to be the kind of person who has to learn the same lesson over and over again. I have confessed already that I continue to struggle with the consistency of my compassion and commitment to those suffering in dire circumstances. I have to work hard at maintaining a tender heart and letting my heart *continue* to be "broken by the things that break the heart of God." A few years ago God dealt with me again on this issue—this time speaking through my wife's sharp elbow (something that has often been a powerful teaching tool in my life).

It was the closing night of a three-day conference on the urgent need for the Christian community to respond to the widows and orphans of the AIDS pandemic. I was the closing speaker at the final dinner for about three hundred people. My goal was to challenge them to do something, to get involved. In fact, we had cleverly positioned the photo of a child who needed to be sponsored at each place setting so that I could provoke everyone in the room to support the one child whose framed picture stood on the table right beside their chocolate mousse. I spoke for thirty minutes and gave what I thought was quite an inspiring call to action. Then, as the music played and people considered how to respond, I sat down at my table and bowed in prayer, praying that we would receive a strong response to my call for support.

That's when I felt Reneé's elbow. I glanced toward her and found her pointing to the photo of the child in front of us. I whispered that my call to action was not for us but for everyone else. I reminded her that we already sponsored a dozen kids through World Vision and that we certainly couldn't pick up another at every event. Then I bowed again in prayer. The second time the elbow was more insistent, and when I looked up, she handed me the response card and pen and gave me "the look." I've seen this look often in our marriage, so I knew what I had to do; I reluctantly filled out the card, and we became the new sponsor of a young boy named Morgan, from Zambia. My college-aged son, Andy, had come down from school to attend the event, and he decided to sponsor the child at his place (I think to impress his girlfriend, who was also there). It turned out to be Morgan's brother Jackson.

The conference ended, and we all went home. Honestly, I didn't give much thought to these two boys over the next couple of years. Reneé is the one who writes letters to our kids and sends them cards. I just pay the bills. But about two years after the event, I was planning a trip to Zambia when my staff reminded me that I had two sponsored boys who lived there.

"Oh yeah," I said. They then told me they thought we should film me meeting the two boys, and that we could tell their story in one of our TV specials. So a few weeks later I found myself walking across a field in Zambia to meet Morgan and Jackson, who lived with their grandmother, Mary Bwalya.

When she saw me, Mary ran to greet me, grabbed my hand, and bowed almost to the ground, thanking me profusely for what I had done. She said, "When I learned two years ago that a family in America had decided to sponsor Morgan and Jackson, I knew that God had replaced the parents these boys had lost! If I had wings, I would have flown to the airport to greet you." I was stunned and embarrassed. Mary was not eager to thank me because I was the president of World Vision; she wanted to thank the American sponsor who had rescued her grandsons. She saw me as a new father for two boys who had lost their own father to AIDS. I then sat and talked with her and the boys, and I learned just how dire their situation had been. Both of their parents had died within the same year. There were four siblings, Jackson being the oldest. They had literally nursed their parents on their deathbeds, watching their painful and horrible deaths as they wasted away, consumed by sores that covered their bodies. Jackson, thirteen at the time, knew that he would have to care for his three younger siblings, so he quit school and tried to find work and food. (Mary lived several hundred miles away and had not yet heard of the deaths of her son and daughter-in-law.)

But Jackson was not able to support them, so all four left school and began to scavenge and beg for food. "There were days we lay all day on the floor of our hut because we were too weak from hunger. We sometimes went a week with no food, and I feared that Morgan would not survive," Jackson told me.

Finally, their grandmother learned of the deaths and managed to take a bus across the country to rescue her grandchildren, taking them back with her. But a poor widow herself, Mary could not manage to feed and support four young children. Soon they all began to sink deeper into hunger and despair. They hit bottom when a storm wrecked the little mud hut they lived in, adding homelessness to their desperate conditions.

Here Mary picked up the story. "That was when I learned the joyous news—that an American family had decided to sponsor Morgan and

Jackson—and I thanked God that He had raised someone up to help us."

I felt so ashamed. That night two years earlier at the banquet, I had filled out a card and dutifully written down my credit card number—*only* because my wife had made me. I had not thought about the lives involved, that my decision might have been a matter of life or death. It had only been a transaction to me, costing me just two dollars a day. But to Mary and those boys, it was an answer to prayer that literally may have saved their lives. If you watch the TV special that features my meeting with Morgan and Jackson, you will see me crying as I tell their story. God had broken my heart again with something that broke His heart too. If you don't think a small gesture of compassion can make a difference, think again.

A WIDOW'S MITE

> *But the king replied to Araunah, "No, I insist on paying you for it. I will not sacrifice to the LORD my God burnt offerings that cost me nothing." So David bought the threshing floor and the oxen and paid fifty shekels of silver for them.* —2 Samuel 24:24

A few years ago Raul Hernandez, one of our World Vision representatives in Florida, responded to a phone call from an elderly woman in Miami who asked if he could come to her apartment to discuss a gift. When he returned, he e-mailed the rest of us at World Vision about his meeting. Here is his account:

The apartment complex was situated in a poor Latino neighborhood of Miami. As I knocked at the door, I noticed the humble surroundings. She opened the door. Ana[10] is a wonderful 91-year-young Colombian lady.

"Come on in, you are the person World Vision sent to receive my gift?" She invited me to her humble one-bedroom apartment. No air conditioning. But the room was filled with excitement and the refreshing presence of the Holy Spirit. Her smile reminded me of the sweetness of my own grandmother who was instrumental in my salvation. We started a long and vivid conversation that I wished wouldn't end.

I was told about her coming to the U.S. in 1954 (even before I was born) with her husband, her struggle to raise up her three children, her long working hours to meet the basic family needs, her striving to keep the values she was taught in her native Colombia and to keep the unity of the family. Then she told me about her terrible time of sickness, almost totally paralyzed, immobilized, strangled by pain, limited by the mercy of others to move her around. Until she met Katherine Kuhlman and through her she met the Lord and His healing power that sustains her until today. I have to confess that I was ashamed that I need more medication than she needs.

After many marvelous stories she stood up and said, "Let me bring my gift to the children that World Vision is serving." She went to a little night table and brought an envelope to the table where we were seated. She opened the envelope with care as if it was a ceremony of mercy and love. She passed to me five clipped lumps of twenty-dollar bills. "Count them, please," she said. "I want to be sure I counted correctly."

I counted them, and it was one thousand dollars. She then said, "I have been saving this for a long time with the intention to give it to World Vision for the poor children in the world. Every time someone gave me a gift for my birthday, or for Christmas or New Year, I saved it for the poor children. You see, I have this apartment, it's the only possession I have, but then I am so blessed by the Lord that I want to bless those who are less fortunate than me. I used to sponsor a girl from Guatemala since she was a little baby, but then she graduated and World Vision transferred my sponsorship to another girl in Colombia whom I still sponsor. But I was thinking, I will soon start my travel to my Celestial Home, to my Father; I need to do something soon on behalf of those suffering children, that was why I called to World Vision to send me someone to receive this gift. I want to keep this anonymous, God knows. My prayer is that as Jesus took two fish and five loaves of bread and multiplied them to feed the thousands, that He will do the same with this, my gift. It's not much, but it is everything I have."

I was crying inside, such generosity is only possible by the work of the Holy Spirit. I felt I was blessed beyond my imagination. The humid heat of Miami, in this small apartment without air conditioning, was totally forgotten under the refreshing breeze I felt coming from above as I enjoyed this visit with a World Vision donor. I was wondering, as I drove back home, how many Anas World Vision has the privilege to be blessed with; she is not a major donor, she is a heavenly donor.

World Vision has received multimillion-dollar gifts, but I am almost certain that Ana's gift caused equal rejoicing in heaven, because Ana gave what she could.

My hope is that as you have read these past few chapters, you have developed a better understanding of what you, uniquely, have to offer. Most of us greatly underestimate the potential value of our time, treasure, and talents in terms of what they can add to the beautiful mosaic of what God is doing in our world. Many of us sit on the sidelines because we don't appreciate what we have to offer. Others know *what* they have to offer, but they don't know *how*. To speak to this, let me quote my pastor, Earl Palmer: "God can't steer a parked car." If we sit in the parking lot with our engines turned off, just waiting for a voice from the sky, we'll never get anywhere in our quest to solve the world's problems. We need to at least "start our engines."

We may not be clear on just how God wants to use us. But that's no excuse for doing nothing. Just jump in, and start doing. Austin Gutwein shot free throws and built a school for orphans. The widow Ana saved her quarters and dollars for years and offered them to God to help children. And Bill Gates started a foundation to improve global health and education.

What will *you* do?

CHAPTER TWENTY-SIX

A Mountain of Mustard Seeds

*The one who says it can't be done should get out of
the way of the one who is doing it.*

—CHINESE PROVERB

Make your life a mission—not an intermission.

—ARNOLD GLASGOW

One way to conclude a book like this would be to cast a utopian vision of
a world without poverty, injustice, and suffering—a "happily ever after"
ending that trivializes the height and depth of the problems facing our
world. But I am more of a realist than that. And yet I want these last pages
to excite you with the possible.

As you contemplate just how you might become involved, how you
might change the status quo in the face of all that I have presented in this
book, it would be easy to make one of two mistakes. You could become so
overwhelmed by the magnitude of the challenges in our world that you turn
away, hopeless, convinced that nothing you could do will ever make a difference. Or you could dive in with naive enthusiasm, underestimating the
problems, only to burn out from discouragement after the first few setbacks.
But if you truly want to follow Christ and carry the good news in tangible
ways throughout our world, neither of these approaches is very useful. The
pessimist here sees only obstacles. The optimist sees only opportunities. But

the *realist* sees the possibilities between the two. And that's who we must be. We must be *people of the possible*.

Robert Kennedy once said, "There are those who look at things the way they are, and ask why . . . I dream of things that never were, and ask why not?" Isn't it all a matter of perspective? What do you see when you look at the pain and suffering in the world? Do you see a malnourished child—or a future farmer? A child without schooling—or a potential teacher? Do you see a frightened child huddling in a refugee camp—or do you see a prospective leader? When you look into the faces of the poor, the marginalized, and the downtrodden, do you see hopelessness—or people made in the very image of God, with the prospects of a hope-filled future ahead of them? We, as Christians, can look at our broken world, shrug our shoulders, and say, "That's just the way things *are*." Or we can instead embrace a vision of what *could be*—if we'd each pitch in. Isn't it better to light a candle than curse the darkness? And what could be accomplished if we lit not one candle but many? The light of even one challenges the gloom, but the light of a million could obliterate it.

Moving Mountains

"I tell you the truth, if you have faith as small as a mustard seed, you can say to this mountain, 'Move from here to there' and it will move. Nothing will be impossible for you" (Matt. 17:20). I used to read that verse and think that it was just an exaggeration that Jesus was making in order to make a point about the power of faith. *We can't* literally *move mountains . . . can we?* But then I saw it in a different way. What if Jesus meant for millions of His followers to each put their faith into action by grabbing a shovel—and challenging the mountain *one shovelful at a time*? Any mountain can be moved—even the one called Poverty, or Hunger, or Injustice—*if* we have enough people "shoveling."

Jesus actually compared the coming of the kingdom of God on earth to the tiny mustard seed: "The kingdom of heaven," He said, "is like a mustard seed, which a man took and planted in his field. Though it is the smallest of all your seeds, yet when it grows, it is the largest of garden plants and becomes a tree, so that the birds of the air come and perch in its branches" (Matt. 13:31–32). Like the petite mustard seed, this kingdom may seem small and powerless, but once it is planted and takes root, it grows exponentially in power, size, and influence. If a single mustard seed can multiply so dramatically, try to imagine the power of a mountain of mustard seeds—the impact of God's people, called by God and working collectively through faith to spread the gospel.

"The kingdom of God is within you." —Jesus Christ, in Luke 17:21

This gospel that we have been given—the whole gospel—is God's vision for a new way of living. It inaugurates the reality of God dwelling within us, His followers, no longer in a temple in Jerusalem. And it calls for us to join Him in saving the world that He loves so much. The power of this gospel was announced by Jesus in a synagogue in Nazareth, when He made an audacious claim—and an outrageous promise that the good news would be preached to the poor and that justice would be restored. The poor would be helped by the rich; the powerful would protect the powerless; the hated would be loved; the brokenhearted would be comforted; the oppressed would be liberated; the downtrodden would be lifted up. God's kingdom was going to begin on earth through the changed lives of His followers, and its hallmarks would be forgiveness, love, compassion, justice, and mercy. There would be no Jew or Greek, slave or free, male or female—all would be equal in God's eyes. This was the essence of the good news of the gospel, *the whole gospel*.

Jesus was to be the firstborn of this new kingdom. He would teach His first followers new kingdom values and give them a vision of a different kind of world. And that's what He did. This new community of "Jesus followers" began to grow and flourish as they, in turn, spread the good news of this new kingdom to others and demonstrated it through their lives. Jesus called this new community the Church and said that the gates of hell would not prevail against it. Then He went to the cross to defeat death and evil in the spiritual realm and to throw open the gates of heaven. Man and God could now be reconciled.

And then . . . Jesus rose again, showing Himself to those who loved Him, and giving them a charge to set the gospel in motion while He was away. Then He ascended, right before their eyes, to heaven, so He could prepare a place for all who would be saved through the lives and work of those who call Him Lord. Jesus had changed everything.

This was God's plan to change the world—He chose His followers to be the change—He chose you, and He chose me. We are the ones who will bring the good news to the poor, bind up the brokenhearted, and stand up for justice in a fallen world. We are the revolution. We are God's Plan A . . . and He doesn't have a Plan B.

SMALL THINGS WITH GREAT LOVE

We can do no great things, only small things with great love. —Mother Teresa

It starts with you. In the end, God simply calls you to be faithful to the things He has given you to do. He doesn't require you to be a superstar, just faithful and obedient, by praying, loving, serving, giving, forgiving, healing, and caring—doing small things with great love.

As I write these words, I am looking out a window in my house. I see the beauty of God's creation—lush green trees, blooming flowers, bright blue skies, and snowcapped mountains in the distance. I can hear a dog barking, an airplane flying overhead, and the thrum of cars on the highway nearby. And yet I know that somewhere, perhaps not very far away, there is pain and suffering—someone crying out to God for help. A neighbor has been diagnosed with cancer. A father has lost his job. A family has lost their home. Somewhere else there is a child without a mother, or a parent grieving for a child. There are children without food to eat or water to drink. There are girls and boys exploited by evil people who curse God as they carry out their evil schemes. In yet another place desperate thousands have been driven from their homes by calamity or war. There are lonely people without comfort or hope, with no one to turn to. Sickness and death stalk millions who have no doctors or medicine. Yes, not too far away, and distant too, there are broken people in this broken world. Broken and bruised. I know that.

But I also know the power of the gospel—the gospel *without* a hole— that we are charged to carry. I have seen it with my own eyes.

Ten years ago I took one small step of faith, and God has privileged me to glimpse the revolutionary power of the gospel in our world. I have traveled more than a million miles to dozens of countries around the globe. I have felt the "wind at my back" of millions who pray and give what they are able, and faithful churches determined not just to speak of the gospel but to demonstrate it. I have witnessed the faith of hundreds of anonymous "Mother Teresas," who serve as Christ's hands and feet in the dumps and slums, the brothels and the refugee camps. Yes, I have seen the power of these "small things" done with great love. I have also seen the impact of the kingdom of God—a mountain of mustard seeds—transforming people's lives. I have seen the possible.

I've seen the hungry fed and people taught to fish and farm. I've watched wells being drilled and cisterns being built—the thirsty given water. I have seen the sick healed, the lame walk, and the blind given back their sight. I have met refugees who have been resettled, disaster victims who've been restored, and captives who have been released. I've seen widows comforted, orphans cared for, children freed from slavery and abuse, schools built, clinics opened, babies vaccinated, loans lifting the poor out of poverty—I've witnessed these things with my own eyes. But even greater than these, I have seen the very gaze of Christ staring back at me through the eyes of the poor, and the love of Christ demonstrated to them through the lives and deeds of His faithful servants. Best of all, I've watched them find new life in the One who created them. I have been an eyewitness to these things—to this amazing, full gospel, transforming the most broken of lives and flooding the darkest of places with the radiant light of hope. I know these things to be possible.

CATCH THE VISION!

Picture a different world. Imagine one in which two billion Christians embrace this gospel—the whole gospel—each doing a part by placing his or her piece into the puzzle and completing God's stunning vision of a reclaimed and redeemed world—the kingdom of God among us. Visualize armies of compassion stationed in every corner of our world, doing small things with great love. Imagine the change. Might the world take notice? Would they ask new questions? *Who are these people so motivated by love? Where did they come from? Why do they sacrifice so to help those the rest of the world has forgotten? Where do they find their strength? Who is this God they serve?* And most important, *Can we serve Him too?* Can you imagine this different vision for our world? Can you glimpse just now what God longs to see?

WHAT DO *YOU* SEE?

Where are you right now, and what do you see? Are you commuting to work on a train, reading in bed, or perhaps just sitting in your own living room? How do you see the world around you? Do you see people who need God's love, suffering that breaks God's heart, evil that goes unchallenged? Do you see problems that can't be solved and mountains that can't be moved, or do you see light dispelling the darkness and the kingdom of God advancing with force? Do you see the opportunities and the possibilities, or just the obstacles? What gospel have you embraced:

- a revolutionary gospel that is truly good news for a broken world? or . . .
- a diminished gospel—with a hole in it—that's been reduced to a personal transaction with God, with little power to change anything outside your own heart?

And when you close this book, what will you do now? What does *God* expect of you? Are you willing to be open to His will for your life? Do you have the faith of a mustard seed? Do you believe what Jesus said, that "the kingdom of God is within you" and that He wants to enlist you in His great work of advancing His kingdom on earth?

He is calling you right now to do that which He created only you to do. Can you hear Him? I can.

You, Me, let's go. We have work to do, and it's urgent. Join Me . . .

TO LEARN MORE

If you were motivated by the information in this section and want to dig even deeper, visit www.theholeinourgospel.com for more resources. On this site you'll find:

- tangible things you can do that make a difference for the poor;

- a place to share your own stories and experiences with others on the same journey;

- more stories of people here and around the world whose lives have been changed because they got involved;

- resources for churches that want to get involved in a deeper way;

- videos that show what's being done around the world to help those in need;

- An extensive book list by categories, such as poverty, social justice, foreign policy, spiritual growth, Christian life, charitable giving, and others;

- Links to other resources and Web sites of interest.

To find out more, visit www.theholeinourgospel.com

Q&A WITH RENEÉ STEARNS

What is one of the encouraging things God has done in your life since *The Hole in Our Gospel* was released?

Since Rich's book was published, I have had numerous opportunities to travel around the country and speak to churches and women's groups about what God expects of us in light of the needs that exist in our world today. And when I do, people of all ages and stages of life share with me their own personal stories of how God has challenged them to step out in faith—stories of great sacrifice, creativity, and obedience. I've spoken with young moms who want to know how to instill in their children compassion for those in need, and on one occasion I remember well, I met with a grandmother who wanted my advice about how to discern God's call on her life in regard to the poor. At age seventy, she still was on the lookout for God's direction. She still wanted to know what He, at that very moment, expected of her. What an encouragement that was to me. After many years of being a stay-at-home mom, sometimes I think it's too late to ask the question, "What does God expect of me now?" But of course, it's not too late at all. As Paul reminds us in Ephesians 2:10, "For we are God's workmanship, created in Christ Jesus to do good works, which God prepared in advance for us to do." He has a plan for the world, and He has invited us to participate with Him in accomplishing that plan. The Creator of the universe, who numbers the stars and calls them all by name, has called my name, too, asking me to be His co-laborer. What a privilege!

What was it like for your children to make a U-turn from a life of privilege to one in which addressing poverty became the main priority?

World Vision's work has always been very important to our family. Long before Rich came to World Vision as president, we sponsored children and supported projects. Every time we received a World Vision video, my youngest son would run upstairs to get his piggy bank before we began to watch so that he would be ready to immediately respond to the need. As a family, we all had a real sense that what God was doing around the world through the work of World Vision was important and that we were a part of it. So we saw it as a real honor for Rich to be considered as a candidate for the presidency of World Vision.

When he was chosen, all of my kids were incredibly encouraging. As Rich agonized over the decision, my oldest daughter reminded us that if this was where God wanted us to be, we wouldn't be happy anywhere else. My son with the piggy bank challenged us to fast and pray, and so we did. And then, finally, we packed up the house, said goodbye to friends, and headed to Seattle.

Not everything went smoothly, as anyone who has ever packed up five kids and moved them cross-country to a new home has experienced. We were asking a lot of them. But one of the things that I think people miss when they inquire about the transition to World Vision is something we won't know this side of Heaven, something that perhaps God will share with us when He calls us home. We know about leaving behind the house, the school, the job, the friends, and even the blue Jaguar. What we don't know about is all that God may have spared us from by allowing us to make this move. Who knows what our life would have been like if we had stayed where we were?

And rather than an insulated life of privilege, our kids have had the opportunity to see firsthand what God is doing around the world and to participate in His work in bringing help and hope to those in need. They have met wonderful Christian men and women doing remarkable things with very little. They have been challenged and encouraged and motivated to make the world a better place for all of God's children. Even today, some of them are doing that through their chosen vocations, some of them as they continue to support the work of World Vision through prayer and giving.

Since childhood, you dreamed of helping the poor. How does your life today fit that dream?

Ever since I was a little girl, I wanted to help poor people. It seemed so unfair to me that, for no better reason than an "accident of latitude" (as Bono calls it), some people in the world had so much and others had so little. And maybe because, as a young girl, I watched too much of the old TV show *Perry Mason*, I thought that the best way to help was to become a lawyer. So after law school, I took a legal services job and began representing under-resourced clients. At first, I loved what I did, but increasingly, it became obvious to me that while I could help with the kinds of legal issues that go along with a lack of money, the people coming into my office had problems that went way beyond anything I had learned how to fix in law school. My legal advice was a bandage on the wound, but it didn't come close to curing the disease. What was needed, I thought, was a more holistic approach to poverty, the kind that took into account the whole person— not just the physical but the mental and the spiritual as well. As it turns out, I have discovered that it's the same kind of holistic approach World Vision brings to the work it does around the world.

Rich vividly describes his first face-to-face encounter with developing-world poverty. What was yours, and how did it affect you?

My first encounter with international poverty came on a trip I took to Guatemala in 1998. After spending several days in the countryside, we returned to Guatemala City to visit some World Vision projects there. A morning spent with preschoolers at a daycare center was followed by a trip to the Guatemala City dump, a sprawling display of the refuse created by a city of more than two million people. And among the garbage hundreds of families foraged, scavenging for pieces of recyclable plastic or a leftover bite of a sandwich.

I stood at the edge of the dump with a young woman and her two small children. As I watched the little boy eating contentedly from a dirt-encrusted yogurt cup he'd found among the garbage, I thought of my own children back home, about to sit down to a hot lunch in the school cafeteria. Here we were, two women separated by culture, language, and economics, and yet, as I bent to admire her beautiful little boy and girl, I was struck not so much by what separated us as by what we had in common. As I watched, I could see in her smile the pride she had in that little family, the pleasure she took in seeing her children the focus of my attention. I know those feelings. I'm a mom too. I also know the dreams a mother has for her children's future, and I wondered back then if we shared those as well. Could a woman living in the dump dream of a life without hunger and poverty and disease? Could she call a tin shanty home and still imagine a future filled with hope? In the years since that first encounter with poverty, I have come to understand that the answer to those questions is a resounding yes. Men and women all over the world have hopes and dreams and expectations for their children's futures that go far beyond their immediate circumstances—

whether it's in the Guatemala City dump, a triage tent in famine-plagued Niger, or a war zone in northern Uganda. What's more, I've learned that through the work of World Vision we can help make those dreams a reality.

What is your top travel tip for women traveling to the developing world?

My advice is simple: travel light. While my husband lives by the motto, "Be prepared," I am a minimalist. I believe in making do. Why fill the suitcase with things you might not use and that, in fact, take up valuable space that could otherwise transport home the treasures you receive during your travels?

Everywhere we've traveled, we've been blessed with gifts of love from people whose lives have been touched by the work of World Vision—a clay pot from a woman who'd been given a microfinance loan, a dress from a young girl who was taught how to sew, a needlework sampler from a mother whose son had been given computer training. We understand full well that these gifts are not really for us. They aren't even for the thousands of World Vision donors and staff that we represent during our visits. Rather they are gifts lavished on Jesus out of their poverty.

It occurs to me that people who are most useful to God travel light. God can't use me if I'm overwhelmed with excess baggage. If I insist on dragging around the heavy burdens of security, possessions, recognition, or whatever else there is that might get in the way of my serving God, I'm limited in the ways I can serve Him. But it's never too late to put them aside to follow the call of Jesus. He invites us to put down our own overwhelming, unwieldy baggage and pick up His. "Come to me, all you who are weary and burdened, and I will give you rest. Take my yoke upon you and learn from me, for I am gentle and humble in heart, and you will find rest for your souls. For my yoke is easy and my burden is light" (Matt. 11:28–30).

You're often the heroine in Rich's stories, the "conscience" keeping the two of you on track in so many crucial moments of testing and trial. How did that trust and sense of shared accountability develop between you?

First, I have to say that Rich has a very kind and generous memory. Although he is too thoughtful to mention them in the book, there of course have been countless times in our thirty-five years of marriage when, far from being a voice of wisdom, I was the one who needed some good advice. But whether on the giving or the receiving end of wise counsel, we both recognize that it is God who is the ultimate source of all wisdom and direction, and it is Him we turn to when we find ourselves at a crossroad. And He is faithful! Being confident in who we are, as people saved by God's grace, and knowing that the ultimate source of authority in our home is God Himself, allows us the freedom and the boldness to both challenge and encourage one another to be all God intends for us to be.

Do people often ask you the same question they pose to Rich after reading the book: "What do I do now?" If so, what's your response?

Most of us have a fairly limited perspective on the larger world around us. I often say about my family and friends that they are great people, but for the most part they live in a very small world, understandably limited by their own personal experiences. And honestly, if the way I spend my time is any measuring stick, even I sometimes act as if my world were only as big as the space between my house, the grocery store, the mall, and my church!

When we ask ourselves the question "What do I do now?" it's important to step back and take a wider view of things, to look beyond our individual circumstances and remember that there's a great big world out there that God wants us to engage! I think it's important for us to see ourselves as part of a larger community, navigating shoulder-to-shoulder through life, supporting one another, encouraging one another, and celebrating one another's successes.

Not everyone can pick up and travel to the places of most need around the world. But everyone can buy a map and brush up on geography. We should find where the places in the news are located and learn more about them. We should read about the people affected by the events going on around the world. These are real people with real problems, and the more we know about them, the more we will be able to understand their needs.

I also encourage people to take advantage of programs that highlight the cultural diversity of their own communities—and get their children involved. Here in the Seattle area, there are puppet shows, ethnic dance recitals, and musical events that showcase people and cultures around the world. I'm sure there are those same kinds of events in other areas as well.

I live in a city where almost one in every three people was born outside of the United States. There are eighty-one different languages spoken by students in our local public schools. God has brought the world to our doorstep—we need to make every effort to get to know them!

And, in the words of World Vision founder Bob Pierce, "Don't fail to do something because you can't do everything." Remember the story of Mary, the sister of Martha and Lazarus, who broke open an alabaster jar of fragrant perfume to wash the feet of her Lord? Perhaps in the larger scheme of things it was a small gesture. And yet Jesus said of her, "I tell you the truth, wherever the gospel is preached throughout the world, what she has done will also be told, in memory of her" (Mark 14:8–9). A small act, done with great love by ordinary men and women, can change the world.

WHAT ARE YOU GOING TO DO ABOUT IT?

For me, the experience of writing a book and putting it out to market has been akin to building a kite out of old newspapers, sticks, and string. When the kite is finished, the builder takes it outside, perhaps to the top of a hill, and lifts it up, just hoping God will put a little wind underneath it to lift it into the sky. The one thing a kite builder cannot provide is that wind—and without it, the kite cannot soar. I have been grateful for the wind God has provided to take my little book to places I never dreamed it could go.

Since writing *The Hole in Our Gospel*, I've crisscrossed the country, speaking to groups as small as two and as large as fifteen thousand. I've had the chance to speak with hundreds of people who read the book, from teenagers to U.S. senators, and I have been deeply touched by their passionate determination to do more—to make themselves available and do something tangible to demonstrate the "whole" gospel to those who desperately need it.

Many have decided to sponsor a child as a place to start. Others have committed to volunteer their time to find more sponsors or to adopt a child into their homes. Several have targeted a project, like a water well or a school, helping to raise money and participate in its accomplishment. Still others are exploring ways their business or professional skills might be deployed to make a difference. For example, readers with medical skills have promised to spend a few weeks abroad every year to help the poor with their medical needs. A group of Washington farmers is exploring ways to ship container-loads of lentils from their farms to famine areas. A group involved in helping refugees here in the United States reported a surge in volunteers from people who have read the book. Still others have been inspired to do something totally unrelated to global poverty by visiting the sick or elderly in their communities or by helping local food banks.

Perhaps the most heartening response has been from pastors and churches. Small groups and whole congregations have decided to read *The Hole in Our Gospel* and collectively undertake a project or make a commitment. Some churches have adopted "sister communities" and are pledging to walk with them for a period of years.

It is very encouraging to see the creativity and conviction of those who are already "off and running." But I have discovered that there is an even larger group of readers who want to help but just don't know how they can make a difference. "So what do I do now?" That's the question I hear most frequently from people. Maybe that describes you. You're motivated, you're convicted—but you're not sure what to do next.

I wish there was an easy answer. God's call looks different in every person's life. Not everyone experiences God's calling as I did—with a two-by-four to the head! Only you can seek and find God's will for *you*. The best way I know to discover His leading is to turn a listening ear to that still, small voice and offer up a willing heart. Remember, when you're doing something for God, you can't know the end at the beginning. The good news is, you don't need to. It's God's plan, perfectly designed for *you*. He just needs you to be willing to take that first step.

I encourage you to seek God's will through prayer, reading Scripture, and seeking counsel from wise and godly people who know you. But after you've done that, it's time for action. Put yourself in play. Take some tangible steps. As my pastor once said, "God can't steer a parked car." Consider what you're passionate about, get busy learning about that area of interest, and offer up your time, talent, and treasure. God might want a dramatic change of scene for you, or a dramatic heart change that opens opportunities where you already are. When we are fully devoted to Christ—whether we serve as a missionary, a stay-at-home mom, or a CEO—we are *all* in full-time Christian service.

On the next several pages, I've compiled a list of various ways you can act on your faith—by learning, praying, taking action, giving, and speaking up. My hope is that these suggestions will help you find that specific thing that you, your family, or your church or small group can do. At the very least, I hope these things spark your own imagination. Who knows? You may be the next Leon McLaughlin, the shoe-shine guy who brought clean water to Bolivia, or Austin Gutwein, the teenager who used basketball to help AIDS orphans. You might even be the next Bob Pierce, who was asked in 1947, "What are you going to do about it?" . . . and then started World Vision.

LEARN

It can be difficult to feel a connection with people you've never met, who live in places you've never visited—or maybe never even heard of. Yet these are the people who are never far from God's heart. Here are some ways to deepen your understanding about people who live in extreme poverty in distant countries. Individuals, parents with their children, small groups, Sunday school classes, or Bible studies could use these as a starting point for their own creative ideas.

Buy a world map. Post it in a prominent place, and when a crisis happens—such as an earthquake in Haiti, a tsunami in Samoa, or a hurricane in El Salvador—use pushpins or stickers to note where they are and remind you to learn about them and pray for the people.

Tune in to poverty. Instead of playing music in your car, spend your commute time listening to educational radio programs. National Public Radio's excellent programming covers diverse topics in thoughtful ways. Or you can seek out *World Vision Report*, a weekly radio program about the people behind global issues affecting the world's poor. It airs on hundreds of radio stations and you can listen online or download podcasts at www.worldvisionreport.org.

Sponsor a child. By sponsoring a child, you can experience a new country, culture, and context through the eyes of a little boy or girl. Seek to learn about him or her through letters and your own research. Watch as your own children begin to see the world in a different way. On your world map, add a pushpin for your sponsored child so you remember to pray often. World Vision is among several charities offering child sponsorship (www.worldvision.org/thiog); to find them on the Web, search for "sponsor a child."

Form friendships. God has brought world cultures to our neighborhood. Get to know them. Visit ethnic churches in your area to get to know Christians from other places. Look for local programs providing refugee resettlement; World Relief, a Christian organization, works through local churches to provide this ministry. If you have a college or university in your town, get acquainted with international students from developing countries and offer to help them with things like English skills.

Learn and teach. Consider how you might equip young people to become compassionate global citizens by teaching your children or youth group about poverty issues. Encourage them to learn about how the lives of children in other countries may differ from theirs, the challenges they face, and to discover other cultures and traditions. Find free educational resources, along with issue-related materials, DVDs, and more at www.worldvisionresources.com.

Embark on a "Six-Week Quest." If this book has provoked you to read this section, then perhaps you're ready for a forty-two-day journey of discovery. *The Gospel Quest* is a companion study guide to this book that will help you discover the answer to the question "What now?" It comes with a six-lesson DVD featuring me, Reneé, Max Lucado, Philip Yancey, Lynne Hybels, and others. Find out more at www.thegospelquest.com.

Explore music. Listen to traditional music from other countries (those you hear about on the news or the country where your sponsored child lives). You can find music from Afghanistan to Zimbabwe at National Geographic World Music (http://worldmusic.nationalgeographic.com).

Join or start a campus group. College students can join World Vision ACT:S, a network of students committed to exploring what faith says about justice. Check out if your campus has a chapter, and if not, start one. Learn more at www.worldvisionacts.org.

Read and start a book club. There are many wonderful books that help us understand poverty and justice at a deeper level. Some are factual and others tell real, human stories of struggle and triumph. Commit to reading some of these books, and start a book club with a few friends who share your interests. See the list of recommended books on page 303, or visit www.theholeinourgospel.com for a more extensive list.

Watch a movie. Films are a powerful and influential medium in our culture. Watch movies such as *Blood Diamond* to learn about child soldiers and the diamond trade; *Hotel Rwanda* to see courage in the face of genocide; or *Slumdog Millionaire* to understand the plight of street children in India. Discussing the movies with others afterward enhances the experience. Go to www.theholeinourgospel.com for a list of other thought-provoking films.

Get a reality check. If you think you're not rich, just compare yourself to someone who lives on less than a dollar a day. A Web site, www.globalrichlist.com, quickly shows you, based on your income, where you rank on a global scale of wealth. It's an eye-opener.

PRAY

I believe prayer is a form of social action. A colleague of mine at World Vision, John Robb, once wrote, "Wherever in the world there is significant development—people coming to Christ, health improvements, economic opportunities, adoption of kingdom values—it is the direct result of Christians praying." If you want to be a prayer warrior on behalf of the suffering and oppressed, this involves time and a commitment to stay informed about what's happening in the world so you can pray with specificity and timeliness. It also means welcoming discomfort and pain (see the Franciscan blessing below) or asking, as World Vision founder Bob Pierce prayed, for your heart to be broken by the things that break God's heart.

Intentional intercessory prayer can be done individually or in groups, through regular devotions or as often as the Holy Spirit moves you. Many people find it helpful to incorporate prayer into ordinary tasks you do every day. Along those lines, here are seven steps toward integrating prayer for the poor in your daily life:

1. When you take your morning shower, pray for families in poor countries who do not have access to clean water, forcing mothers to spend hours collecting inadequate water and causing children to suffer and even die from water-related diseases.
2. When you pack your lunch or your child's lunch, pray for the one billion people who are chronically hungry in the world today.
3. As you commute to your job, pray for the adults around the world who can't find consistent work to feed their families, or pray for the millions of children forced into harmful or exploitative labor.
4. When you drop off your child at school, pray for children around the world who cannot get an education because of poverty or discrimination.
5. As you take a vitamin, pray for the families without adequate

health care, leaving them and especially their children vulnerable
to preventable diseases.

6. When you arrive home after work, pray for the children and families
   who are homeless due to poverty, conflict, or natural disasters.

7. As you tuck your children into bed, guide them to pray for the
   millions of children who have lost their parents around the world—
   especially the fifteen million AIDS orphans around the world, many
   of whom must survive without guardians.

This is one of my favorite prayers. I encourage you to pray this
Franciscan benediction, and to reflect on the message of hope contained
within:

May God bless you with a restless discomfort
about easy answers, half-truths, and superficial relationships,
so that you may seek truth boldly and love deep within your heart.

May God bless you with holy anger at injustice, oppression,
and exploitation of people, so that you may tirelessly work for
justice, freedom, and peace among all people.

May God bless you with the gift of tears to shed with those who suffer
from pain, rejection, starvation, or the loss of all that they cherish, so that you
may reach out your hand to comfort them and transform their pain into joy.

May God bless you with enough foolishness to believe that
you really can make a difference in this world, so that you are able,
with God's grace, to do what others claim cannot be done.

And the blessing of God the Supreme Majesty and our Creator,
Jesus Christ the Incarnate Word Who is our Brother and Savior,
and the Holy Spirit, our Advocate and Guide, be with you
and remain with you, this day and forevermore. Amen

ACT

You might remember the popular Nike slogan from a few years ago:
Just do it. There probably isn't a more pithy way to exhort people to get up,

get going, get active. And that applies to serving the poor. You don't have to have money and power or education and advanced skills to make a difference. Everyone can do something. Those "small things with great love" (in Mother Teresa's words) bring great joy to our Father. Here are some ways you can act, whoever you are, wherever you live.

Volunteer in your own backyard. If you look around your own city or town, there are plenty of things you can do that require little more than time. Volunteer at a soup kitchen or AIDS hospice; give to, or volunteer at, a food bank; teach English to refugees; mentor an at-risk child; serve at the local Ronald McDonald House (www.rmhc.org); visit lonely patients at a nursing home.

Get something started in your church. You can work through and with your church to increase involvement with the poor. Start a ministry if there isn't one for serving or praying for local or global needs. Get your small group to take on a service project. Talk to your pastor about holding a "Hope Sunday," encouraging people to sponsor children. The point is, if a poverty-focused ministry isn't happening at your church, don't wait—you can be a force for change.

Take a short-term mission trip. These up-close-and-personal experiences can open your eyes and put you on a path to greater involvement. Many churches have opportunities to serve a poor community in hands-on ways. If yours doesn't, check out some other groups such as Habitat for Humanity (www.habitat.org) or Cross-Cultural Solutions (www.crossculturalsolutions.org), or for young people, Youth with a Mission (www.ywam.org).

Do your best work pro bono. Developing countries often have a shortage of highly trained professionals such as doctors, dentists, contractors, or business consultants. When you volunteer your time, you make a big investment in God's kingdom. Look for opportunities through your church or professional association. Also, a great contact for Christian medical professionals is Medical Teams International (www.medicalteams.org).

Raise funds for your favorite charity. I don't know a charity or nonprofit that couldn't use enthusiastic volunteers to help them meet new supporters and raise money to support their work. World Vision, for example, has a Child Ambassadors program for passionate child sponsors to speak from their experience in various forums in order to sign up new sponsors. Vicki Casper, a flight attendant from Oceanside, California, and a sponsor for twenty-five years, does just that. Everywhere she goes (and that's a lot of places!), she keeps sponsorship information ready. What if you could help even one child every month find a sponsor? Find out how at www.worldvision.org/achildiswaiting.

Look for on-the-job ways to serve. You don't have to work for a faith-based organization to do the Lord's work. Perhaps you've got access to people who would give to a cause if you asked. A fun example: Ted Mettelstaedt, the community services supervisor of Bellevue, Washington, used his position in the Parks and Recreation department to coordinate the collection of more than five thousand soccer balls from around Washington state. The new and lightly used balls were sent overseas to children who otherwise would have had to improvise with balls made out of plastic bags and string.

Use your athleticism. Running a marathon or climbing a mountain is a great accomplishment in itself, but by incorporating a cause, you can make the experience even more meaningful. Through World Vision, you can join Team World Vision to raise awareness and money for the poor through such events. For example, a team of eight students from Wheaton Academy in Warrenville, Illinois, climbed Mt. Rainier, raising $1 for each of the mountain's 14,410 feet, for drilling wells in a water-starved area of Zambia—and the students beat their goal, raising nearly $20,000. In the 2009 Chicago Marathon, more than 1,200 Team World Vision runners raised more than $800,000 for children in Africa. For more information and inspiration, visit www.worldvision.org/teamworldvision.

Join an assembly line. Many organizations collect new or used goods to send overseas; all of those items need to be organized and packaged. You can volunteer to sort and pack at warehouses or collection centers. Also, World Vision has two programs that are great opportunities for churches, companies, and other groups to assemble vital supplies: Caregiver Kits and SchoolTools. Caregiver Kits are sent to volunteers in rural Africa who selflessly care for their AIDS-affected neighbors. These kits contain basic items such as latex gloves, soap, and antifungal cream. SchoolTools are packs of school supplies for kids around the world and here in the United States who don't have pencils, notebooks, and other basic educational items. Learn more about these programs at www.worldvision.org/caregiverkits or www.worldvision.org/schooltools.

Go hungry. Most of us think we know what hunger means. But if you spend thirty hours without food—all the while serving others or learning about poverty in the developing world—it makes an impression. The 30 Hour Famine (www.30hourfamine.org) is a popular youth movement to fight hunger and raise awareness. No matter what age you are, you can use this approach to benefit any organization. Simply set a fasting goal, ask others to support you with pledges by the hour, and donate the money you raise to your favorite charity.

Students: Use creative activism to bring issues to life. These events raise awareness in memorable, meaningful ways that get people's attention. For example, World Vision ACT:S—a network of students committed to exploring what our faith says about poverty and injustice—uses experiential campaigns to respond to critical issues, such as the Broken Bread Poverty Meal, the Human Wrong initiative to stop child slavery, the "Lives Are on the Line" AIDS campaign, and Night of Nets (www.nightofnets.org) to end malaria. Learn more about creative activism at www.worldvisionacts.org or by calling 1-888-876-2004.

GIVE

In the New Testament story about the feeding of the five thousand, Jesus asks, "How many loaves do you have?" That's still a relevant question today. What do you have that Jesus could use, and what could He do with it? Each of us has resources beyond money that can be used in creative and compassionate ways to serve the poor. Here are some examples of how ordinary people took what they had in their hands and saw amazing things happen when they gave it to Jesus.

Set a new giving goal. Whether you already tithe or you don't, determine a percentage of your income you will give this year to God. Then next year, increase it a little. You might also designate an annual pay raise or bonus to this purpose.

Give beyond the grave. You can designate your favorite charity in your will so that your treasure will continue to be used in compassionate ways after you've passed from this life. World Vision's Gift Planning program (www.worldvision.planyourlegacy.org) offers help with this, as do other organizations and charities.

Give at the office. Many companies match charitable donations—does yours? It's an easy way to give twice as much. Or you can rally your fellow employees to raise money for a cause, adopt a charity, or sponsor a child as a group. Equip and inspire your colleagues with facts and stories related to the cause. If you're a CEO and you haven't already taken the plunge into corporate philanthropy, start now—it's good business. An example: Larry Dahl, owner of Oil Stop oil-and-lube stores in California, invites his customers to donate an additional $1 for digging wells in West Africa through World Vision. He matches it . . . and the Conrad N. Hilton Foundation matches it again—raising more than $6,000 a week.

Find treasure in trash. Fundraising ideas can come from anywhere. Tara Paul of San Diego had a "duh!" moment when her twelve-year-old daughter wrote an essay suggesting that funds from recycling bottles and cans be used for worthy causes. So Tara started a ministry called DUH—Desperate, Underprivileged, and Hungry—and organized her church, The Rock, to bring their bottles and cans in with them each Sunday. The ministry raises about $4,500 monthly and currently sponsors 100 children. Not only do they collect at church, they are proactive in supporting and collecting at other Rock community outreach events.

"Sell" your time. After all, time is money—and you can creatively auction it for a good cause. A great example: Instead of spending his Thanksgiving leave with his family, a Marine from North Carolina "sold" the hours for $25 per hour to raise money for a local homeless shelter. He spent the four days living among the people the shelter serves. You can auction your time and skills to the highest bidder and donate the proceeds to your favorite charity.

Tax yourself for little luxuries. This is an ingenious idea from The Journey Church in San Jose, California, a congregation of 225. The church printed "Luxury Tax" cards based on the board game Monopoly and asked members to "tax" themselves based on luxuries they take for granted, such as the number of water taps or toilets in their homes. They've raised more than $25,000 for Limpopo, an AIDS-devastated community in Zimbabwe.

Give meaningful gifts. Let's face it: We all have more stuff than we need. At Christmas and other major holidays, do your loved ones really need another gadget or gizmo from you? Instead, give them something meaningful. Many charities have alternative-giving catalogs; probably you've seen the one from Heifer (www.heifer.org). Through the *World Vision Gift Catalog* (www.giftsofhope.org) you can give goats, soccer balls, fruit trees, part of a water well, and much more. This type of giving is educational; teachers like Amy Brailey in Lake Station, Indiana, use the catalog to help students understand and care about the needs of the poor. After serious consideration, Amy's eighth graders—who are low-income themselves—raised money to pay for a year of schooling for an AIDS orphan and to provide safety for a sexually exploited girl.

Donate a day's wages. Whether your daily wages amount to a big number or a small one, anyone with a job can do this. Eugene and Minhee Cho, a pastor and his wife in Seattle, invited their family, friends, and the rest of the world to donate one day's wages and to renew that pledge every year on their birthdays. For this they created the Web site www.onedayswages.org, which includes information on global poverty and a handy wage calculator. Using the power of the Internet and social media, they've garnered nearly eight hundred thousand fans on Facebook.

Donate something of value—make it even more valuable. Many of us have expensive possessions sitting around our house that we could live without, but we're hesitant to part with them. That was Art Tascone, a North Carolina doctor and self-described "motorhead" who had twelve rare automobiles in a warehouse near his house. But one day, Art had a revelation when he thought, "What am I doing with these things? I could be doing something better." He donated the most prized vehicles in his collection—a 1960 Lincoln Continental, a 1961 Cadillac, and a 1962 Ford Thunderbird—to World Vision to sell to help the poor. He now drives a Toyota minivan and has no regrets.

Give up a regular expense. This could be your morning latte or a deluxe car wash—the point is to give the money to a good cause instead. A creative example comes from a stay-at-home mom who decided to give up her usual lunch for a year and donate the money to World Vision. Instead, she's eating a bowl of cornmeal porridge—highly nutritious but not very tasty, she says on her blog. She's humbled by the daily reminder that this porridge is the only food many people have, and they walk miles to get it.

Pets vs. Children. Living in an affluent society, it's easy to fall into spending patterns that don't hold up when compared to the dire poverty in the world. For example, I love my dog, but I spend a lot on her care, food, and kennel costs. Another reader of my book commented, "My dogs eat better and are better taken care of than most children." Commit to giving as much to help the less fortunate as you spend on your pets. You may be surprised that it substantially boosts your giving to the poor!

Create a different kind of gift registry. If you have a special event, such as a birthday, wedding, anniversary, graduation, or retirement coming up, it's the perfect opportunity to raise funds for a favorite charity in lieu of presents you probably don't need. For example, the Web site www.global-giving.com offers a gift registry that you can set up, choosing from a wide range of charitable projects, including poverty relief.

SPEAK

You might think you're the last person on the planet who is qualified to speak up for anything, much less advocate for those who live in extreme poverty. Would you think that a guy who had been living in hiding for forty years after he killed someone could stand up to the most powerful ruler in the world? That was Moses. Would you think that one pretty girl could save her people from annihilation by speaking up when she hadn't been spoken to? That was Esther. Neither of them felt qualified to speak on behalf of God, and truthfully, neither of them particularly wanted to get involved. But as Esther's uncle, Mordecai, told her, maybe you're right where you are for "such a time as this" (Esther 4:14).

Being an advocate is a powerful way to pursue justice for the poor, and it can take many forms. In this wonderful democracy we live in, you and I can influence elected officials—when we speak, they listen. With the right message and the right tools, you can speak through the media. Or you can raise awareness about poverty in your own community. Here are some ideas on speaking up for the world's poor:

Send a message to Congress. Voice your support to political leaders for funding or legislation alleviating global poverty. The three best ways to deliver a message are sending e-mails, writing letters, and making phone calls. You can find up-to-date information and sample letters and phone scripts at www.worldvision.org/advocacy, World Vision's advocacy Web site. Or churches, students, and other groups can support hunger legislation through Bread for the World's "Offering of Letters" events (www. bread.org).

Organize an in-district or a town hall meeting. Coordinate a gathering between elected officials and fellow constituents to discuss issues facing the poor (locally or even globally). World Vision's *A Citizen Guide to Advocacy* can provide you with advice for an effective meeting. Download a free PDF of this guide by visiting www.worldvision.org/advocacy.

Seek media coverage. If you're passionate about a cause and you want to talk about it to the widest audience possible, there's nothing better than the mass media. The three best ways to generate news coverage are pitching a human-interest story, writing opinion editorials (op-ed pieces), and writing letters to the editor. You can get local media to cover your story by showing them that local people are actively working to be part of the solution.

Use social media. You can use a blog, your Facebook profile or MySpace page, Twitter, or YouTube to spread the word about poverty. Join Facebook fan pages. Comment on the blogs of other advocates, and tweet about them. Consider posting videos of your youth group, small group, or friends advocating on behalf of the world's poor. Post a link to your video to your other social networking sites for maximum exposure.

Speak or invite a speaker to your professional or social organizations. Charities or other organizations in your area have knowledgeable people who can speak from deep experience on global or local poverty issues. World Vision can provide you with talking points and resources to share with your audience. If you would like to invite a World Vision spokesperson, send a request to the Speakers Bureau at speakersbureau@worldvision.org.

Join an advocacy group or network. This is a great way to receive education and updates, meet like-minded people, and find out about opportunities to get involved. There are networks around issues as well as geographic regions. On a national level, get connected with advocacy organizations such as Bread for the World (www.bread.org), the ONE Campaign (www.one.org), or Results (www.results.org).

Can Poverty Be Defeated?

As I've outlined in this book, extreme poverty is the most devastating problem facing the human race. It condemns nearly half the world's population to hunger, disease, and oppression—often with little hope for the future. These are human beings made in the image of God, yet they are tragically prevented from realizing their God-given potential. But it doesn't have to be this way. The reality of poverty can be overwhelming, but we must understand that this age-old adversary can be defeated.

With forty thousand staff working in nearly one hundred countries, World Vision is one of the largest international relief and development nonprofits in the world. Through our sixty years of experience, we've developed a practical and proven approach to help children and families emerge from poverty into a brighter future. I hope the following questions and answers will give you a better understanding of our approach and encourage you to be part of the solution.

What does it take for an impoverished community to become self-sufficient?

Earlier in the book, I mentioned the famous proverb "If you give a man a fish, he'll eat for a day, but if you teach a man to fish, he'll eat for a lifetime." Experience shows that the best way to fight poverty is to empower people to shape their own future—to treat the causes of poverty and not just the symptoms. To do this, we have to make a long-term investment in communities. World Vision partners with local people—seeking to understand their unique circumstances and identifying lasting solutions tailored to their unique needs. It's about listening and equipping—not dictating answers or "fixing" the problem ourselves. We help the community to own their own future—because the best way to change a child's life is to change the world they live in.

When it comes to poverty, there are so many complicating factors. Why not just pick the biggest need and focus on that?

Meeting one need isn't enough. Shelter is a good thing, but having a new home doesn't necessarily put food on the table. Food security is crucial, but food without medical care is insufficient for good health. Access to healthcare is key, but without clean water and sanitation, people will continue to get sick. Water is foundational to life, but without schools and education, or economic opportunities and access to capital, communities remain mired in poverty.

Jim Collins writes that "good is the enemy of great." Single-sector efforts, like feeding the hungry or building schools, are "good." They're key pieces of the puzzle. But "great" demands that we go deeper and meet the entire range of a community's needs—including water, food, healthcare, education, and economic opportunity. When we address these needs simultaneously, communities gain the momentum they need to reach self-sufficiency and defeat poverty.

Why does World Vision focus on children?

Because poverty delivers the heaviest blow to the youngest, most vulnerable members of society. I believe it's our collective responsibility to ensure these children are loved, protected, and empowered to realize their full potential. After all, they are the future leaders of their communities.

Jesus opened His arms to children (Matt. 19:14), and He calls us to do the same. That's why we're committed to helping every child enjoy good health, be educated and cared for, participate in their community, and love God and their neighbors.

What makes child sponsorship so effective?

Child sponsorship is a long-term commitment—exactly what impoverished communities need. We know there's no "quick fix" for poverty; that's why our community development projects last ten to fifteen years, on average. Linking sponsors to individual children helps ensure a consistent base of funding for the ongoing transformation in the community. And since we combine sponsorship gifts with other significant sources of funding—including gifts from individual donors; government grants; and corporate gifts like clothing, books, and pharmaceuticals—the sponsor's impact is multiplied several times over.

Another reason we link sponsors with children is the impact it has on both sides. Children experience physical, spiritual, and emotional transformation, and sponsors come to understand poverty through the eyes of their sponsored child.

How does World Vision integrate its Christian faith in its work?

Every day, we encounter challenges such as corruption, flawed value systems, and broken relationships that underscore the words of the Apostle Paul: "Our struggle is not against flesh and blood, but against . . . the powers of this dark world" (Eph. 6:12). Yet we have seen how biblical principles such as honesty, integrity, faithfulness, and the sanctity of life can transform families and entire communities.

Being a witness to Christ is central to who we are and what we believe. At the same time, we don't want to coerce, manipulate, or proselytize those we serve—and we shouldn't need to. Our charge is to ensure that our lives, deeds, and words give a testimony to the gospel that naturally points people to the love of Christ.

In Christian-majority contexts, where our witness can be fully expressed, we work to meet people's material needs and encourage spiritual maturity—for example, we partner with local churches to provide opportunities for children and families to experience life in Christ.

In contexts where Christianity is not the majority faith, we are guided by 1 Peter 3:15:

Always be prepared to give an answer to everyone who asks you to give the reason for the hope that you have. But do this with gentleness and respect.

We strive to show respect to those who follow other faiths—and we are frequently honored by being asked to explain what motivates our compassion for the poor. The answer, of course, is the gospel: "We love because [Christ] first loved us" (1 John 4:19).

Fighting poverty isn't easy. You might even say that it *is* rocket science—but poverty can be defeated. More importantly, serving the poor is an inherent part of our calling as Christians. God didn't leave us the option of being apathetic toward the needs of the poor. My prayer is that all of us will embrace these words of instruction and encouragement from the Apostle Paul:

Let us not become weary in doing good, for at the proper time we will reap a harvest if we do not give up (Gal. 6:9).

RESOURCES FOR YOUR JOURNEY

There are many good resources to assist your quest to discover what *you* can do. To get started, check out this list, and if you are interested in more resources, visit www.theholeinourgospel.com for an extensive list.

RECOMMENDED BOOKS

The End of Poverty: Economic Possibilities for Our Time by Jeffrey Sachs, New York: The Penguin Press, 2005.

The Life You Can Save: Acting Now to End World Poverty by Peter Singer, New York: Random House, 2009.

The Bottom Billion: Why the Poorest Countries Are Failing and What Can Be Done About It by Paul Collier, New York: Oxford University Press, 2007.

Rich Christians in an Age of Hunger: Moving from Affluence to Generosity by Ronald J. Sider, Nashville, TN: Thomas Nelson, 2005.

Revolutionary Generosity: Transforming Stewards to Be Rich Toward God by Wesley K. Willmer, editor, Chicago: Moody Publishers, 2008.

Philanthro-Capitalism: How the Rich Can Save the World by Matthew Bishop and Michael Green, New York: Bloomsbury Press, 2008.

When Helping Hurts: How to Alleviate Poverty Without Hurting the Poor . . . and Yourself by Steve Corbett and Brian Fikkert, Chicago: Moody Publishers, 2009.

Beyond Humanitarianism: What You Need to Know About Africa and Why It Matters, Princeton N. Lyman and Patricia Dorff, editors, New York: Council on Foreign Relations Books, 2007.

Hot, Flat, and Crowded: Why We Need a Green Revolution—And How It Can Renew America by Thomas L. Friedman, New York: Farrar, Straus and Giroux, 2008.

The Volunteer Revolution: Unleashing the Power of Everybody by Bill Hybels, Grand Rapids, MI: Zondervan, 2004.

Up and Out of Poverty: The Social Marketing Solution by Philip Kotler and Nancy R. Lee, Upper Saddle River, NJ: Wharton School Publishing, 2009.

The CEV Poverty & Justice Bible, New York: American Bible Society, 2009.

Good News About Injustice: A Witness of Courage in a Hurting World (updated 10th anniversary edition) by Gary A. Haugen, Downers Grove, IL: InterVarsity Press, 2009.

The Irresistible Revolution: Living as an Ordinary Radical by Shane Claiborne, Grand Rapids, MI: Zondervan, 2006.

Halftime: Changing Your Game Plan from Success to Significance by Bob Buford, Grand Rapids, MI: Zondervan, 1997.

Surprised by Hope: Rethinking Heaven, the Resurrection, and the Mission of the Church by N. T. Wright, New York: HarperOne, 2008.

Stewards in the Kingdom: A Theology of Life in All Its Fullness by R. Scott Rodin, Downers Grove, IL: InterVarsity Press, 2000.

Glocalization: How Followers of Jesus Engage in a Flat World by Bob Roberts Jr., Grand Rapids, MI: Zondervan, 2007.

Half the Sky: Turning Oppression into Opportunity for Women Worldwide by Nicholas D. Kristof and Sheryl WuDunn, New York: Borzoi Books, 2009.

Strength in What Remains: A Journey of Remembrance and Forgiveness by Tracy Kidder, New York: Random House, 2009.

Stones into Schools: Promoting Peace with Books, Not Bombs, in Afghanistan and Pakistan by Greg Mortenson, New York: Viking Adult, 2009.

Under the Overpass: A Journey of Faith on the Streets of America by Mike Yankoski, Sisters, OR: Multnomah Press, 2005.

Voices of the Poor—Can Anyone Hear Us? by Deepa Narayan, New York: Oxford University Press, 2000.

Take Your Best Shot: Do Something Bigger Than Yourself by Austin Gutwein with Todd Hillard, Nashville, TN: Thomas Nelson, 2009.

Warrior Princess: Fighting for Life with Courage and Hope by Princess Kasune Zulu, Downers Grove, IL: InterVarsity Press, 2009.

MOVIES

Hotel Rwanda (MGM/United Artists, 2004), *Blood Diamond* (Warner Brothers, 2006), *Slumdog Millionaire* (Fox Searchlight Pictures/Warner Brothers, 2008), *Invisible Children* (Invisible Children, Inc., 2003), *Amazing Grace* (Samuel Goldwyn Films, 2006), *The Constant Gardener* (Focus Features, 2005), *City of God* (Miramax, 2002), *Beyond Belief* (Principle Pictures, 2006), *Lost Boys of Sudan* (Actual Films/Principle Pictures, 2004), *The Kite Runner* (Dreamworks, 2007).

STUDY GUIDE

As you read this book, you may have thought to yourself, *What can I do to make a difference?* This study guide is designed to help you delve more deeply into the ideas behind *The Hole in Our Gospel*, to discover more about your own heart, and to reflect on actions *you* can take to help alleviate poverty and injustice in the world. As you begin to study, you may find it useful to keep a journal in which to make notes, write out ideas stimulated by the book, and to record your prayers. You can use this guide for personal reflection or group study as you read, study, reflect, and prayerfully consider the question: What does God expect of *me*?

In addition to this study guide, additional resources are available to help you go even deeper on your journey. Visit www.theholeinourgospel.com, where you will find a free, downloadable, and expanded version of this study. Additional resources are available at this site as well. Or, to bring the message of *The Hole in Our Gospel* to your church or small group with a breakaway campaign, *The Gospel Quest* is a six-week, small-group curriculum that will help transform your church, instilling congregants with compassionate hearts for the poor. The church launch kit includes:

- a copy of the book *The Hole in Our Gospel*
- 5 six-week study guides
- a six-week study DVD
- 5 six-week personal action journals
- six-weeks' worth of sermon outlines and PowerPoint presentations
- 6 weekend service promo video bumpers
- a quick-start guide
- a 2' x 5' vertical banner and free banner stand
- sample outreach tools

Launch kits, bulk quantities, and additional campaign materials are available at www.thegospelquest.com or by calling 1-800-946-5983. A free sample curriculum kit is available to church leaders (shipping and handling not included).

PROLOGUE AND PART 1

THE HOLE IN MY GOSPEL—AND MAYBE YOURS

1. Rich Stearns says that until he went to Rakai, Uganda, he lived in a bubble, insulated from anything too raw or upsetting (prologue, pages 7–8). Can you identify with this? If so, what factors do you think contribute to the existence of your bubble?

2. Do you agree that poverty and suffering in the world have been—and are—drowned out by "choruses of praise music in hundreds of thousands of churches across our country" (prologue, page 11)? Why or why not? What is your church doing to help the poor? How can you help it do more? Brainstorm ideas (and create an action list) with other members of your church.

3. What is the "bingo card" gospel (chapter 1, pages 16–20), and what's wrong with it? Do you agree that the gospel requires more of us than just believing the right things? Might there be "holes" in your own interpretation of the gospel? Brainstorm with friends about what those areas might possibly be in your lives or, perhaps, in the life of your church.

4. Thinking of Jim Wallis's experiment with his Bible (chapter 1, pages 23–24), are there passages in the Bible that you would prefer to overlook or ignore? What are they, and why do you want to ignore them?

5. Rich described his journey through unemployment and the lessons he learned from those times (chapter 2, pages 28–29). We've all faced hard times. How have such times in your life broken you? How did those times change you?

6. The story of the rich young ruler goes deeper than money alone (chapter 3, pages 36–38). What are you blessed with that you might be withholding from God? Your time or talent? Other things? Discuss this question and ways to break through any reluctance to give all to the Lord.

7. Rich writes that "Sometimes, in fact often, God's blessings often come through our sufferings . . ." (chapter 3, page 42). As Christians, we are often quick to praise God when good things happen, but what about when bad things happen? What Scriptures can you find that speak to this?

Take action: Most of us have a list of conditions we present to God before surrendering completely to Him (chapter 3, pages 38–39). On a sheet of paper, make a list of things that might prevent you from serving God unconditionally right now.

Pray: Are you struggling to be completely open to God's will for your life? Pray that you will become open to Him, and that you will be increasingly sensitive to hearing His voice and understanding His call on your life.

PART 2

THE HOLE GETS DEEPER

1. In the seventh century BC, God criticized the Israelites' attempts to get back into His good graces through prayers and religious ceremonies (chapter 4, pages 54–55). Think about the priorities of your church and compare them with the focus of the Israelites. How would your church stand up to Isaiah's criticisms?

2. Think about your experience of working with the poor and marginalized in your community—or anyone you have helped through a tough time. Have there been moments when you, like Mother Teresa, saw "Christ, in his most distressing disguise" (chapter 4, page 60)? Describe that situation and what it's teaching you upon reflection. Pray that God will show you what He requires of you, and that you will have an open heart as He shows you His will throughout this book.

3. Is it possible to love God and not love your neighbor (chapter 5, pages 65–67)? Why are the two commandments so inextricably connected?

4. What are the ways in which you and your church have taken on the "mission of God" by showing your love to your neighbors (chapter 5, page 69)? Which is more important: telling people about Christ or demonstrating His love through acts of kindness, compassion, and justice? Why do you believe this? Are there times when we should do one but not the other?

5. Do you see a connection between Rich's difficult childhood and his

later resistance to believing in Christ (chapter 6, pages 74–76)? What was it? In what ways do your childhood experiences and relationship with your parents affect your openness to or resistance to God?

6. People like Rich need intellectually rigorous books to help them move from agnosticism to faith (chapter 6, pages 80–82). Why might people like him be offended to be told that you—or others—were praying for them? What are better ways to share your faith?

7. Do you believe it's true that every follower of Christ was made for a purpose (chapter 7, page 92)? Even you? Explain why or why not. What would you say God's purpose for your life is? What are you currently doing to live out that purpose? What could you begin to do this week to move in that direction?

Take action: Discerning our unique calling is not always a simple undertaking. Rich mentions seven things we must do in order to hear God's still, small voice (chapter 7, page 93). What are they? What would you add to the list? Which are you currently doing—and which could you begin this week?

Pray: Walk through your neighborhood, praying for each household and thinking of ways you could most effectively show love to your neighbors. Peruse an atlas or globe, and pray for your global neighbors in need and consider what you can do to help them.

PART 3

A HOLE IN THE WORLD

1. Due to the repeated images of poverty and adversity bombarding us through the media, have you experienced "compassion fatigue" (chapter 8, pages 107–110)? Think back on the most recent global disasters you've witnessed in the news. Did you and/or your church respond to them with urgency? If not, why not? What can you do to avoid becoming detached and indifferent toward these images of suffering?

2. Even the president of World Vision confesses that he struggles to mourn over dying children on another continent as he would his own (chapter 9, page 109). Is this tendency something that we can overcome? What can you do to maintain a feeling of urgency for the plight of children in far-off lands?

3. Does the story of Rich's encounter with the child in India (chapter 9, pages 111–113) bring to mind any personal encounter you've had with someone in need? What was it, and how did you respond? How do you wish you had responded?

4. What could you do now to make your financial contributions more personal (chapter 9, page 113)? What are some ways that you and your family could have some regular contact with those in need? List the first three steps you could take to make it happen.

5. What were your first associations with the words *poor* and *poverty* (chapter 10, pages 115–120)? What prejudices were you brought up with about people who are poor? Which stereotypes about people who are poor do you still find lingering in the back of your mind?

6. In 2 Corinthians 8:13–15, Paul urges the Corinthian church to help the Jerusalem church so that there would be more equality between them (chapter 10, pages 122–123). What steps might your church—and you personally—take to strive toward greater equality with the poorest of the poor?

7. In which of these programs (or similar programs) do you and your church participate?
   • Take short-term mission trips
   • Support shelters for the homeless
   • Budget to give regularly to local charities
   • Budget to give regularly to international relief organizations
   • Help run or serve in a food kitchen
   • Spend time every week in a charity program
   • Sponsor a child (or children) through World Vision or another organization
   • Partner with a church in a poor area or developing country
   Work with at-risk young people
   • Other (please list)
   How would you rate the long-term effectiveness of each of these

efforts? How might you refocus your efforts, based on what you've read in chapter 11?

8. Rodrick of Zambia said, "God has been good to us, and with His continued blessings, I hope to build a school" (chapter 11, page 130). With this sense of giving back, in light of God's blessings in your life, how would you end this sentence? *God has been good to me, and with His continued blessings, I hope to . . .*

9. What have you seen in the news in the past few years about what the U.S. government is spending to combat AIDS in Africa? If you don't remember, look it up on the Internet. How much have we designated for this cause? Do you think this is an appropriate amount, too much, or too little? On what do you base your opinion? Consult chapter 12 for more background on how hunger, illness, dirty water, and preventable diseases impact people who are poor.

10. By this point in the book you may be feeling overwhelmed by the challenges facing the poor. If we believe the two statements that (1) every one of the challenges has a solution, and (2) every one of us can make a difference (chapter 13, page 151), what more do you think concerned Christians should be doing? What changes could you make in your life?

11. Until now, what has been your belief about the power of prayer as a weapon against the pain of the world?
   • Prayer is the most important weapon.
   • We could pray, but what is really needed is our money.
   • Prayer is an equally important weapon to be used alongside the work of churches, relief organizations and government aid.
   Explain or discuss this with friends.

12. Consider repeating Reneé Stearns' experiment of going without water for a day. Put a sticky note on every faucet and water related appliance saying "not available to 1 billion people." At the end of the day write down your feelings and emotions.

Take action: Reflect on the times when you have been the answer to someone's prayers. Make a list beginning with *I am an answer to someone's prayer every time I . . .*

Pray the prayer of World Vision's founder, Bob Pierce: "Let my heart be broken by the things that break the heart of God." In addition, pray for people caught in the web of poverty and consider how you might influence your church to take action to meet the needs of the poor.

PART 4

A HOLE IN THE CHURCH

1. Rich says that the American church in his parable was oblivious to the suffering of the church in Africa, because it was preoccupied with its own programs (chapter 15, page 177). List the programs, according to priority, that you think your church is preoccupied with. (You might start by looking at your church bulletin.) What changes do you feel should be made to their relative priorities?

2. Would you describe your church more as a "spiritual cocoon," where Christians retreat from a hostile world, or a "transformation station," whose primary objective is to change the world (chapter 15, page 179)? Why? How is that manifested? What could you as an individual or study group do to help lead your church to have an outward vision to become salt and light in the world?

3. Do a little research about your church's missions commitments. Find out how much your church gives to missions programs (that focus on the poor) every year. Then ask what percent of its total budget that number is. Do you think this percentage is high enough (chapter 16, page 185)? What would be required to add one or more percentage points to that total for missions?

4. Does your church support or partner with another church or churches in a developing nation (chapter 16, page 189)? If so, what can you do to learn more about it and increase your members' involvement with that church? If not, what can you do to begin such a program in your church?

5. What was your reaction to the results of the Barna Group survey results on the willingness of Christians to help people affected by AIDS

(chapter 17, pages 195–196)? What other "justice blind spots" might the church have today that future generations will see clearly?

6. In the "faith vs. works" debate (chapter 17, pages 198–202), where have you and your church traditionally stood? What were your reasons? Does Rich's perspective on this make sense to you? Why or why not? If you are in a church that associates social action with liberal theology, how would you now define social action in a way that is consistent with your theology?

7. If "money is power, and power competes with God for supremacy in our lives" (chapter 19, page 212), which or who is winning that competition in your life? In what kinds of situations do you feel that power struggle most keenly, and how have you handled it?

8. Read Malachi 3:8–12 again (chapter 19, page 214). Have you experienced God pouring out blessings on you as a result of your giving your money to Him and His Church? In what ways? What dangers lie in leaning too heavily on this passage as a motivation to give?

9. Read Rich's "Letter to the Church in America" (chapter 20, pages 213–225) and underline the sentences that you think you and your church especially need to heed.

10. List some things your church is known to be *against* (chapter 21, pages 228–229). In another column list the things your church is known to be *for*. Which list is longer?

11. Read Mark 1:40–45 (chapter 22, page 239). Since the Church is the living body of Christ, re-read the passage, replacing all references to Jesus with "my church." What insight did this reading bring to you?

Take action: If it's true that "it's not our money—it all comes from God; we are not entitled to it but entrusted with it; and God expects us to use it in the interest of His kingdom," then what can you do to move from your current attitude toward your money to this scriptural view (chapter 18, page 207)? Make a list of three or four steps you could take toward that goal and implement them.

Pray: In your prayer time, ask God to show you what "great omissions" He sees in your life (chapter 16). Make a note of His answers in your journal.

PART 5

REPAIRING THE HOLE

1. To repair the hole in our own gospel requires an "intentional decision. It doesn't just happen" (chapter 23, page 244). What changes could you decide to make in your life in order to become a change agent for Christ?

2. "This gospel we embrace and this Jesus we follow are dangerous" (chapter 23, page 246). What is dangerous about Jesus and the gospel? What frightens you about this danger? What exhilarates you?

3. Do you agree that God's image and identity are defaced by the continued existence of poverty and injustice in the world (chapter 24, page 255)? Why or why not?

4. Identify one or several "impossible dreams" you or your church could accomplish for the poor in your community and the world—one stone at a time (chapter 24, page 256). Are you a leader with Nehemiah's organizational skills? If so, begin now to write out action plans that could lead to the dream—one step at a time.

5. "We are God's Plan A . . . and He doesn't have a Plan B" (chapter 25, page 277). What does this mean in relation to what you, your small group, or your church might commit to do as a result of this study? If you don't do it, who will?

Take action: In your journal or on a whiteboard, summarize what you and/ or your small group or church have decided to do to bring the whole gospel to your community and world as a result of this book and study. Then go to www.theholeinourgospel.com and share your ideas, actions and results as an encouragement to others who are on the journey with you.

Pray: Ask God to bless and use your gifts of time, talents, and treasures to bring hope and justice to a world in need.

NOTES

INTRODUCTION

1. Johnny Cash, "No Earthly Good."
2. Throughout this book I will use the Bible in an authoritative way. I believe that the Bible is the anchor of truth that we must always look to as we seek God's will for us. Truth is not a relative concept but an absolute. When we base our beliefs on our culture, our own worldview, or even the opinions of the majority, we become a boat with no anchor, making it possible for anything to be true.

PROLOGUE

1. "HIV/AIDS in Uganda," Uganda AIDS Commission official Web site, http://www.aidsuganda.org/ (last accessed October 13, 2008).
2. http://www.avert.org/aidsorphans.htm.
3. United Nations Development Programme, *Human Development Report 2007/2008* (New York: Palgrave MacMillan, 2007), 25.
4. Joint United Nations Programme on HIV/AIDS (UNAIDS), *2008 Report on the Global Aids Epidemic* (Geneva: UNAIDS, 2008), 163.

PART 1

CHAPTER 1

1. *Dictionary.com Unabridged* (v 1.1), s.v., "gospel," http://dictionary.reference.com/browse/gospel (accessed March 20, 2008).
2. David Kinnaman and Gabe Lyons, *UnChristian: What a New Generation Really Thinks about Christianity . . . and Why It Matters* (Grand Rapids: Baker Books, 2007), 72.
3. United States Geological Survey, "Earthquake Hazards Program," Department of the Interior, http://neic.usgs.gov/neis/eq_depot/2001/eq_010126/index.html.
4. Atul Tandon, a native of India, was World Vision's senior vice president of Donor Engagement, having recently joined the ministry after a distinguished career with Citicorp. With his baseball cap, blue jeans, and World Vision logo shirt, these men surely mistook him for one of "the Americans."
5. Jim Wallis is the founder of *Sojourners* magazine and a speaker and author on issues of biblical justice.
6. The British and Foreign Bible Society, 2008. See http://www.povertyandjusticebible.org/.
7. Jim Wallis, *God's Politics* (New York: HarperSanFrancisco, 2005), 212–213.
8. *The American Heritage Dictionary of the English Language*, 4th ed., s.v., "hole."

CHAPTER 2

1. At times it was even a bit risky, and of course, I would have been horrified if my own kids had ever tried this. But I grew up in the days when kids played in the streets without a thought of any sinister consequences.
2. Bob was subsequently appointed by President Clinton to serve as America's first ambassador for International Religious Freedom, a position in which he served with distinction for the next several years.

CHAPTER 3

1. Bob Buford, a Texas businessman, coined this phrase in his wonderful book *Halftime: Changing Your Game Plan from Success to Significance* (Grand Rapids: Zondervan, 1997), to describe a different goal for people who have succeeded in their secular careers.
2. Bruce Wilkinson, *The Prayer of Jabez: Breaking Through to the Blessed Life* (Sisters, OR: Multnomah, 2000).
3. Excerpt from The Fellowship of the Ring by J.R.R. Tolkien. Copyright © 1954, 1965 by J. R. R. Tolkien. Copyright renewed by Christopher R. Tolkien, Michael H. R. Tolkien, John F. R. Tolkien and Priscilla M.A. R. Tolkien. Reprinted by permission of Houghton Mifflin Harcourt Publishing Company. All rights reserved.
4. Bill told me later that after my answer he knew I was the right person for the job because I was the only one who had answered his question honestly. He said anyone who *was* "comfortable" with that kind of suffering was probably the wrong person for the job.

PART 2

CHAPTER 4

1. There has been much debate over the identity of those referred to in Matthew 25 as "the least of these brothers of mine." Some commentators argue that this did not mean all the poor and needy but was a specific reference to those who are disciples of Christ, and that the sheep and goats are judged based on how they treated Christ's followers or disciples. Some argue for an even narrower definition that encompasses only Christ's disciples involved in spreading the gospel as missionaries. I will not repeat those arguments here. My own belief is that Christ's meaning here encompassed any who were poor or needy. The passages leading up to this scene of final judgment in Matthew 25 paint a picture that supports the notion that God will judge people based on the authenticity of their profession of faith, using the evidence of a lifestyle of obedience. In Matthew 23, Jesus castigated the Pharisees in the strongest language as hypocrites whose actions and lives were inconsistent with their supposed piety. "Woe to you, teachers of the law and Pharisees," He said, "you hypocrites! You give a tenth of your spices—mint, dill and cumin. But you have neglected the more important matters of the law—justice, mercy and faithfulness. You should have practiced the latter, without neglecting the former" (v. 23). Then, in Matthew 24 and 25, we find a series of warnings and parables about the end of the age, whose purpose is to exhort the believer to be ready for the Master's return. In the parable of the talents, just preceding the vision of the final judgment, the master returns to inspect what his servants have done while he was away. The two that had acted in accord with the master's expectations were commended and rewarded. The servant who had done nothing with what the master had entrusted to him was chastised and thrown into darkness. Taken together, these passages suggest that Matthew (and Jesus) intended to suggest that the genuineness of a person's professed faith would ultimately be judged by the "fruit" evident in a lifestyle consistent with the teachings and commands of Christ. Certainly, demonstrated concern for the poor would have been at the top of any list of Christ's teachings.
2. For more information, see Michael Gerson, "To End a Nightmare: Balancing Peace and Justice in Central Africa," *Washington Post*, October 17, 2007, A17, http://www.washingtonpost.com/wp-dyn/content/article/2007/10/16/AR2007101601520.html.
3. Camilla Olson and Melanie Teff, "Northern Uganda: Give Displaced People Real

Options," Refugees International, http://www.refugeesinternational.org/policy/ field-report/northern-uganda-give-displaced-people-real-options. IDPs are internally displaced people who have fled their homes and come to live in sprawling camps in deplorable conditions. They struggle to live without sanitation, health care, or adequate food until it is safe for them to return to their homes. In Gulu, some had lived in camps twenty years and seen their children and their grandchildren born there.
4. Not their real names.

CHAPTER 5

1. *Poverty and Justice Bible* (Swindon, UK: The British and Foreign Bible Society, 2008).
2. Not to be confused with Jeffrey Geoghegan and Michael Homan's *The Bible for Dummies*, published in 2003.
3. N. T. Wright, *Surprised by Hope: Rethinking Heaven, the Resurrection, and the Mission of the Church* (New York: HarperCollins, 2008), 208, italics in original. Reprinted by permission of HarperCollins Publishers.

CHAPTER 6

1. John R. W. Stott, *Basic Christianity* (Downers Grove, IL: InterVarsity Press, 1958).

CHAPTER 7

1. The Internet Movie Database, "Memorable quotes for Chariots of Fire," IMBD. com, http://www.imdb.com/title/tt0082158/quotes.
2. John Ortberg, *If You Want to Walk on Water, You've Got to Get out of the Boat* (Grand Rapids: Zondervan, 2001).
3. Brainy Quote, "Mother Teresa Quotes," BrainyMedia.com, http://www. brainyquote.com/quotes/quotes/m/mothertere114249.html.

PART 3
CHAPTER 8

1. Jimmy Carter for the Nobel Foundation, "Text from the Nobel lecture given by the Nobel Peace Prize Laureate for 2002," Jimmy Carter Library and Museum, http://www.jimmycarterlibrary.gov/documents/jec/nobel.phtml.
2. Ibid.
3. Jeffrey D. Sachs, *The End of Poverty: Economic Possibilities for Our Times* (New York: Penguin Press, 2005). Used by permission of The Penguin Press, a division of Penguin Group (USA) Inc.
4. "Annual Television Set Sales in USA," http://www.tvhistory.tv/Annual_TV_Sales_39-59.JPG.
5. Planned Giving Design Center, LLC, "U.S. Charitable Giving Estimated to Be $306.39 Billion in 2007," http://www.pgdc.com/pgdc/us-charitable-giving-estimated-be-30639-billion-2007.
6. Although the term was likely coined earlier, it was made especially popular by Susan D. Moeller's book, *Compassion Fatigue: How the Media Sell Disease, Famine, War and Death* (New York: Routledge, 1999).
7. Bureau of the Census, *Statistical Abstract of the United States 1939* (Washington, DC: United States Government Printing Office, 1939), 433.
8. Bureau of the Census, *Statistical Abstract of the United States 1950* (Washington, DC: United States Government Printing Office, 1950), 522.

9. Bureau of the Census, *Statistical Abstract of the United States 2008* (Washington, DC: United States Government Printing Office, 2008), table 1242.

10. Bono, in Sachs, *The End of Poverty: Economic Possibilities for our Times*, foreword.

CHAPTER 9

1. Global Issues, http://www.globalissues.org/article/715/today-over-26,500-children-died-around-the-world.

2. Moeller, *Compassion Fatigue*, 22.

3. Peter Singer, *Practical Ethics*, 2nd ed. (Cambridge, UK: Cambridge University Press, 1993), 229. Reprinted with the permission of Cambridge University Press.

4. Ibid.

5. Peter Singer, "Famine, Affluence and Morality," *Philosophy and Public Affairs* 1, no. 1 (Spring 1972).

CHAPTER 10

1. Keith Epstein, "Crisis Mentality," *Stanford Social Innovation Review* (Spring 2006).

2. Ibid.

3. Family Care Foundation, "If the World Were a Village of 100 People," http://www.familycare.org/news/if_the_world.htm (accessed August 5, 2008).

4. U.S. Department of Commerce, Bureau of Economic Analysis, "Per Capita Personal Income by State," Bureau of Business and Economic Research, University of New Mexico, http://www.unm.edu/~bber/econ/us-pci.htm (accessed August 5, 2008).

5. United Nations Development Programme, *Human Development Report 2007/2008* (New York: Palgrave MacMillan, 2007), 25.

6. "The World's Billionares: A New Count, A New Record," by Sam Pizzigati, http://www.alternet.org/workplace/79993/ (last accessed October 20, 2008).

7. Anup Shaw, "Poverty Facts and Stats," Global Issues, http://www.globalissues.org/article/26/poverty-facts-and-stats#src18.

8. United Nations Development Programme, *Human Development Report 2007/2008*, 25.

9. Ibid.

10. Sachs, *The End of Poverty*, 28.

11. Jimmy Carter for the Nobel Foundation, "Text from the Nobel lecture given by the Nobel Peace Prize Laureate for 2002," Jimmy Carter Library and Museum, http://www.jimmycarterlibrary.gov/documents/jec/nobel.phtml.

12. Poverty is not our fault in the sense that most of us have not actively and intentionally endeavored to perpetuate poverty or oppress the poor. We are, though, complicit in sustaining poverty through our apathy and our unwitting support of systems that do oppress the poor. When we purchase clothing manufactured in a sweatshop by child laborers or buy coffee from a system that fails to appropriately reward the hardworking farmers who grow and harvest the coffee, we become part of the systems that perpetuate exploitation and poverty. In that sense our sins, with regard to the poor, are more the sins of omission than commission.

CHAPTER 11

1. Dr. Jayakumar Christian is the national director of World Vision India and author of *God of the Empty-Handed: Poverty, Power, and the Kingdom of God* (Monrovia, CA: World Vision International, 1999).

CHAPTER 12

1. Marc Lacey, "Across Globe, Empty Bellies Bring Rising Anger," *New York Times*, April 18, 2008.
2. United Nations Children's Fund, *The State of the World's Children 2007* (New York: United Nations, 2006), 24.
3. "Hunger Facts," World Food Program, http://www.wfp.org/aboutwfp/facts/hunger_facts.asp?section=1&sub_section=5 (last accessed October 20, 2008).
4. Robert Black, Saul Morris, and Jennifer Bryce, "Where and Why Are 10 Million Children Dying Every Year?" *The Lancet* 361:2226–34 (2003).
5. World Food Programme, "What Is Hunger?" http://www.wfp.org/aboutwfp/introduction/hunger_what.asp?section=1&sub_section=1.
6. Ibid.
7. ActionAid International USA, "25,000 Empty Plates Mark Daily Hunger Death Toll," OneWorld.net, http://us.oneworld.net/node/158162.
8. Deepa Narayan, *Voices of the Poor—Can Anyone Hear Us?* (New York: Oxford University Press, 2000), 45.
9. Jan Eliasson and Susan Blumenthal, "Dying for a Drink of Clean Water," *Washington Post*, September 20, 2005, http://www.washingtonpost.com/wp-dyn/content/article/2005/09/19/AR2005091901295.html.
10. "World Security Depends on Averting Water Wars," Environment News Service, March 22, 2002, http://www.ens-newswire.com/ens/mar2002/2002-03-22-01.asp.
11. "Global Water Crisis Basic Facts Sheets," Water Partners International, http://www.water.org/FileUploads/WPMidCurricFULL.pdf, (last accessed October 20, 2008).
12. Isha Seshay, "Inside Africa: Marking World Water Day," transcript from an interview with Lucy Liu, March 22, 2008, http://transcripts.cnn.com/TRANSCRIPTS/0803/22/i_if.01.html.
13. Eliasson and Blumenthal, "Dying for a Drink of Clean Water."
14. Donald G. McNeil Jr., "Child Mortality at Record Low; Further Drop Seen," *New York Times*, September 13, 2007, http://www.nytimes.com/2007/09/13/world/13child.html?_r=1&oref=slogin.
15. United Nations Children's Fund, *The State of the World's Children 2008* (New York: United Nations, 2007), 116–17.
16. Bono, in Sachs, *The End of Poverty: Economic Possibilities for our Times*, foreword.
17. Associated Press, "U.S. life expectancy tops 78 for the first time: Federal report cites decline in heart disease, other major causes of death," June 11, 2008, http://today.msnbc.msn.com/id/25097931/.
18. CNN, "U.N.: Life expectancy in sub-Sahara Africa hit hard by AIDS," October 28, 1998, http://www.cnn.com/HEALTH/9810/28/aids.report.01/index.html.
19. Central Intelligence Agency, "Rank Order: Life Expectancy at Birth," *World Factbook* (Date of information, 2008 est.), https://www.cia.gov/library/publications/the-world-factbook/rankorder/2102rank.html.
20. World Health Organization, *World Health Statistics 2007* (Geneva: World Health Organization, 2007), 19.
21. United Nations Children's Fund, *The State of the World's Children 2008*, 8 (pie chart).
22. World Health Organization, "Malaria," http://www.searo.who.int/en/Section10/Section21/Section334_4008.htm (accessed August 6, 2008).
23. Michael Finkel, "Stopping a Global Killer," *National Geographic*, July 2007.

24. Ibid.
25. Roll Back Malaria, "Children and Malaria," World Health Organization, http://www.rbm.who.int/cmc_upload/0/000/015/367/RBMInfosheet_6.htm (accessed August 6, 2008).
26. Ibid., http://www.rbm.who.int/cmc_upload/0/000/015/363/RBMInfosheet_10.htm.
27. Melinda Gates, "Malaria Forum Keynote Address," Bill & Melinda Gates Foundation, http://www.gatesfoundation.org/MediaCenter/Speeches/Co-ChairSpeeches/MelindaSpeeches/MFGSpeechMalariaForum-071017.htm, October 2007.
28. World Health Organization, "Tuberculosis: The Startling Facts," WHO, http://www.searo.who.int/LinkFiles/Tuberculosis_right8.pdf (accessed August 6, 2008).
29. World Health Organization, *Global Tuberculosis Control* (Geneva: World Health Organization, 2008), 3.
30. Division of Tuberculosis Elimination, "A Global Perspective on Tuberculosis," Centers for Disease Control, http://www.cdc.gov/TB/WorldTBDay/resources_global.htm (accessed August 6, 2008).
31. Left untreated, HIV will be passed on through childbirth in about one-third of the cases. However, there are highly effective and affordable treatments for pregnant women and their infants that can reduce the transmission to almost zero if administered on a timely basis. Advances in antiretroviral drug therapy have not "cured" AIDS but have made it manageable as a chronic disease if the patient has access to these therapies. Americans and Europeans, for example, can live virtually normal lives by faithfully taking their medicines, but until recently these drugs have not been widely available in poor countries.
32. Joint United Nations Programme on HIV/AIDS (UNAIDS), *Report on the Global Aids Epidemic* (Geneva: UNAIDS, 2008), 16.
33. Ibid., 30.
34. Ibid., 15.
35. Ibid., 39–40.
36. "India World's Second in AIDS Crisis," IBN Live, December 1, 2006, http://www.ibnlive.com/news/indias-story-got-aids-dont-know/27443-3.html.
37. OSI, "HIV/AIDS Policy in Ukraine: A Civil Society Perspective," Open Society Institute, October 2007, http://www.soros.org/Staging/initiatives/health/focus/phw/articles_publications/publications/ukraine_20071015?skin=printable.
38. UNAIDS, *Report on the Global AIDS Epidemic*, Annex 1.
39. Ibid., 16.
40. Ibid., Annex 1.
41. *Orphan* is defined as a child who has lost one or both parents. Usually if one parent has died, the other is soon to follow, as the disease has been passed from one parent to the other.
42. Edward C. Green, *Rethinking AIDS Prevention* (Westport: Greenwood Publishing Group, 2003), 143.
43. Ibid.
44. Ibid.
45. Joint United Nations Programme on HIV/AIDS (UNAIDS), 07 *Aids Epidemic Update* (Geneva: UNAIDS, 2007), 11.

CHAPTER 13

1. Four years later I visited them both. Because of the intervention of World Vision's

Zambia staff, Maggie was in a private school. She was dressed in her clean school uniform, shoes and all. Finedia was living much more comfortably in a new house built for her by World Vision; she even had a couch and two stuffed chairs.

2. Narayan, *Voices of the Poor*, 53.

3. 2003 Environmental Scan, a report to the OCLC membership, "Worldwide Education and Library Spending," Online Computer Library, http://www.oclc.org/reports/escan/economic/educationlibraryspending.htm (accessed August 7, 2008).

4. United Nations Development Program, *Human Development Report 2003* (New York: Oxford University Press, 2003), 92.

5. Bonded labor is a form of modern-day slavery wherein a desperately poor family is offered a loan in exchange for the daily labor of one of their children. The promise is that the child's labor will pay back the debt over a period of time, and then the child will be released. However, the interest rates are so high that the child is never released. There are hundreds of thousands of children trapped today in these immoral bonded-labor schemes.

6. United Nations Children's Fund, *The State of the World's Children 2008* (New York: United Nations, 2007), 147.

7. Ibid., 22.

8. Central Intelligence Agency, "The 2008 World Factbook: Niger," CIA, https://www.cia.gov/library/publications/the-world-factbook/print/ng.html (accessed August 7, 2008).

9. Ban Ki-Moon, Children and the Millennium Development Goals, United Nations Children Fund (New York: UNICEF, 2007), 58.

10. United Nations, *The Millennium Development Goals Report 2007* (New York: United Nations, 2007), 16.

11. CARE, *Women's Empowerment*, http://www.care.org/newsroom/publications/whitepapers/woman_and_empowerment.pdf, 1. See also http://www.minuhemmati.net:80/gender/womenland.htm.

12. International Council on Women's Health Issues, http://www.icowhi.org/.

13. Commission on the Status of Women, "No Tool for Development More Effective than Empowerment of Women, Says Deputy Secretary-General, as Women's Commission Opens 50th Session," United Nations, http://www.un.org/News/Press/docs/2006/wom1539.doc.htm (accessed August 7, 2008).

14. The World Revolution, "Peace, War & Conflict," http://www.worldrevolution.org/projects/globalissuesoverview/overview2/PeaceNew.htm (accessed August 7, 2008).

15. The International Rescue Committee, "Special Report: Congo," http://www.theirc.org/special-report/congo-forgotten-crisis.html (accessed August 7, 2008).

16. United Nations Development Programme, *Human Development Report 2007/2008*, 321.

17. Anup Shah, "World Military Spending," Global Issues, http://www.globalissues.org/Geopolitics/ArmsTrade/Spending.asp#WorldMilitarySpending (accessed August 7, 2008).

18. Development Co-operation Directorate, "Debt Relief Is Down: Other ODA Rises Slightly," Organisation for Economic Co-operation and Development, http://www.oecd.org/document/8/0,3343,en_2649_33721_40381960_1_1_1_1,00.html (accessed August 8, 2008).

19. Sachs, *The End of Poverty*, 295.

CHAPTER 14
1. Adapted from Loren Eiseley, *The Star Thrower* (New York: Harvest, 1979).
2. United Nations Development Programme, *Human Development Report 1990* (New York: Oxford University Press, 1990), 17; and United Nations Development Programme, *Human Development Report 2007/2008*, 232.
3. Ibid., 264.
4. United Nations Children's Fund, *The State of the World's Children 2008*, foreword.
5. UN Millennium Project 2005, *Halving Hunger: It Can Be Done*, summary version (New York: The Earth Institute at Columbia University, 2005), preface.
6. United Nations Development Programme, *Human Development Report 1990*, 23; and United Nations Children's Fund, *The State of the World's Children 2008*, 14.
7. United Nations Development Programme, Human Development Report 1990, 17; and United Nations Development Programme, *Human Development Report 2007/2008*, 272.
8. "Millennium Development Goals," Millennium Promise, http://www.millenniumpromise.org/site/PageServer?pagename=press_mdg. This page features a digital clock in the upper right-hand corner, with a countdown to the year 2015. See also the UN Millennium Project Web site, Historic site, http://www.unmillenniumproject.org/; and in particular, their "About MDGs: What they are" page, http://www.unmillenniumproject.org/goals/index.htm.

PART 4
CHAPTER 15
1. Narayan, *Voices of the Poor*, 136.

CHAPTER 16
1. "Pastor Poll," The Barna Group, Ltd., 1999.

CHAPTER 17
1. Dee Alexander Brown, *Bury My Heart at Wounded Knee* (New York: Picador, 1976).
2. Rev. James H. Thornwell, "The Worcester Fanatics—Progress of Socialism, Abolition, and Infidelity," *New York Herald*, October 29, 1850.
3. Martin Luther King Jr., "Letter from Birmingham Jail." April 16, 1963, available online at MLK Online, http://www.mlkonline.net/jail.html.
4. Ibid.
5. Ibid.
6. "Omnipoll," The Barna Group, Ltd., 2002.
7. John Stott, *Human Rights and Human Wrongs* (Grand Rapids: Baker Book House, 1999), 83–84.
8. J. Wesley Bready, *England: Before and After Wesley* (New York: Harper, 1938), 327.

CHAPTER 18
1. LovetoKnow Corp., "American Dream definition," www.yourdictionary.com/american-dream (accessed August 11, 2008).
2. Lexico Publishing Group, LLC, "gospel.Dictionary.com Unabridged (vol. 1.1)," based on the *Random House Dictionary*, Random House, Inc. 2006, http://dictionary.reference.com/browse/american%20dream (accessed August 11, 2008).

CHAPTER 19

1. Randy Alcorn, *Money, Possessions and Eternity* (Carol Stream, IL: Tyndale House, 2003), 16–17.
2. R. Scott Rodin, *Stewards in the Kingdom* (Downers Grove, IL: InterVarsity Press, 2000), 205–6.
3. Global Rich List, "How Rich Are You?" Poke, http://www.globalrichlist.com/ (accessed August 26, 2008). This site bases its calculations on figures from the World Bank Development Research Group. In making individual calculations, Poke assumes a world population of six billion and an average worldwide annual income of five thousand.
4. The Donella Meadows Archive, Voice of a Global Citizen, "State of the Village Report," the Sustainability Institute, http://www.sustainer.org/dhm_archive/index. php?display_article=vn338villageed (accessed August 27, 2008). See also Joyce Dargay, "Vehicle Ownership and Income Growth, Worldwide: 1960—2030," New York University, http://www.econ.nyu.edu/dept/courses/gately/DGS_ Vehicle%20Ownership_2007.pdf (accessed August 12, 2008).
5. David B. Barrett and Todd M. Johnson, *World Christian Trends, Ad 30 –Ad 2200: Interpreting the Annual Christian Megacensus* (Pasadena, CA: William Carey Library Publishers 2003), 1.
6. It would cost about $65 billion per year according to Sachs, *The End of Poverty*, 295.
7. Barrett and Johnson, *World Christian Trends*, 400.
8. The Barna Group, "New Study Shows Trends in Tithing and Donating," http:// www.barna.org/FlexPage.aspx?Page=BarnaUpdate&BarnaUpdateID=296 (accessed August 11, 2008).
9. Ibid. See this site for Barna's definition of "born again."
10. Ibid. The Barna Group defines "Evangelical Christians" as people who are born-again, plus they meet seven other conditions: (1) they say their faith is very important in their life today; (2) they believe they have a personal responsibility to share their religious beliefs about Christ with non-Christians; (3) they believe that Satan exists; (4) they believe that eternal salvation is possible only through grace, not works; (5) they believe that Jesus Christ lived a sinless life on earth; (6) they assert that the Bible is accurate in all that it teaches; and (7) they describe God as the all-knowing, all-powerful, perfect deity who created the universe and still rules it today. Being classified as an evangelical is not dependent upon church attendance or the denominational affiliation of the church attended. Respondents were not asked to describe themselves as "evangelical."
11. State of Church Giving Through 2005, "Giving Research," Empty Tomb, Inc., http://www.emptytomb.org/fig2_05.html (accessed August 11, 2008).
12. Ibid., http://emptytomb.org/scg05pressadv.html.
13. Bureau of Economic Analysis, "State Personal Income 2007," http://www.bea.gov/ newsreleases/regional/spi/spi_newsrelease.htm (accessed August 11, 2008). Based on U.S. per capita income of $38,611.
14. I want to acknowledge that I have sympathy for poor families who struggle to tithe their incomes and still support their families. For them, this is not an easy command to follow. I also want to add that those of us who *have* been blessed financially can and should give more than the minimum 10 percent.
15. Pam Danziger, "Luxury Consumer Confidence Bounces Back as Affluent Consumers Spend More on Luxury Indulgences," Unity Marketing, http:// www.unitymarketingonline.com/events/index.php (accessed August 11, 2008).

16. Associated Press, "Wardrobes for Teens Include Luxury Items," *Champaign News-Gazette*, August 9, 2007.
17. Ken Gassman and Cheryl Russell, "IDEX Online Research: Americans Haven't Stopped Spending," International Diamond Exchange, http://www.idexonline.com/portal_FullNews.asp?id=30257 (accessed: August 12, 2008).
18. Tom Tulloch, North American Association of State & Provincial Lotteries, e-mail inquiry.
19. Office of the Director of U.S. Foreign Assistance, "International Affairs FY 2009 Budget," U.S. Department of State, http://www.state.gov/f/releases/factsheets2008/99981.htm (accessed August 12, 2008).
20. Joel Stein, "It's a Dog's Life," *Time* magazine, May 19, 2003.
21. American Society for Aesthetic Plastic Surgery, "11.7 Cosmetich Procedures in 2007," http://www.surgery.org/press/news-release.php?iid=491 (accessed August 12, 2008).
22. A. Scott Moreau, "Putting the Survey in Perspective," Linda J. Weber and Dotsey Welliver, eds., *Mission Handbook 2007-2009* (Wheaton, IL: Evangelism and Missions Informational Service, 2007), 12–13.
23. Sachs, *The End of Poverty*, 295.
24. United Nations Development Programme, *Human Development Report 1998* (New York: Oxford University Press, 1998), 37.
25. Global Issues, http://www.globalissues.org/article/715/today-over-26,500-children-died-around-the-world.

CHAPTER 20

1. The scriptures used in this letter are based on the NIV rendering, but with additions and minor changes to improve readability. Verses used: Rev. 2:1–2; James 5:5; Rev. 2:4; Isa. 5:8–9; Haggai 1:5–6; James 5:2–3; Rev. 3:17; James 2:5; Matt. 6:19–21, 33; 2 Cor. 8:9; Luke 6:46; James 1:22; John 14:21; Micah 6:8; Gal. 5:14; Deut. 15:11; Ps. 82:3; Isa. 58:4–7; 1 John 3:17; Joel 2:12–13; Eph. 4:1–2; Rom. 12:2; Isa. 55:2; 58:9–11; 1 Cor. 15:58; Rev. 22:12.

CHAPTER 21

1. My mother was a lapsed Roman Catholic, excommunicated after marrying my father, a twice-divorced man. She always considered herself a Catholic and a Christian despite the fact that she no longer went to church. Her view would have been that people were born into their faith (Christian, Jew, Muslim, etc.), and unless they rejected it later in their lives, they were permanent members of that faith. Faith, in other words, was not something one typically chose.
2. Kinnaman and Lyons, *UnChristian*, 24–25.
3. Ibid., 26.
4. Ibid., 34.
5. Ibid., 47.

CHAPTER 22

1. The statistic turned out to be incorrect. It was actually closer to 17 percent at the time. In 2008, it was 28 percent.
2. Eileen W. Lindner, ed., *Yearbooks of American & Canadian Churches 2008* (Nashville: Abington Press, 2008), 381.

PART 5

CHAPTER 23

1. Bob and Pam started International Health Services, which is growing and active today. Read about them at www.internationalhealthservices.org.

CHAPTER 25

1. The MCA was established by President Bush and approved by Congress to channel assistance to nations that meet certain positive criteria for development. Basically it is intended to reward developing nations that act responsibly.

2. David Beckmann, president of Bread for the World, is a friend of mine. Bread for the World is a Christian organization that focuses on influencing government policies to alleviate hunger and poverty through advocacy and letter writing.

3. Bread for the World, "Your Letters Make a Difference," *Bread* (newsletter), September 2004. Copyright © 2008 Bread for the World.

4. J. Wilbur Chapman, *The Life and Work of Dwight Lyman Moody* (New York: Bradley-Garretson, 1900). Note: This book is also available online at http://www.biblebelievers.com/moody/index.html.

5. For example, try these Web sites: http://www.umc.org/site/c.lwL4KnNlLtH/b.1355371/k.9501/Spiritual_Gifts.htm
http://www.churchgrowth.org/cgi-cg/gifts.cgi?intro=1
http://www.christianet.com/bible/spiritualgiftstest.htm

6. Johnathan Sim was a faithful World Vision staff member who died tragically at age thirty-three. His wife, Kelly, had a dream to build a school in his name. Austin became her partner in that dream.

7. Austin Gutwein, "History," Hoops of Hope, http://www.hoopsofhope.org/index.php?page=history. See also Liz Werner, "One: 13-Year-Old Humanitarian," *Need* magazine, 11, http://www.hoopsofhope.org/uploads/File/NEED03_ONE.pdf.

8. Based on drilling one borehole well at a cost of $12,500 to serve five hundred people for about twenty-five years.

9. Jeff Raderstrong, "Filtering out a global problem," *Seattle Times*, July 14, 2008.

10. Not her real name.

Scripture Index

Exodus
  3:9–14, 90
  4:1–3, 90–91
  4:10–14, 91
  32:9, 64
  33:3, 64
  33:5, 64
Leviticus, 211, 212
  19:18, 66
  23:22, 123
  27:30, 211
Deuteronomy
  6:5, 66
  8:10–18, 204–205
  9:13, 64
  14:29, 211
Joshua
  24:15, 36
2 Samuel
  24:24, 271
1 Kings, 65
2 Kings, 65
1 Chronicles, 65
  4:9–10, 40
  29:11–16, 205–206
2 Chronicles, 65
Nehemiah
  1:3, 254
  1:4, 254
  2:17, 255
Job
  29:11–17, 6
Psalms
  50:10, 206
  82:3–4, 116
Proverbs
  19:17, 152
Isaiah
  1:10–17, 183–184
  1:13, 220
  1:16–17, 186
  10:1–2, 132
  29:13, 179
  53:3, 9

58, 54–57, 67
58:6–7, 186
61:1, 22
61:1–3, 175–176
Jeremiah
  22:16, 151
Ezekiel
  11:19, 116
  16:49, 119–120
Daniel
  7:13–14, 58
Amos
  5:11–12, 127
  5:21–24, 127
Jonah
  2:8, 89
Micah
  6:8, 53
Malachi, 216
  3:8–12, 214
Matthew
  5:3–10, 16
  5:9, 158
  5:13–14, 16, 164, 202
  5:15, 202
  5:16, 202, 220
  6:10, 5, 20, 179
  6:21, 43
  6:24, 212
  6:33, 203
  7:3–5, 197
  7:16, 199
  7:19–23, 85–86
  9:37–38, 18
  10:42, 111
  11:12, 70
  11:25, 65
  12:28, 2
  13:13–15, 197
  13:31–32, 275
  13:33, 16
  14:16, 252
  14:18–20, 252–253
  14:21, 252

17:20, 275
19:16–20, 36–37
19:22, 38
19:24, 2
21:32, 2
21:43, 2
22:34–40, 66
22:40, 67
23, 315–316n1
23:4, 66
23:13, 66
23:13–33, 65
24, 315–316n1
25, 57–59, 67, 86,
  315–316n1
25:14–15, 206
25:20–23, 207
25:26, 207
25:28, 207
25:30, 207
25:31–46, 58
25:36, 152
25:40, 16, 60, 152, 249
25:43, 152
25:45, 152
28:16–20, 67
28:19, 20
28:19–20, 72
Mark
  1:15, 2
  1:40–41, 239
  4:1–20, 18
  4:26–29, 18
  6:34, 251
  6:35–36, 251
  6:37, 252
  6:38, 252
  7:6–8, 194
  8:34–36, 39
  10:14, 106
  10:21, 37
  14:33–34, 244
  14:50, 244

Luke
  2:10, 7
  4, 23, 24, 53–54, 68, 179
  4:14–21, 21
  4:18, 11, 21
  4:18–19, 22, 63, 219
  4:19, 68
  6:37, 229
  6:41–42, 197
  6:43–44, 85, 200
  6:46, 85
  6:46–48, 247
  6:49, 80
  9:11, 251
  9:23–24, 40
  9:57–62, 39
  10:1–3, 18
  10:25–37, 100
  12:16–21, 174
  12:34, 210
  15:32, 63
  16:19–21, 187
  16:22–23, 187
  17:21, 17, 276
John
  3:16, 2
  4:35–38, 18
  10:10, 20
  14:6, 82
  16:33, 161
  20:21, 68
  20:24–28, 74
Acts
  1:11, 69
  2:44–45, 208
  2:47, 208
  22:1–11, 74
Romans
  1:16, 6
  8:19, 241
  10:14–15, 70
  12:6–10, 264
1 Corinthians
  1:26–29, 77
  1:27, 46
  8:13–15, 97
  12:1–12, 264
  12:28, 264

  13:1–3, 67
  15:58, 69
2 Corinthians
  4:7, 257
  5:17, 245
  5:20, 3, 237
  8:1–4, 177–178
  8:8–9, 178
  8:9, 120
  8:13–15, 122–123, 178
  8:21, 194
  9:6–15, 123–124
  9:13, 16–17
  11:23–27, 40–41
  12:9, 90
Galatians
  1:6–7, 23
Ephesians
  1:17–18, 197–198
  2:8–9, 198–199
  2:10, 199
  4:11, 264
  6:12, 164
1 Timothy
  1:15, 73
  6:17–19, 215
James
  1:22, 86, 230
  1:26–27, 185
  1:27, 10
  2:14–19, 86
  2:18, 2, 198
  4:17, 186, 187
  5:1–5, 216–217
1 Peter
  4:12–14, 42
1 John
  2:3–4, 59–60
  2:3–6, 87
  2:6, 26
  3:16–20, 87
Revelation
  2:7, 223
  2:18–19, 231
  3:15–16, 221–222
  3:17, 222
  3:18–20, 222
  6:5–6, 132

GENERAL INDEX

Africa. *See also specific countries*
  diseases and health care in, 105, 141,
    144–145
  HIV and AIDS in, 99, 105, 146, 147,
    148–150, 157, 188–189, 231–237,
    265–266, 325n1 (chap.22)
  imaginary church in, 174–176
  moral responsibility to help, 104–105
  mortality rates and life expectancy, 140
  stereotypes about poverty, 117
  water and waterborne diseases, 138–140
afterlife, focus on, 17
AIDS. *See* HIV and AIDS
American Dream, 203–204, 205
Ana, 271–273
Andes Mountains, 164–169
Annan, Kofi, 157
Armenia, 154
Asia, 221–223, 247–249
awareness, access, and ability to help our
  neighbors, 101–105

Basic Christianity (Stott), 80
Beatitudes, 15–16, 21
Beatrice and Rodrick, 128–130, 153
Beckmann, David, 261, 325–326n2
beliefs, basis for, 314n2. *See also* faith
Bible
  as anchor of truth, 314n2
  passages that address poverty, justice,
    and oppression, 23–24
Bill and Melinda Gates Foundation, 144, 273
bingo card gospel, 16–20
Bolivia, 268
bonded labor, 155, 321n5
Bongani, 233
Bono, 104–105, 140, 198, 263
Bread for the World, 261, 325–326n2
Brentwood Baptist Church, 234
Bryce, Bill, 30–32, 33
Buford, Bob, 315n1
Bush, George W., 234, 261, 325n1 (chap.1)
Bwalya, Mary, 270–271

Cambodia, 70–72

Campus Crusade, 18, 78, 129
Cape Town, South Africa, 99
careers, 93
Caribbean countries, 148
Carter, Jimmy, 97–98, 99, 100, 105, 122
Chambers, Robert, 118
Chapman, J. W., 262
Chariots of Fire, 92
children
  bonded labor and, 155, 298n5
  child-headed households, 10
  compassion for the sick and poor,
    108–113
  deaths of from health predators, 141–
    142
  deaths of from poverty-related causes,
    106–107, 114–115
  diseases and health care, 140–142
  education of, 155, 157
  emotional distance from suffering of,
    107–109
  girls, challenges faced by, 156–157
  hunger and malnutrition, 132–135, 150,
    163, 218
  Jesus' love for, 10
  moral responsibility to help, 110–111
  mortality rates and life expectancy,
    140, 163
  orphans, sponsorship of, 268–271
  orphans left by AIDS pandemic, 10–11,
    50, 148, 195–196, 269–271, 320n41
  suffering of because of cowardice,
    49, 50
Children of War Center, 62–63, 159–160
Chilulu, Morgan, 180, 235–237
China, 149, 247–249
Christian, Jayakumar, 128
Christian Family Church, 235–237
Christians
  America as Christian, 226–227, 325n1
    (chap.21)
  conversion of, 19
  perceptions of, 227–230
  public expression of faith by, 2, 57, 202
  radioactive Christians, 245–247, 249

role in changing the world, 1–5
successful Christians lives, 36–37
what being Christian means, 1
Christian service. *See also* disciples
doing our part, 251–256, 274–279
what we have to offer, 257–273
Church
budgets and spending of, 180
Church of God's Blessings, 173–174,
176–177
Church of the Suffering Servant,
174–176, 188
criticism of, 171–172
cultural blindness of, 190–198
disparity between rich and poor, 122–
124, 172–179, 186–189
faith and works, integration of, 198–202
importance of role of, 179–180
Letter to the Church in America,
223–225, 325n1 (chap.20)
orphans, care for by churches, 10–11,
171
pastor poll of priorities, 185
pastors' challenging jobs, 172
resources to help end the suffering,
122–124, 177–179, 188–189, 206–208,
237–240
social issues, track record on, 190–194,
196–197
superficial and shallow faithfulness of,
183–186
wealth of, 216
work and deeds of, 172, 198–202
civil rights, 191–194, 196
Clinton, Bill, 118–119
Clinton Global Initiative, 118
coin flip bike rides, 26–27, 315n1
Colson, Chuck, 41
commandments, greatest, 66–69, 74, 186
commission, sins of, 185–186
compassion fatigue, 102, 317n6
Compassion Fatigue (Moeller), 107, 317n6
Conrad N. Hilton Foundation, 138
Courageous Leadership Award, 232
cultural blindness, 190–198

Damascus Road, 74, 264
David, 45, 205–206, 250, 259

Democratic Republic of Congo, 157
disciples
absolute surrender of, 37–39
as change agents, 244–245, 277–279
command to make disciples, 67–69, 72,
164
definition of, 68
hardship and suffering of, 40–42
people God chooses, 45–46, 73, 89–94,
250–251, 277–279
proclaiming and spreading gospel by, 16
purpose God has for us, 92–94, 250–253
talents of, 264
transformation from cowardly to
courageous, 244–245
what we have to offer, 257–273
diseases and health care, 105, 140–150
Doctors Without Borders, 141

education
cost of providing, 218
HIV and AIDS infection rates and,
150, 157
literacy and, 155, 163
equality, 178
Esther, 264
Ethiopia, 132–133
Evangelical Call to Civil Responsibility
(National Association of
Evangelicals), 202
evangelical Christians, 216, 227, 324n10
evangelism
dictate to proclaim and spread the
gospel, 18–20
harvest metaphor, 18–20
missions programs, support for, 181–
183, 234
Evangelism Explosion (Campus Crusade), 18
Ezekiel, 119–120
Ezra, 254

faith
authenticity of, 59–60, 84–85, 185–186
demonstration of through actions,
84–87, 179, 198–202, 218–220, 230,
237–240
faith and works, integration of, 198–
202

outward expression of, 2, 57, 202
power of faith in action, 22–23, 275–276
salvation by faith alone, 198–199, 201
sharing and spreading of, 16–20
superficial and shallow faithfulness, 54–55, 85–86, 183–186
Finedia, 152, 321n1
Finney, Charles G., 200
Fish Hoek Baptist Church, 99, 231–234
Florencio, 168
Four Spiritual Laws (Campus Crusade), 18, 78
Francisco, 165, 168
Francis of Assisi, Saint, 23
Frist, Bill, 261
fruit-bearing trees metaphor, 85–86, 199–200

Garden of Gethsemane, 244
Gates, Bill, 267, 273
Gates, Melinda, 144–145
Gbum Gbum, Northern Ghana, 138–139
gender issues, 156–157
gifts, spiritual, 264
girls, challenges faced by, 156–157
God
    absolute commitment to, 36–39, 49–50, 82–84, 94
    blessings from, 40–42, 214–215
    broken heart of, 9, 108–110, 116, 255
    calling by, 92–94, 279
    dependence on, 211–212
    expectations of us by, 1–3, 4, 37–39, 53–54, 57–61, 66–69, 279
    God's game, 208–209
    idols that compete with, 37–38, 42–44, 89
    love for, 66–68, 69, 186
    misunderstanding and disobeying, 64–65
    obedience to, 85–87
    as owner of riches, 206–208
    pencil in the hand of, 94
    people God chooses, 45–46, 73, 89–94, 250–251, 277–279
    prayers, answering of, 56–57, 165–167
    prayers, listening to, 55, 184, 185

promise to people who obey, 56–57
purpose God has for us, 92–94, 250–253
relationship with God, 212
as source of prosperity, 204–208
superficial and shallow faithfulness to, 54–55, 85–86, 183–186
good news. See gospel
Good Samaritan, 100
Gordon-Conwell Theological Seminary, 30
gospel
    bingo card gospel, 16–20
    definition of, 11, 15
    dictate to proclaim and spread, 18–20
    hole in, 11
    power to change the world with, 4, 57, 73–74, 234, 275–279
    recipients of the good news, 21–22, 60, 62–63, 70–72
    role in changing the world, 2–3
    understanding God's truth, 64–70
Graham, Billy, 18, 186, 259, 262
Great Commission, 67–69, 72, 164
Green, Ted, 150
Gujaret, India, 22–23, 111–113, 314n4
Gulbranson, Gary, 87
Gulu, Uganda, 61–63, 316n3
Gutwein, Austin, 265–266, 273, 326n6

Habitat for Humanity, 22–23, 97
Haggai, 254
Haiti, 133
Ham, Mordecai, 262
health care and diseases, 140–150
Hernandez, Raul, 271–273
Hilton, Steve, 138–139
HIV and AIDS
    Christian community's response to, 194–196
    education, availability of teachers and, 149, 155
    education and rates of, 150, 157
    Hoops of Hope and, 265–266
    life expectancy and, 140
    ministry in Malawi, 188–189
    ministry in South Africa, 99, 231–237, 325n1 (chap.22)
    orphans left by pandemic, 10–11, 50, 148, 195–196, 269–271, 320n41

threat from, 105, 146–150
treatments for, 320n31
Ugandan pandemic, 7–8, 9–11, 146
Hoelkeboer, Tena, 248
hole, definition of, 24
Hoops of Hope, 265–266
Hope Teams, 235–236
hunger and malnutrition, 132–135, 150, 163, 218
Hybels, Bill, 45, 92, 179, 315n4
hypocrites, 228, 229

Ibrahim, Sahabi, 141
idols that compete with God, 37–38, 42–44, 89
illiteracy, 155, 163
income statistics, 121–122, 215, 323n3
India, 22–23, 111–113, 147, 149, 314n4
internally displaced people (IDPs), 316n3
International Health Services, 325n1 (chap.23)
Isaiah, 41, 197
Israelites, 64–65, 90–91, 204–205

Jackson and Morgan, 269–271
Jacob, 92
Jerusalem, 253–256
Jesus Christ
    absolute commitment to, 36–39, 49–50, 82–84, 94
    attributes of, 230
    care for those in need as care for Christ, 58, 60, 67
    crucifixion and Resurrection of, 244–245, 276–277
    expectations of us by, 2–3
    feeding the five thousand, 251–253
    Great Commission, 67–69, 72, 164
    His most distressing disguise, 60, 61–63
    love for children, 10
    messianic prophecy, 20–21
    mission statement of, 20–22
    money, discussions about, 210, 212
    religious leaders' conspiracies against, 65
    signs of the coming of God's kingdom, 57
    teaching of God's truth by, 65–69
    whole person, care for, 20
    W.W.J.D., 26–27
JESUS Film (Campus Crusade), 18, 129
Johnathan Sim Legacy School, 265–266, 326n6
John Paul II, Pope, 186
John the Baptist, 20, 41, 57
Jonah, 89
Joseph and Michael, 61–63
Jubilee, 22, 211
Judah, 65, 183–184
judgment day, 57–60, 292–316n1
Judges, 65
judgmental behavior, 228, 229, 235
justice and oppression. See poverty, sickness, and justice
Justo, 165, 168

Kamaleson, Sam, 68
Kennedy, Robert, 275
Kimball, Edward, 261–262, 263
Ki-moon, Ban, 260
King, Martin Luther, Jr., 127, 192–193, 196, 198
kingdom of God
    coming of, 15–16
    justice and concern for the poor and, 15–16, 22, 55–57, 120
    mustard seed comparison, 275–276
    transformation of world into, 2–5, 57, 68–69, 276–277
    world order of, 15–16, 56–57, 68–69, 243–244
Kony, Joseph, 61
Korea, 101, 249, 260

Laodicea, 221–223
Latin America, 147–148
Lazarus, 186–187
Lenox, 8, 29, 46–48
lepers, 119, 239–240
Letter to the Church in America, 223–225, 325n1 (chap.20)
Liddell, Eric, 92
life expectancy, 140, 163
literacy and education, 155, 163
Living Hope, 232–234

Living Hope Health Care Centre, 232
Lord of the Rings, 42–44
Lord's Prayer, 5, 20
Lord's Resistance Army, 61–62, 159
love, 66–68, 69, 71, 186
Lugar, Richard, 261

Maggie, 152, 321n1
malaria, 105, 142–145, 150
Malawi, 149, 188–189
malnutrition. *See* hunger and malnutrition
Maluzi, Bakili, 149
Mamane, Saa, 141
Margaret, 159–160, 164
Mary, 250
McLaughlin, Leon, 267–268
Meyer, F. B., 262
Michael and Joseph, 61–63
microfinance industry, 153–154
military spending, 158
Millennium Challenge Account (MCA), 261, 325n1 (chap.1)
Millennium Development Goals (United Nations), 163–164, 322n8
Milton, 235, 236
missions
    missionaries, attributes of, 258–259
    support for missions programs, 181–183, 234
Moeller, Susan, 107, 317n6
money. *See* wealth and money
Moody, Dwight L., 262
moral responsibility, 104–105, 110–111
Morgan and Jackson, 269–271
mortality rates and life expectancy, 140, 163
Moses, 45, 90–91, 92, 204–205, 251, 259
mountains, moving, 275
Museveni, Yoweri, 150
mustard seed, 275–276

Native Americans, 190–191, 196
Nehemiah, 253–256
neighbors
    awareness, access, and ability to help, 101–105
    love for, 66–68, 69, 71, 99–100, 186
    poverty-stricken people as, 99–101
Niger, 141, 156

Octaviana, 165–169
omission, sins of, 178–179, 185–186, 187
oppression. *See* poverty, sickness, and justice
Ortberg, John, 93
Ourng, Roth, 70–72

Palmer, Earl, 273
pastor poll of priorities, 185
Paul, 40–41, 45, 73, 92, 122–124, 164, 177–178, 197–198, 259, 264
people of the possible, 274–275
Peru, 164–169
Peter, 250, 264
Pierce, Bob, 9, 101, 109–110, 116, 152, 247–249, 250
poverty, sickness, and justice
    accomplishments and progress in efforts to help, 163–164
    awareness, access, and ability to help distant neighbors, 101–105
    Bible passages that address, 23–24
    care for those in need as care for Christ, 58, 60, 67
    causes of, 125–128, 130
    commitment to justice for, 22, 196–198, 200
    compassion for the sick and poor, 9, 21–22, 108–113, 119–120, 164, 237–240, 248–249
    compassion for the sick and poor and judgment day, 57–61, 86, 187, 315–316n1
    cost of lifting poor out of extreme poverty, 216, 218, 323n6
    deaths of children from poverty-related causes, 106–107, 114–115
    depersonalization of through statistics, 114–116
    diseases and health care, 105, 140–150
    disparity between rich and poor, 97–99, 100–101, 121–124, 172–179, 186–189, 215–216
    doing our part to transform the world, 251–256, 274–279
    economically poor, 152–154
    fixes for, 130
    gender issues, 156–157

giving things to the poor, 126
hunger and malnutrition, 132–135, 150, 163, 218
illiteracy, 155, 163
kingdom of God and justice for the poor, 15–16, 22, 55–57, 120
marred identity of the poor, 128
opportunities for the poor, 117–119, 128–130
orphans, care for, 10–11
perpetuation of poverty, our role in, 318n12
poverty-stricken people as our neighbors, 99–101
principles to remember, 151–152, 161–162
realist's approach to helping the poor, 274–275
recipients of the good news, 21–22, 60, 62–63, 70–72
refugees and war, 157–160
resources to help end the suffering, 122–124, 177–179, 188–189, 206–208, 237–240, 251–253, 257–273
responsibility to help the poor, 122–124, 151–152, 161–163, 164, 201–202
stereotypes about poverty, 116–117
water and waterborne diseases, 135–140, 150, 163, 218, 267–268, 326n8
whole person, care for, 20, 22, 248–249
Poverty and Justice Bible, 24
Prayer of Jabez (Wilkinson), 40, 41–42
prayers
    answering of by God, 56–57, 165–167
    listening to by God, 55, 184, 185
Priggen, Mariah, 261
prisoners, 22
prodigal sons, 63
prosperity gospel, 39, 40
public expression of faith, 2, 57, 202
Pumla, 233
purpose God has for us, 92–94, 250–253

radioactive Christians, 245–247, 249
Rakai, Uganda, 7–8, 9–11, 50
realist's approach to helping the poor, 274–275
refugees and war, 157–160

Richard, 7–8, 9–10, 50
Robin Run Retirement Community, 261
Rodin, R. Scott, 212–213
Rodrick and Beatrice, 128–130, 153
Rokia, 115
Rosamaria, 165
Russia, 149
Ruth, 123

Salisbury, Dean, 268
Sargsyan, Lida, 154
Seiple, Bob, 30, 315n2
Sim, Johnathan, 326n6
Sim, Kelly, 326n6
Singer, Peter, 110–111
slavery, 191, 196, 200
sleeper cells, 246–247
Slovic, Paul, 115
Small, Deborah, 115
Snyder, Bob, 246, 325n1 (chap.23)
Snyder, Pam, 246, 325n1 (chap.23)
social justice. See poverty, sickness, and justice
South Africa, 99, 231–234, 325n1 (chap.22)
Southeast Asia, 117, 141, 146
spiritual gifts, 264
starfish parable, 162
statistics, 114–116
Stearns, Andy, 25–26, 269
Stearns, Grace, 60
Stearns, Karen, 76
Stearns, Pete, 50, 145
Stearns, Reneé
    absolute commitment of, 49–50
    career and life of, 27–28
    children and health care, 140–141
    dating relationship with Richard, 76–79, 84
    engagement and marriage to Richard, 8–9, 84
    missions conference attendance, 48–49
    missions works, talk about, 258–259
    money, discussions about, 213–214
    orphans, sponsorship of, 269, 271
    as radioactive Christian, 245–246, 247
    Seattle trip, 25–26
    temptation before World Vision decision, 46–47

volunteer work, 60
water insufficiency experience, 137
Stearns, Richard
 career and life of, 8–9, 27–29, 34–35,
  42–44, 93
 childhood of, 26–27, 29–30, 74–76,
  315n1
 Christian journey of, 4, 8–9, 27–29,
  88–89
 college plans and attendance, 75, 76–79
 conversion of, 8–9, 18, 80–84, 88
 dating relationship with Reneé, 76–79, 84
 engagement and marriage to Reneé,
  8–9, 84
 missions conference attendance, 48–49
 missions programs, support for, 181–
  183
 missions works, talk about, 258–259
 money, discussions about, 213–214
 orphans, sponsorship of, 268–271
 as radioactive Christian, 245–246, 247
 successful Christians life, 36–37
 temptation before World Vision
  decision, 46–48
 World Vision leadership position, 9,
  25–26, 30–35, 44–50, 93–94, 259
Stearns, Sarah, 60
Stevenson, Rob, 33–34, 35, 44, 45, 48, 50
Stewards in the Kingdom (Rodin), 212–213
Stott, John R., 80
study guide, 305–313
success to significance, 38, 315n1
Sunday, Billy, 262
Surprised by Hope (Wright), 69

Tada, Joni Eareckson, 41, 259
talent, 263–266
talents parable, 206–207
Tandon, Atul, 23, 314n4
Teresa, Mother, 60, 94, 186, 198, 259
territory, enlargement of, 40–41
Thomas, 74, 83
Thomas, John, 231–234
time, 259–263
tithe, 210–215, 216–220, 324n14
Toms, Paul, 258
treasure, 266–273
truth, Bible as anchor of, 314n2

tuberculosis, 105, 145–146, 150
Tutu, Desmond, 186, 196, 198

Uganda
 AIDS pandemic in, 7–8, 9–11, 50, 146,
  150
 child-headed households in, 10
 education spending, 155
 Gulu, 61–63, 316n3
 Lord's Resistance Army, 61–62, 159
 war atrocities in, 158–160
Ukraine, 147
United Nations Millennium Development
 Goals, 163–164, 322n8
United States
 America as Christian, 226–227, 325n1
  (chap.21)
 diseases and health care in, 141, 148
 education spending, 155
 income of people in, 121–122
 military spending, 158
 mortality rates and life expectancy, 140
 opportunities for the poor, 117–118
 stereotypes about poverty, 116–117
USAID, 22–23, 234

Vikas, 112–113

walking the walk, 24, 59
Wallis, Jim, 23–24, 314n5
war and refugees, 157–160
water and waterborne diseases, 135–140,
 150, 163, 218, 267–268, 326n8
wealth and money
 American Dream, 203–204, 205
 of the Church, 216
 disparity between rich and poor, 97–
  99, 100–101, 121–124, 172–179,
  186–189, 215–216
 financial resources to help end the
  suffering, 122–124, 177–179, 206–
  208, 237–240, 266–273
 financial unfaithfulness, consequences
  of, 214–215, 216–217
 getting in the game, 208–209
 God as owner of, 206–208
 as idols that compete with God, 37–38,
  42–44, 89

income statistics, 121–122, 215, 323n3
Jesus' discussions of, 210, 212
missions programs, support for, 181–183, 234
obedience to God and, 87
relationship with money, 210, 212–213
source of prosperity, 204–208
successful Christians lives, 36–38
time, value of, 260
tithe, 210–215, 216–220, 324n14
Wesley, John, 200
What Would Jesus Do (W.W.J.D.), 26–27
White Jade, 247–249
whole gospel
    in action in Cambodia, 70–72
    compassion and justice for the poor, 60, 248–249
    power to change the world with, 234, 276
    proclaiming and spreading, 22, 24
    promise to people who obey, 56–57
whole person, care for, 20, 248–249
Wick, Connie, 261, 263
Wilberforce, William, 196, 263
wilderness experience, 28–29
Willow Creek Leadership Summit, 232
women, challenges faced by, 156–157
world
    awareness, access, and ability to help distant neighbors, 101–105
    broken world, compassion for, 9, 21–22, 108–113, 116, 119–120, 164
    challenge of new millennium, 97–99
    doing our part to transform, 251–256, 274–279
    income statistics, 121–122, 215, 323n3
    kingdom of God world order, 15–16, 56–57, 68–69, 243–244
    our role in changing, 1–5
    population of, 121
    responsibility for tackling problems of, 3–4
    social revolution to change, 22
    transformation of by power of the gospel, 4, 57, 73–74, 234, 275–279
    transformation of through tithing, 217–220
    turning away from, 2, 3, 68, 161, 179–180

World Health Organization, 103, 142–143
World Relief, 258
World Vision
    awareness-raising activities of, 101
    beginning of, 247–249
    in Cambodia, 70–71
    Children of War Center, 62–63, 159–160
    Courageous Leadership Award, 232
    financial gifts to, 271–273
    HIV and AIDS projects, 99, 149, 188–189, 235
    Indian earthquake, rebuilding after, 22–23, 314n4
    information about, 281
    leadership of, 8–9, 25–26, 30–35, 44–50, 93–94, 259
    microfinance projects, 153, 154
    pastor poll of priorities, 185
    in Peru, 165–169
    scope of work of, 249, 281
    water distribution and filtration projects, 268
    water projects, 138–139
Wright, N. T., 69

Yunus, Muhammad, 153

Zambia, 128–130, 152, 235–237, 265–266, 269–271, 321n1, 325n1 (chap.22)

Zechariah, 254

ABOUT THE AUTHOR

RICHARD STEARNS has been president of World Vision U.S. since June 1998, bringing with him twenty-three years of corporate experience. After growing up in a broken home with limited financial means and parents who didn't attend high school, Stearns earned scholarships to two Ivy League schools. He went on to a successful corporate career that led him on a journey across multiple companies and industries with stints at Gillette, Parker Brothers Games, and Lenox, America's finest tableware and gift company. He was named president of Parker Brothers Games at the age of thirty-three and subsequently president and CEO of Lenox, Inc. He holds a bachelor's degree in neurobiology from Cornell University and an MBA from the Wharton School at the University of Pennsylvania. Following a sense of God's call on his life, he resigned his position at Lenox in 1998 to become World Vision's U.S. president. As a spokesperson for World Vision, he has appeared on CNN, Fox, ABC, NBC, and PBS. Rich and his wife, Reneé, live in Bellevue, Washington, and have supported World Vision since 1984. They have five children of their own plus millions more around the world.

World Vision, serving in nearly one hundred countries, is a Christian humanitarian organization dedicated to working with children, families, and their communities worldwide to reach their full potential by tackling the causes of poverty and injustice.

About World Vision

WHO WE ARE:
World Vision is a Christian humanitarian organization dedicated to working with children, families, and their communities worldwide to reach their full potential by tackling the causes of poverty and injustice.

WHOM WE SERVE:
Motivated by our faith in Jesus Christ, World Vision serves alongside the poor and oppressed as a demonstration of God's unconditional love for all people.

WHY WE SERVE:
Our passion is for the world's poorest children whose suffering breaks the heart of God. To help secure a better future for each child, we focus on lasting, community-based transformation. We partner with individuals and communities, empowering them to develop sustainable access to clean water, food supplies, health care, education, and economic opportunities.

HOW WE SERVE:
Since 1950, World Vision has helped millions of children and families by providing emergency assistance to those affected by natural disasters and civil conflict, developing long-term solutions within communities to alleviate poverty and advocating for justice on behalf of the poor.

YOU CAN HELP:
If you want to put your faith into action today, become a World Vision child sponsor to connect with one special child who will know your name, write to you, and feel your love and prayers. Your monthly sponsorship gift will provide a child with things such as: clean water, nutritious food, health care, educational opportunities, and spiritual nurture.

Sponsor today at www.worldvision.org/thiog